D1631318

111599

Lives of
Career Women
Approaches to Work,
Marriage, Children

Lives of Career Women

Approaches to Work, Marriage, Children

Edited by

Frances M. Carp, Ph.D.

Wright Institute
Berkeley, California

With a Foreword by
Robin B. Kennedy, J.D.

With a Prologue by
Albert I. Rabin, Ph.D.

✳ INSIGHT BOOKS
Plenum Press • New York and London

Library of Congress Cataloging in Publication Data

Lives of career women: approaches to work, marriage, children / [edited by] Frances
M. Carp; with a foreword by Robin B. Kennedy; with a prologue by Albert I. Rabin.
    p.   cm.
    Includes bibliographical references and index.
    ISBN 0-306-43960-3
    1. Women in the professions—Case studies.
HD6054.L58   1991   91-18066
305.43—dc20   CIP

ISBN 0-306-43960-3

© 1991 Plenum Press, New York
A Division of Plenum Publishing Corporation
233 Spring Street, New York, N.Y. 10013

An Insight Book

Printed in the United States of America

Contributors

Frances Merchant Carp, Ph.D., Research Psychologist, Wright Institute, Berkeley, California 94704

Nancy McCall Clish, M.D., Founder, San Jose Women's Medical Group, Inc., San Jose, California 95124

Wilma Thompson Donahue, Ph.D., Director Emeritus, Institute of Gerontology, University of Michigan, Ann Arbor, Michigan 48109

Josephine Rohrs Hilgard, M.D., Ph.D., Psychiatrist Emeritus, Stanford University Hospital, Stanford, California 94305

I. M. Hulicka, Ph.D., Distinguished Professor of Psychology, State University of New York, Buffalo, New York 14222

Jacquelyne Johnson Jackson, Ph.D., Professor of Sociology, Duke University Medical School, Durham, North Carolina 27706

Jacquelyn Boone James, Ph.D., Research Associate, Henry A. Murray Research Center, Cambridge, Massachusetts 02138

Lois Mailou Jones, Distinguished Artist, Meridien House International, Washington, D.C. 20009

Robin B. Kennedy, J.D., Staff Attorney, Office of the General Counsel, Stanford University, Stanford, California 94305

M. Powell Lawton, Ph.D., Director of Research, Philadelphia Geriatric Center, Philadelphia, Pennsylvania 19141

Helena Znaniecka Lopata, Ph.D., Professor of Sociology, Loyola University, Chicago, Illinois 60626

Lisa Redfield Peattie, Ph.D., Professor Emeritus, Department of Urban Studies and Planning, Massachusetts Institute of Technology, Cambridge, Massachusetts 02139

Albert I. Rabin, Ph.D., Professor of Psychology Emeritus, Michigan State University, East Lansing, Michigan 48824

Catherine Scofield Rude, Retired Teacher, Public School System, Nyack, New York 10960

Margaret Collins Schweinhaut, State Senator, Maryland State Legislature, Annapolis, Maryland 21401

Beverley L. Thomas, R.N., Retired Administrator, Sacred Heart Hospital, Eugene, Oregon 97401

Marie McGuire Thompson, Retired Commissioner, United States Public Housing Administration, Washington, D.C. 20005

Ruth B. Weg, Ph.D., Professor of Biology, Ethel Percy Andrus Gerontology Center, University of Southern California, Los Angeles, California 90089

Vivian Wood, Ph.D., Professor of Social Work Emeritus, University of Wisconsin, Madison, Wisconsin 52706

Shirley F. Woods, Archdeacon, Episcopal Diocese of California, San Francisco, California 94108

Foreword
Viewpoint of a Young Woman Lawyer

Robin B. Kennedy, J.D.

A story is told about the singer Connee Boswell. In her seventies, long after her heyday as a singer with the big bands of the 1930s, a reporter asked her what it had been like to be a star in the Swing Era. "Geez, honey," replied Boswell, "If I'd known it was an era, I would of paid more attention!"

The stories that follow reveal two extraordinary things about the contributors' lives and work. First, they lived those stories in an era in which traditional gender roles went unchallenged, feminist ideology was unknown, and society provided no infrastructure for educating or employing professional women; everything they did, they did on their own, against horrendous obstacles and in contravention of societal norms and expectations. Second, they were apparently unaware that they were establishing themselves as role models for a later generation. They pursued intellectual and professional excellence for its intrinsic value, not to change the world or to teach anyone else a lesson.

Few female high-school graduates in the class of 1990—black or white—would be thought unusual if their goals included attending college and ultimately pursuing independent professional careers. The early decades of the century did not afford the luxury of such expectations to young women. Yet the sixteen whose stories are portrayed here defied the ordinary and the usual in their pursuit of skills and education and in their trust in the capacity to use the serendipitous.

Through the words of one of the contributors we are asked to believe that "much credit is due to Lady Luck." Perhaps. But these women have more in common than having been in the right place at the right time. They had the courage, imagination, and tenacity to embrace Lady Luck when she appeared at the door and to stay the course when she had apparently abandoned them. They were motivated not by hunger for recognition and success but by their passion to be effective in the service of humanity and the correction of social inequities. They did not necessarily set out to establish careers, but were energetically opportunistic and ready to follow each bend in an unknown road. They had no role models nor even a conscious yearning for any. Neither they nor their husbands were exposed to feminist theory — a body of literature that did not appear until their careers were well launched — so these unusual women had to teach concepts of equality to understandably resistant mates while they were in the process of recognizing and articulating such concepts for the first time.

To invent gender equality while living it, to resist the safe conventions of one's community, to "not hesitate to walk in" when an unknown door opened, to withstand the lonely humiliation of gender and racial bias all required a special gift. Nearly universally, these women tell us that the nature of the gift was the confidence to believe in themselves, and that the givers of the gift were their parents. Their parents believed them to be special, treated them no differently than they did their male children, set high standards of excellence, and, perhaps most importantly, did not impose a ceiling on expectations.

In these stories we come to understand that the parents'

confidence was well placed. We recognize that if these women could conduct such interesting and worthy lives in their era—an era they did not recognize as such at the time—we honor them best by doing so in our own.

Acknowledgments

Heartfelt thanks to the many persons who cheerfully helped locate and recruit chapter authors and to the many others who provided material for chapter introductions, the majority of them men. This is logical in that most persons in the career fields represented are men. It is a favorable sign for the future of women in these fields that so many men went to considerable effort to help bring this book to completion. Because most wanted it so, these persons remain anonymous, with a few exceptions. In particular I am grateful to those exceptions: the Right Reverend William E. Swing, bishop of the Episcopal Diocese of California, who provided most of the introduction to Woods' chapter; Robert N. Butler, M.D., first director of the National Institute on Aging, who wrote the conclusion of the introduction to Donahue's chapter; and M. Powell Lawton, Ph.D., who wrote the introduction to my chapter.

I am grateful, too, to the young women in the Introduction of the volume who allowed publication of their very personal dilemmas and hope that somewhere in the book each will find information helpful to her situation. Most admirable of all are the women who laid out their lives for anyone to read, in hopes that their experiences will be enlightening to young women and to researchers attempting to rectify the inequity in information about men and women.

Special recognition is due the three persons who read sixteen chapters in preparation for writing their own contributions: Robin B. Kennedy, J.D., whose Foreword was written from the viewpoint of a young career woman; Albert I. Rabin, Ph.D., whose Prologue reflects the vantage point of a man in later maturity, who has an eminent international career in the field of personality research and theory; and Jacquelyn Boone James, Ph.D., a young investigator who, in Chapter 18, reviews the sixteen chapters in terms of their potential impact upon future research.

Contents

Foreword: Viewpoint of a Young Woman Lawyer vii
Robin B. Kennedy, Attorney

Prologue: View of a Man Who Has Spent a Lifetime
   on Personality Research and Theory 1
Albert I. Rabin, Personality Psychologist

Chapter 1
Introduction 9
Frances Merchant Carp, Psychologist

Chapter 2
A Survivor's Career 23
Wilma Thompson Donahue, Social Gerontologist

Chapter 3
The Career of an African-American Woman Artist 43
Lois Mailou Jones, Artist

Chapter 4
The Political Life 55
Margaret Collins Schweinhaut, State Senator

Chapter 5

Washington, D.C.—To the Wild West
   and Back Again 71

Marie McGuire Thompson, Housing Commissioner

Chapter 6

My Life as a Professional, a Wife, and a Mother 85

Josephine Rohrs Hilgard, Psychiatrist

Chapter 7

The Other Journey 103

Shirley F. Woods, Archdeacon

Chapter 8

Disorder or Congruence? 125

Frances Merchant Carp, Psychologist

Chapter 9

A Woman in Academe: Adventure,
   Fulfillment, Disillusion 143

Ruth B. Weg, Biologist

Chapter 10

A Professor's Story 159

Vivian Wood, Social Worker

Chapter 11

Not a Career: A Life 173

Lisa Redfield Peattie, Anthropologist/Community Planner

Chapter 12

Occupation: Sociologist 191

Helena Znaniecka Lopata, Sociologist

Chapter 13
The Once-Reluctant School Teacher 209
Catherine Scofield Rude, Elementary School Teacher

Chapter 14
A Woman Physician Looks Back 225
Nancy McCall Clish, Physician

Chapter 15
Serendipity and Adaptiveness: The Lucky Planner? 235
I. M. Hulicka, Psychology Professor

Chapter 16
A Career in Nursing 257
Beverley L. Thomas, Registered Nurse

Chapter 17
This Sho' Nuff Ain't Been No "Zombie Jamboree" 275
Jacquelyne Johnson Jackson, Medical Sociologist

Chapter 18
Implications for Future Research 299
Jacquelyn Boone James, Research Psychologist

Chapter 19
Summary 307
Frances Merchant Carp, Psychologist

Index 313

Lives of Career Women

Approaches to Work, Marriage, Children

Prologue
View of a Man Who Has Spent a Lifetime on Personality Research and Theory

Albert I. Rabin, Ph.D.

Narratives of women's lives, biographies and autobiographies of and by women, have appeared in print rather infrequently until recent years. Some writers have speculated about the reason for such scarcity. It seems that in a man's world the comings and goings of men and their adventures and misadventures were considered of greater consequence and worth recording. Women had taken (or have been relegated to) a backseat, so to speak, in the public life of society, and the resulting meager literary record reflected this state of affairs (Heilbrun, 1988).

Trends have changed and are changing rapidly, as the accounts presented in this volume will testify. Many more stories and records of women's lives have been published in

Lives of Career Women: Approaches to Work, Marriage, Children, edited by Frances M. Carp. Plenum/Insight, New York, 1991.

recent years, and the present collection illustrates and further contributes to this growing literature.

The sixteen autobiographical essays that comprise this book have been solicited by the editor with a practical purpose in mind. This book has been designed as a response to the needs of the younger generation of men and women to learn about lives of women who "made it." It is about women who were able to combine career and family with varying degrees of success and about the ingredients that contributed to their success. What is most interesting is how the women tell their story and their view of how their lives have unfolded, with the perspective gained in later maturity. To be sure, each life course and its corresponding story is unique in many ways and evolves its own pattern. Yet, there are some configurations of relationships, circumstances, and events, as well as modes of coping with them, that have some commonalities. These may serve as a basis for generalization and for the elicitation of general relevant principles regarding the lives of women in the latter half of the twentieth century.

Questions regarding the fidelity and truthfulness of personal life narratives have been raised from many quarters. From the psychoanalyst's perspective we are told that in the narratives there are two kinds of truth, "the narrative truth and the historical truth" (Spence, 1982). The former is seen as a considered, coherent, often consistent and more comprehensive story. It is an "adequate" story in terms of prevailing social standards. On the other hand, the historical truth is more accurate and factual. This distinction, which stems from the scrupulous analysis of interview material, applies to written narratives, such as autobiographies, as well—perhaps even more so. To paraphrase a wag's comment in a different context, autobiographies are like statistics: What they reveal is interesting; what they conceal is vital. This is, perhaps, an exaggeration and an unfair generalization of the nature of autobiographies, however, the autobiography highlights the defensiveness and selectivity of material that often characterizes the narrative process. Prepared and structured written life stories about oneself are even more vulnerable to the criticism mentioned above than stories obtained in several interviews in which most points, inconsistencies, and denials can be attacked and ultimately dissolved.

Much of the criticism detailed above concerns the use of autobiographies in the study of personality and its development, the extensive and intensive exploration of psychodynamics and motivation in interaction with the biosocial sphere. The following brief autobiographical essays were not expected to reveal all; the aim of the enterprise was more circumscribed and more focused. The women were asked to reflect upon their life course in terms of career building and its interaction with the private life from the vantage point and perspective of later maturity.

Some interesting data and observations on career changes of younger women have been reported recently in a series of studies (Rosenwald & Wiersma, 1983; Wiersma, 1988). The initial accounts given by the women studied in the early interviews, whose aim was to obtain autobiographical material, were of the nature of press releases. Press releases are described by the investigators as well-rehearsed official stories regarding career decisions. However, "in joint effort between interviewer and subject, the original account was extended, amended, and revised to yield a more complex personal story (Rosenwald & Wiersma, 1983, p. 214). In a later article Wiersma advocates the use of hermeneutics in interpreting the storied material. She states that "this storied construction of reality has less to do with facts and more to do with meaning" (Wiersma, 1988, p. 207). Her understanding of the press releases is based on their symbolic meaning rather than on their literal meaning.

Undoubtedly, the documents prepared by the contributors to the present volume contain their share of press-release, "prefabricated" statements dictated by culture and zeitgeist. Advanced age does not entirely liberate us from such influences in considering our life course. But, again, it should be pointed out that the aim of the present biographers was not to plumb the depth of personality development or self-formation, but to understand the relationships between different factors and forces that affected their life course.

The style of the autobiographies varies markedly and reflects interestingly the different agendas of their authors. Some contain a number of press releases, whereas others avoid them almost entirely; some are rather psychologically minded, whereas others eschew motivational explanations; some are more strictly career-oriented and career-driven, and others' ambitions are more diffuse. In all of these essays, however, we note the pursuit of what Tomkins called "commitment scripts," which "involve the courage and endurance to invest and bind the person to long-term activity and to magnify positive affect in such activity by absorbing and naturalizing the various negative costs of such committed activity" (Tomkins, 1987, p. 167). The nature of the commitment in this group of women is by and large quite different from those obtained from a group of middle-class men. The plots of the stories by a group of achieving men "emphasize relentless forward movement, are shaped by career culture, which demands constant advancement . . . It expresses men's aggressive self-aggrandizement, while denying their desire for affection and their vulnerability to rejection (Ochberg, 1988, p. 173). One does not get a similar impression from the stories before us of "relentless ambition and drive for ambition" at such great a cost as for Ochberg's male subjects. Yet, we note a great deal of persistence on the part of the women in the pursuit of their careers, especially since this is an older cohort group, and their task, earlier in this century, was a more formidable one.

The possibility of gleaning some insights and common trends in the life course of these women was mentioned at the outset of this prologue. An attempt to follow through on this will be made subsequently. At the same time, the limitation of generalization must be recognized, since no claim for "representativeness" of the sample of women who tell their stories in this volume is made or intended by the author.

In the first place, one must consider the period of historical and cultural changes spanned by the lives of these women. Three wars, the Great Depression, the civil-rights movement, and the feminist movement were all of momentous importance. Of particular interest is the interaction between the historical event and the life stage of the individual (Elder & Caspi, 1990). A few of the women were children during the First World War. At that age they were relatively less affected by the historical context than the adults in their environment, who were active participants or victims of events. Even so, as Elder and Caspi point out, the children are affected by the changes in the adult world. All of the women have experienced the Great Depression, the Second World War, and the Korean War. The effects varied with the age and stage of development at which they were caught up by the events. For some, life turned topsy-turvy; personal or educational plans had to be relinquished or drastically modified. Others found new employment and educational opportunities, such as the GI Bill. These observations dictate the next general point to be made about the biographies.

The first autobiography in this series, that of Donahue, stresses the "serendipitous" nature of her history and, especially, career development. "Serendipity" also appears in the title of Hulicka's essay. Generally, the theme, the factor of "Lady Luck," emerges in a number of other stories. Even those authors who do not mention this issue explicitly often demonstrate that it was somehow involved in their professional and career advancement. A concomitant but necessary characteristic revealed by these women was the flexibility and capacity for shifting orientations and activities and to move into neighboring fields of endeavor. Hence, a number of our autobiographers started out with limited and circumscribed horizons due to restricted family outlook or extant gender biases and cultural structures. The traditional notions that only teaching and nursing were proper professions of women provided a rather limited scope for career development. The authors' adaptability allowed them to move into the relatively new professional fields of psychology, sociology, gerontology, urban planning, and the like. These had not yet and would not become more exclusively male provinces, which had been true of law and medicine. A number of these women sailed in on the wave of nineteenth-century cultural and professional innovations.

Another general issue that is central in this project is the balancing, nay juggling, act that most women had to perform between career and family. A number of these women made constant and frequent adaptations to their husbands' careers. As tradition had structured until recent years, the women moved to different locations, were the victims of institutions' nepotistic rules, and postponed their educations in order to accommodate their spouses. In the instances where women were willing and able to exercise their flexibility and resilience, the marriages were stable and even exemplary. In some instances, when the husband was willing to assume a less aggressive role in favor of the wife's professional and career plans, the marriage also endured. However, when accommodations between spouses could not be made, and the requirements of the two careers could not be negotiated, divorce was inevitable. This last statement is largely speculative and inferential, for the biographies contain relatively little material on intimate relations that bears directly on this issue.

As to the children reared under the conditions prevailing in two-career families, the outcomes are insufficiently clear in view of the limited material available on this point; there simply is not enough information in most of these schematic presentations. It does appear, however, that in those instances where competent and continuous extramaternal child care was available the results were highly satisfactory. Other children were the beneficiaries of a moratorium period when mothers temporarily relinquished full-time outside employment. In still other cases where the outcome was unhappy, even tragic, we are not in a position, because of the scarcity of relevant cues, to even speculate about the possible causes.

Finally, in reviewing their own lives, most of these women beyond or nearing retirement age feel that they have done well under the circumstances and conditions accessible to them. Some are resentful of the racial and gender bias they have experienced. Others resent the antiquated mandatory retirement rules that still govern academic and other institutions. But most are satisfied with a life well spent and continue to be involved in sundry professional and humanitarian activities. They are not sitting back and "listening to their arteries harden." Erikson (1950) characterized the final developmental stage by the dichotomy of "integrity versus despair." "Integrity is the acceptance of one's only life cycle as something that had to be and that, by necessity, permitted of no substitutions" (p. 232). This acceptance obviates despair, the resentment and regret of an unfulfilled life.

All in all, despite the expressed reservations and caveats concerning one's personal narratives, this book is a very person-oriented document that has much to teach us. It demonstrates the idiographic approach and the study of lives, rather than the nomothetic concern with "variables." We have learned about how women, who during this transitional period of the history in gender relationship and cultural change, were able to balance careers with family responsibilities, how they accommodated to different changes in the occupational and personal realms and persisted and coped with them successfully, and how they emerged in later maturity with an integrated self-concept. The newer generation of women (and men) are living, arguably, beyond the transitional historical phase in gender relationships. Yet, they may learn much from the life histories presented in this volume.

The editor and contributors to this volume are to be congratulated upon producing a unique work. It substantially expands our understanding of the evolution of women's status and gender relationships in our society and, at the same time, makes a methodological contribution to the field.

8   Albert I. Rabin

References

Elder, G. H., & Caspi, A. (1990). Studying lives in a changing society: Sociological and personological explorations. In A. I. Rabin, R. A. Zucker, R. A. Emmons, & S. Frank (Eds.), *Studying persons and lives* (pp. 201–247). New York: Springer.

Erikson, E. H. (1950). *Childhood and society.* New York: W. W. Norton.

Heilbrun, C. C. (1988). *Writing a woman's life.* New York: Ballantine Books.

Ochberg, R. L. (1988). Life histories and the psychosocial construction of careers. *Journal of Personality, 56* (1), 173–204.

Rosenwald, G. C., & Wiersma, S. (1983). Women, career changes and the new self: An analysis of rhetoric. *Psychiatry, 46,* 213–229.

Spence, D. P. (1982). *Narrative truth and historical truth: Meaning interpretation in psychoanalysis.* New York: W. W. Norton.

Tomkins, S. S. (1987). Script theory. In J. Aronoff, A. I. Rabin, & R. A. Zucker (Eds.), *The emergence of personality.* New York: Springer.

Wiersma, J. (1988). The press release: Symbolic communication in life history interviewing. *Journal of Personality, 56* (1), 205–238.

Chapter 1

Introduction

Frances Merchant Carp, Ph.D.

Purpose and Overview

This book was generated by two phenomena: (1) young wo-men's dilemmas about careers, marriage, and children; and (2) growing awareness of inequity in research attention to women as contrasted to men, especially in regard to careers.

In facing major decisions in their lives, young women want to know how real (not fictional) women faced with situations similar to their own met those situations and what were the outcomes. They would like to see alternative courses of action that have been taken and the results, which might enlighten their decisions. Increasing numbers of young women want not just to work but to aspire to careers in their chosen fields. Many of them feel that they are facing an uncharted territory and are not aware of the experiences of career women who preceeded them. Young men contemplating or in relationships with poten-tial career women also express interest in the ways these

Lives of Career Women: Approaches to Work, Marriage, Children, edited by Frances M. Carp. Plenum/Insight, New York, 1991.

situations have been met by others, to provide a preview of what might occur in their lives if one or another course of action were pursued.

Faced with the realities and projections of the population structure and of labor-force participation (Spencer, 1984), policy makers are finding it necessary to consider women's situations. Women's continuing economic inequity reflects the conflict they experience between work and family (Fuchs, 1988). Society has been sensitized to women's issues and has come to realize that the solution or nonsolution of these issues affects us all, men and children equally with women. As women enter the labor force, "Women and their families are undergoing a natural experiment of enormous proportions" (Matthews & Rodin, 1989). Researchers are recognizing the dearth of information on the life courses of women as contrasted to men.

In the next section of this introduction some young women voice their quandaries regarding careers, marriage, and children. The following section deals with the increasing recognition of the need for scientific attention to the development and well-being of women, particularly in regard to careers, that will bring about equity with men. The final section provides the background for the next sixteen chapters, which are career women's accounts of their own approaches to career, marriage, and motherhood.

The authors did not have access to the concerns voiced by these young women and were not asked to write for researchers but focused on their own experiences. Chapter 19 is a brief summary of recurrent patterns and variations among the authors' life patterns. It is hoped that the young women who contributed to this Introduction will find in these chapters material relevant to their perplexities, and that other young women will do so in regard to their own quandaries. The reactions of two young women are included: The Foreword was written by a young woman lawyer and Chapter 18, "Implications for Future Research," by a young woman researcher in women's development and employment. It is also hoped that behavioral scientists will find in this material clues to fruitful investigation and conceptualization of women's well-being in regard to careers, marriage, and children. This notion is supported by both the reactions of the young woman researcher in Chapter 18 and those of the eminent investigator and writer, a man in later maturity, who wrote the Prologue.

Some Dilemmas of Young Women Today

College Seniors Talk about "What Next?"

Students gather for a food break in cramming for finals. "Well, it's nearly over. What's next?" From one, "I can't decide whether to get a job for a while before graduate school. Mom says a dose of reality would do me good, but I'm a little scared of going 'out there.' " From another, "I have to work for a while to earn money, and I'm afraid I'll get stuck and never get back." "Well, I'm going straight to graduate school even though I have to borrow money. I'm not ever going to make coffee for the boss — though going into debt worries me."

"Your mention of making coffee sounds like sexism is on your mind." "It sure is! I don't intend to earn two-thirds of what a man does." From a corner, "I read in the paper that the reason women, overall, make less than men is because of the kinds of jobs most women go into." An interjection, "Or do those jobs get poor pay *because* women are in them? I think it is a chicken and egg thing." The previous speaker resumes, "Anyway, like you, I am aiming for a profession, but I worry about competing with men. Can I do it? Am I capable enough? Tough enough? No matter how capable and 'tough' I am, will it be a fair competition?"

After a pause, "I wonder about that, too, the 'old boy's network.' I've seen it here on campus — supposedly an idealistic ivory-tower place. So won't it be worse in the 'real world'?" Another joins in, "Yesterday I had to go to the dentist, of all things during finals, and in the waiting room I read in a magazine that women hold only two percent of the top executive jobs in the Fortune 500 companies. They have a lot of women employees, even in so-called executive positions, but only a tiny fraction make it to the top." A nod of agreement and, "Yeah, you're talking about what they call 'the glass ceiling,' a subtle barrier that blocks women from the top jobs in most fields, not just the Fortune 500 type."

"I chose an ivory-tower career, thinking that the academic atmosphere and academic freedom must be favorable for women. But I just got this from a friend." She reads aloud:

> Two very significant facts were reported to the Education Committee of the Board of Regents on July 12, 1990 concerning the promotion and retention of women faculty members in the UW system: (1) that from 1983 through 1989, 75 percent of the gains made through new hires were lost by women leaving the System, and (2) that it will take another 65 years to bring the percent of women faculty members to their current availability level. (Swoboda, 1990, p. 1)

"I should explain that 'availability level' is the percentage of Ph.D.'s they award to women. They are saying it will take sixty-five years for them to have as many women on their faculty as they turn out female Ph.D's. So if I go for academia, I'll be one of a very large number of female job-hunters—let alone be in competition with men. Also, why do so many women leave faculty positions? That worries me. Now I don't know what to do."

Hesitantly, "You implied that there may be heavy competition among women in academia. That brought up something that's been bothering me. I've heard that women on the way up in any field are even harder on other women than men are. I wish I knew if it were true. I think I can handle competition with men, but I don't know if I can take it if other women try to climb up over me."

"This is a real switch, but since it seems to be tell-all time, here goes. I'm a Navy brat and planned all my life to follow in Dad's footsteps. Then this morning's paper said two women were raped by crewmates within a week on one Navy vessel. Many other women told about sexual harassment and abuse, verbal and physical, from male crew members. Men on board said the problem is due to the presence of females in the confined quarters of the ship, and the way to stop it is to keep women ashore—and there goes equal chance for advancement. So now I don't know."

"I'm considering politics. It runs in my family, and I held offices in high school and do now in college. And I know we need women in office if we are to get a fair break. But then I look at the odds. Oh, they're better than they were, but . . . how many of the fifty state governors are women? Three. How many women sit in the Congress? Thirty. How many women have been president? Even vice president? So what are my chances? It's a hard decision."

The "hostess" rises, stretches, and begins to pick up remains of the snack. "It's 3:00 and I have an 8:00 final. I wish we could hear from some women who have been through these things."

Issues of Career and Marriage

Several young women meet seeking help with decisions in regard to career and marriage: "The department chairman called me in to tell me I did very disappointingly on the comprehensive exams. He said there must be a reason. There is! I can't sleep on account of it. When the study group met to prepare for the exam I could not keep my mind on the discussion. When we took the exam I could not keep my mind on the questions. It is an awfully hard decision. The department offered me a fellowship to prepare for a career I have dreamed of for years, and just then I fell in love with a wonderful man. So what's the problem?

His job is far from here, and if I marry him I give up the fellowship. If I don't make up my mind soon, I'll lose both."

"My quandary is sort of like yours, except I thought I could have both and now find maybe I can't. We got married in graduate school and dreamed of a perfect two-career marriage. We are about to finish school, and here is my problem: His best offer is across the country from my best offer. Not only that, where he wants to go there are no opportunities in my field. And, to be fair, pretty much the same is true for him if we go where I want to go. So my choice is to go with my husband and put my career in real jeopardy or lose my love." She bursts into tears.

After a while, "What I want to talk about sounds so mundane compared to your problems. My question is simply whether I could handle both a career and marriage. I guess I want to make the decision now so that if it is to be career only I won't put myself in jeopardy of falling in love, at least with marriage in mind. Can two-career marriages work, or is it either-or?"

"I am committed to a career, but my problem is similar to yours—whether to try to combine marriage with it. The main reason I see against that is the high and rising divorce rate. It is hard enough to end a relationship—I know! It must be much more difficult to break up a marriage. Divorce would be more disruptive to a career, it seems to me, than coping with the married state. I sometimes wonder if career women have outgrown the institution of marriage. Or am I just kidding myself? Will I be sorry later on if I don't marry? I just don't know."

"You think you have problems! I have all of them, plus I'm black—Oh! I must remember that it's 'African-American.' It was in the paper that our leaders across the United States agree on that. Anyway, I feel that I *must* accomplish something worthwhile since I have been given this chance for a good education, and I know I will have to work harder on the job. So do I have to give up being married and having a family because I am female *and* a minority?" At last someone responds, "Of course I can't really feel what it must be like for you, but one thing: Don't say or think that you 'were given' this chance for a good education. I know that you are an excellent student." Applause.

"I am a little older, but what many of you say applies to me. My career is really established and taking off, and suddenly my husband wants to move on account of a job offer. It's a good marriage—we've even begun talking about kids. But," she adds bitterly, "we may add to the divorce statistics instead of the birthrate."

Children

"That brings us to my problem—whether or not to have children. Is it fair to bring a child into the world when there is such a high chance you will be divorced and the kid will end up with only one parent? Could I handle single-parenting? And look at what we hear every day about delinquency and stuff. It's always the working mother's fault! But how could I support myself and a child if I quit work, or support my self-esteem if my ex provided financial support?" "Yeah, and what kind of a job could you get when the kids grow up and move out, and child support stops? You'd really be outdated and unemployable."

"My problem is not *whether* but *when* to have children. When is the right time? I see other graduate students lugging infants around, and maybe that's the best way—have them before starting your career. But what if your kid is sick the night before an important exam?" "I wonder if it is fair to the child. All I hear is that during the first months the baby needs to bond with its mother—with a textbook in her other hand?" Someone adds, "Also, most of us students can't afford child care."

A rejoinder, "What makes you think people just out of college have scads of money?" "Yeah, if we wait until we graduate, is it any better? Could I get a job if I was pregnant when I got my degree? Not likely. Not the kind I want, anyway." "No, they'd start you on the 'Mommy track,' *if* they hired you. Have you read about that (Schwartz, 1989)?" Most have read about it in newspapers or magazines. "It's pretty depressing. Having children is an excuse for sidetracking you— shunting you off the track to the top."

"Being pregnant on the job and taking time off when a child is born are real problems especially, I think, in the early years when you are working hard to establish your career and not get on that Mommy track; but I think the worst difficulty, when you have a child, is the double shift at home." There is laughter and, "You are confusing 'double standard' and 'second shift.' " "Well, that's not bad! I think she has something there! Certainly the first is still with us. Have you read *The Second Shift* (Hochschild & Machung, 1989)?" There is discussion, then: "It all boils down to the fact that a wife works about fifteen hours a week longer than her husband, doing housework and child care, after each has put in a full week on the paid job." A surprised, "But that's not fair!" "Fair, schmair. It's true." "And that's why I'm not sure I'll have children, though I want very much to be a mother. Apparently, I have to choose either career or marriage, or else I have to be superwoman or be on the Mommy track or be a bad mother who raises delinquent kids. It's a lousy choice."

"I don't mean to brag, and you'll see I have a serious dilemma, but I managed to get my career well on the tracks and to have one child. My problem is a sibling for Billy. We don't want him to be an 'only,' and I want another child. But could I handle my job and the house and Billy while being pregnant? How would pregnancy and maternity leave affect my career? I'm not sure about timing, biologically and career-wise. My husband and I have talked and talked and discussed ourselves into an impasse."

"I'm in the same boat, and we're considering adoption. But I don't know if it would work. There are lots of pros and cons, but my greatest worry is whether I could truly love an adopted child as I do Emmy. Could we be a real family with one child adopted?"

"Sometimes I think it was the good old days when most women married and were housewives and when the others were teachers or secretaries or nurses. All these difficult decisions we face—are they new? Or have other women faced situations like ours? If so I sure would like to know what they did and how it turned out. That might help me." Nods of agreement, and from one, "You are so right. Look where we get our information: mostly newspapers putting things in to be 'catchy' and sell papers, and magazines that either tell soapy stories of saccharin heroines or report studies—but who knows how accurately." Someone corrects her: "Some of us read the original reports of studies. Statistics are useful, but what I want is some feeling for the *process*, the *person* shaping her own life." "Of course, there is always television." That gets a laugh. "Seriously, I would like to know about real, honest-to-goodness women who made choices like those we have talked about. I'd like to know what they did, and how they felt, and how their lives turned out."

An Issue of Equity

There is growing concern over the inequity in knowledge about the development and well-being of women as compared to that about men. The National Institutes of Health (NIH), which is part of the Public Health Service (PHS) and is the principal federal agency supporting biomedical and behavioral research, has been one target of this criticism. The 1985 report of a Public Health Service Task Force recommended increased research on problems affecting women (Nadel, 1990). In response, NIH established a policy "to ensure that women are included in study populations unless it would be scientifically inappropriate to do so" (p. 2).

Progress seemed insufficient. Finally, pressure was exerted through the mechanism for funding NIH itself. In the 1990 U.S. House of Representatives hearing on the reauthorization of NIH, focus was on the exclusion of women from studies it funded. The opening statement includes: "The result has been a continuous skewing of information, creating a blind spot in our research information" (Waxman, 1990, p. 1). At the same hearing the U.S. General Accounting Office reported that NIH "has made little progress in implementing its policy to encourage the inclusion of women in research study populations" (Nadel, 1990, p. 11). NIH admitted that this "has resulted in significant gaps in knowledge" (p. 2). An example is a study of 22,000 male physicians that found that men who took an aspirin every other day reduced their incidence of heart attacks.

> Institute officials told us women were not included in this study, because to do so would have increased the cost. However, we now have the dilemma of not knowing whether this preventive strategy would help women, harm them, or have no effect. (p. 2)

In response to criticism that women have been excluded routinely from research it funds, NIH created the Office of Research on Women's Health in hopes that this new office will give women's issues the visibility and attention they deserve (Thomas, 1990).

Behavioral science research and theory development, however funded, have been based for the most part on studies of boys and men and have been made "from the standpoint of the Western tradition as it has been created over the centuries largely by men" (Gilligan, Brown, & Rogers, 1990, p. 87). This is clearly true in the area of career development and its interactions with marriage and children. Research was conducted on men, and theoretical constructs were developed from the findings on men.

It is becoming apparent that generalizability to women

cannot be taken for granted. For example, a theoretical model that had been developed from many studies of men performed well in predicting timing of retirement from a set of causal factors and in predicting consequences of retirement in a variety of life arenas—for men. However, the model was not at all successful in predicting either retirement or its consequences among women. According to the investigators, "We need a different theoretical foundation for understanding men's and women's retirement" (Palmore, Burchett, Fillenbaum, George, & Wallman, 1985, p. 121), and they write of "an important agenda for the future": identification of the variables that *can* explain women's retirement and its consequences.

What these investigators found regarding retirement probably holds true in regard to earlier stages of careers and the combination of career with marriage and children. Behavioral scientists may find in the following chapters clues to the ways in which the lives of career women can be studied and hints of the salient variables to include in explanatory models of women's careers, marriages, and children, that predict women's well-being.

Autobiographies of Career Women

The autobiographical approach is appropriate for both purposes of providing information to the young and to the research community. Young women want personal accounts. Research knowledge about women is at a primitive stage compared to that about men. In the early days of the social sciences, the 1930s and 1940s, biographical and autobiographical methods were important in the study of human behavior. With few exceptions, they declined after World War II up through the early 1970s; but recently there has been "a resurgence of interest" in them (McAdams, 1990). Even quantitative-minded investigators see their utility at the "pretheoretical" stage of development of a relatively primitive field such as research on women's lives and careers. It is hoped that researchers of both qualitative and quantitative bent will find in the following chapters clues to fruitful investigation and conceptualization of women's development and well-being, particularly in regard to careers, marriage, and motherhood.

The chapters were written by women identified by peers in their own fields as having successful careers. Authors were selected from a variety of disciplines and arenas to provide a spectrum of career patterns. To ensure a range in regard to the combination of career with marriage and with children, authors were chosen for variety in this area (e.g., never married, married once, married more than once to same/different man; currently divorced, widowed, separated; no children, child or children born/adopted). Their backgrounds are different— wealth and poverty; city, small town, rural; most native-born but two immigrant; most Caucasian but two African-American. They range from daughters of the international intelligentsia to "firsts" in their families or towns to go to college, from priest to atheist.

Patterns of a life cannot be discerned clearly until later maturity, and at that stage a person can look back more dispassionately and report more factually than was possible earlier. One advantage of growing older is increased freedom to express oneself frankly; remarks are no longer inhibited by fear of retribution to husband by his employer or to children by their caregivers or teachers, there are no longer "axes to grind" in what one says: "the older practitioner . . . has no career to build at the expense of others" (Gutmann, 1980). To ensure that the life patterns were well established and clear, and to maximize frankness, authors are beyond or near retirement age.

The chapters exhibit a wide variety of patterns that real career women's lives have taken, in the differing contexts in which these patterns were formed. Therefore, they provide a range of vicarious but realistic experiences for younger persons as they face the building of their own lives and provide material to help investigators devise ways to increase knowledge regarding the development, behavior, and well-being of career women.

To avoid inhibiting the authors' free expression or influencing the book by editorial preconceptions they were given a free hand in writing their personal histories, and no outline was provided. They were asked to record important influences on their lives, particular enablers and/or impediments, major decision points, and how the decisions were made or defaulted. They were asked to assess these influences and decisions and to evaluate the patterns and outcomes of their lives. With the perspective of hindsight, might they do some things differently? Based on the review of their own lives, do they have advice for young women?

Chapters are ordered by authors' dates of birth. This was not anticipated but was possible because everyone spontaneously included dates, contrary to a persistent myth about women. Such ordering provides a look at how the lives of women at various ages were affected by historic events—World War I, the Great Depression, World War II, the Korean War, the civil-rights and feminist movements. The world was different when the first of these authors began her career, different from what it was when the last author set out, and it is vastly different for young women today than it was for any of the authors. This must be kept in mind because the context in which a decision is made influences both the decision and its results. For this reason, authors were asked to include sufficient information about the contexts of their lives so that, in extrapolating to the present, differences due to societal changes and historical events can be taken into account.

References

Fuchs, V. R. (1988). *Women's quest for economic equality.* Cambridge, MA: Harvard University Press.

Gilligan, C., Brown, L. M., & Rogers, A. G. (1990). Psyche imbedded. In A. I. Rabin, R. A. Zucker, R. E. Emmons, & S. Frank (Eds.), *Studying persons and lives* (pp. 86–147). New York: Springer.

Gutmann, D. (1980). Observations on culture and mental health in later life. In J. E. Birren & R. B. Sloane (Eds.), *Handbook of mental health and aging.* Englewood Cliffs, NJ: Prentice-Hall.

Hochschild, A., & Machung, A. (1989). *The second shift: Working parents and the revolution at home.* New York: Penguin.

Matthews, K. A., & Rodin, J. (1989). Women's changing work roles: Impact on health, family, and public policy. *American Psychologist, 44* (11), 1389–1393.

McAdams, D. P. (1990). Unity and purpose in human lives. In A. I. Rabin, R. A. Zucker, R. E. Emmons, and S. Frank (Eds.), *Studying persons and lives* (pp. 148–200). New York: Springer.

Nadel, M. V. (1990). *National Institutes of Health: Problems in implementing policy on women in study populations. Testimony before the House of Representatives.* Washington, D.C.: U.S. General Accounting Office.

Palmore, E. B., Burchett, B. M., Fillenbaum, G. G., George, L. K., & Wallman, L. M. (1985). *Retirement: Causes and consequences.* New York: Springer.

Schwartz, F. N. (1989). Management women and the new facts of life. *Harvard Business Review, 67,* 65–77.

Spencer, G. (1984). *Projections of the population of the United States, by age, sex, and race: 1983–2080.* Washington, D.C.: U.S. Bureau of the Census.

Swoboda, M. J. (1990). Front line news. *University Women, 17* (7). University of Wisconsin System Administration, Office of Equal Opportunity Programs and Policy Studies, Madison, Wisconsin.

Thomas, A. (September 10, 1990). For release. *HHS News.* Washington, D.C.: U.S. Department of Health and Human Services.

Waxman, H. A. (1990). Opening statement. *A hearing on the reauthorization of the National Institutes of Health.* Washington, D.C.: U.S. House of Representatives.

Chapter 2

A Survivor's Career

Wilma Thompson Donahue, Ph.D.

Introduction to Wilma Thompson Donahue

Wilma Donahue took a degree in psychology when that field was still within the philosophy department. She became a clinical psychologist by helping to develop clinical psychology. When demographics on aging were first beginning to strike national consciousness she was a foremost creator of the multidisciplinary field of gerontology. She is equally at home with basic researchers, practitioners in various fields, and political movers and shakers. During three distinct "careers" at the University of Michigan she had great impact upon several governors and the state legislature. She survived her husband's death and her mandatory university retirement by accepting appointment to a White House conference staff. Then she established an international institute in Washington, D.C. In both positions she influenced the nation's administrative and legislative branches. Just as she was beginning to see realization of her dreams for the betterment of life for old people — especially those distressed in mind, body, or estate — the political

Lives of Career Women: Approaches to Work, Marriage, Children, edited by Frances M. Carp. Plenum/Insight, New York, 1991.

tides turned, and funds for social programs dwindled. Still the survivor, she returned to Ann Arbor to establish the Institute on Law and Aging.

Her stature as a gerontologist is acknowledged nationally and internationally. In addition to honorary degrees from St. Thomas' Institute for Advanced Studies in Cincinnati (1965) and Western Michigan University (1970), Donahue has received many awards, including the Gerontology Research Foundation Annual Award for Distinguished Service Work in Gerontology (1957), the Harry S. Kelly Award in Gerontology (1966), the Gerontological Society Achievement Award (1969), the American Association of Retired Persons Distinguished Service Award (1975), the Donald P. Kent Award for Service, Teaching, and Interpretation of Gerontology to the Larger Society (1976), the first University of Michigan Institute of Gerontology Distinguished Service Award (1977), the Association for Gerontology in Higher Education Award for Leadership in the Development of Gerontology in Colleges and Universities (1988), the Ollie A. Randall Award from the National Council on Aging (1982), and the Michigan Women's Hall of Fame Life Achievement Award (1983).

Donahue had a major hand in planning the first National Conference on Aging (1950) as well as the White House conferences on aging in 1961, 1971, and 1981.

She is working with the Michigan Women's Historical Center and Hall of Fame to prepare a videotape to accompany an exhibit of her artifacts and is organizing her papers for the Bentley Historical Library at the University of Michigan. In October 1990 the Institute of Gerontology at the University of Michigan, which she founded, celebrated its twenty-fifth anniversary. She introduced the banquet speaker, Robert N. Butler, M.D., the first director of the National Institute on Aging. He says of her: "She continues to be incisive, even formidable, in intellect and determination. She is one of the great people who have made gerontology grow exponentially in the last twenty-five years."

Readers of yuppie persuasion will find my story boring or amusing or both. I have difficulty sorting out events in my life that would be useful to the sophisticated youth of today. In addition, times are so different than when I set out. A recent incident reminded me sharply of that. A youngish journalist came to interview me. After I had answered her questions for about an hour, and she was preparing to leave, she said, "I suppose you majored in clinical psychology?" With some annoyance I replied, "I was privileged to help develop it." She had not the faintest notion that I had been telling her about events in the early-automobile, pre-radio, pre-etc. society.

To understand the development of a productive life (and I hope mine has been) one must take into account historical events and the prevailing social climate. Regarding my own life, I add luck, good and bad. As I look back my career seems a serendipitous one. I took whatever came to hand, did the best I could with it, and did not mourn or celebrate the consequences. No matter what chance brought me it always seemed the best thing for me to do at the time. As a result, my career appears to have involved "changing" from one role or subject to another. That is true in one sense but not in another. Often, I simply added another enterprise to those underway. Nevertheless, each new one required that I learn the substance and demands of a quite different field. My childhood conditioning is relevant to this pattern.

Growing Up in Iowa (1900–1919)

Describing who I am requires speaking of my parents. My father, born in Ireland, came to the United States with his widowed mother when he was fourteen. He finished high school, and his work life was related to railroads. An outgoing, happy, well-liked person, he provided noncritical consolation if I needed it. My mother, whose family was Virginian, was born in Iowa. When she was two, her mother died, and her father arranged for her adoption by a young farm family. They were a fine couple, and my mother accepted and loved them as if they were her family.

In the tradition of the day, her father believed that girls should not be educated beyond eighth grade. Nor would he let her train to be a nurse, which was her greatest desire. His reason? No decent woman would be a nurse because some patients would be men. Mother had no choice but to accept her situation, so she became an avid self-teacher—a learner for the rest of her life.

My parents were married December 24, 1899, and I joined them December 4, 1900. My mother and I were very close, and she was the major director of the scenario of my development. Brought up to act in her image, I became an avid learner. In fact, we were pal learners. Largely due to her influence, from childhood on I assumed that if I wanted to do something I could, on my own incentive, learn how to do it or how to cause it to come about. When I was small, my mother worked at home as a seamstress—a self-taught skill at which she was an expert— designing as well as making dresses for the wealthy ladies of our town. Later she worked as an accountant for twenty years in a business office and then for a decade on the staff of the state school for girls. After retirement she wasted not a minute. She had always wished to paint, so she painted. Her oils attracted considerable attention from the press, and she received several commissions. As soon as a college offered courses by radio, she enrolled in a succession of them. She assembled a notable collection of geological artifacts. If I had had a choice of mothers I would have taken none other than the lovely, interesting one I was given.

Parents are not the only shapers of the lives of their children. The community plays a role. I grew up in an Iowa town that had begun as a stagecoach station in 1865 and that served a farmer constituency. At the turn of the century a mineral-water spring was found that had medicinal properties. The recently completed Rock Island Railroad brought large numbers of afflicted persons to drink and bathe in the water. Businesses flourished. Hotels were built. Schools, churches, and other public services benefited. The town boasted two banks, two lawyers, two doctors, and so on. It was a good community for those growing up in it.

I became aware of politics when I was twelve. Adventurous, charismatic Teddy Roosevelt was a candidate for president. When anyone promised me his vote (this was before women could vote) I gave him a button to wear. I was quite depressed that my candidate did not win!

My most important career decision turned out to be one I made when I entered high school. Although I could not dream of attending college, I took college preparatory courses. To be safe I also took Normal Teacher Training. My teachers were extraordinary, college-educated old maids who taught us not only book learning but also the values of a good life.

High school was complicated by World War I. Every citizen was expected to help win it. I did Red Cross bandage folding every day after school. On Saturdays I persuaded shoppers to contribute money to the war effort. On evenings I joined the crowd on the railroad platform when the troop train moved by slowly so the soldiers could hand out slips of paper with their addresses and yell, "Please write." My grades were good. I participated in athletics but was second-rate. I had a best friend more gifted than I. My mother made me beautiful dresses for the senior class banquet and for graduation. My proud father strutted a bit. I felt eager to be on with my adult life.

Prelude to the Michigan Years (1919–1922)

World War I ended with exuberance and optimism, although the influenza epidemic swept the country with great loss of life. The suffragists, at long last, won the right of women to vote. The economy flourished. Medical progress was made, especially the bringing of infectious diseases under control. I taught in grade schools. First a country school—one room and eight grades; next, a consolidated school—fifth and sixth grades;

then, eighth grade in a city. I attended Iowa State Teachers College the first two summer vacations and Drake University the third, acquiring credits toward a college degree.

In 1922 I married Lester Joseph Donahue, the only person with whom I had ever wanted to spend a lifetime. A handsome, six-foot-two blond with a quick smile and twinkling blue eyes, he loved people and was very sociable. Now I had a partner who shared all aspects of my life. The commitment lasted forty years until an unexpected heart attack ended the cherished partnership. Our friendship had begun in 1919 on a very hot September afternoon when I was walking from school to the farm where I lived. A hayrack piled high stopped beside me, and a young man called down, "Miss Thompson, would you like a ride?" "Yes, but I can't get way up there." His response, "I will help you." Prophetic words.

When I met Lester he had just been discharged from the Navy, in which he had served all of World War I, mostly in France in an aviation unit. Now he wanted to be a businessman, and I wanted more education. When the Iowa corporation for which he worked promoted him to be its Michigan representative with permission to live in the Michigan community of his choosing, neither of us had any question where that would be— Ann Arbor, where we both could follow our wishes. This was a happy time for us.

The Michigan Years (1923–1970)

The Michigan years began inauspiciously with a train wreck in mid-Iowa, when I was en route to meet my husband who had gone ahead to find a place for us to live. As a consequence I was twenty-four hours late, but after some confusion at the train station we finally found each other, and I saw the beautiful campus of the 1923 University of Michigan.

Education and the Depression (1923–1937)

The university assessed my summer-school credits and enrolled me as a sophomore. Since I had been acclaimed as an artist during high school, teaching days, and at summer schools – winning prizes and recognition – I expected to major in art and aim for a career as a public-school art teacher. I was told to bring samples of my work when I registered. I took two or three that had won prizes. After one look the advisor said, "You have no talent. We cannot admit you to the art school." I went home and threw away all my canvases but one – and that was that!

I had enjoyed a course in psychology at Drake and decided to major in it. Before first semester grades came out I thought I had failed the psychology final exam, so I did not register for the second half of the course. Then I met my psychology teacher on campus. She asked why I was not enrolled, and I explained. She said, "Nonsense! Your grade was the highest. Change your registration and come back." That was a major turning point. I owe much to that teacher. Never again did I needlessly lose self-confidence.

Lester was successful, and we were happily making progress in all ways. Then, suddenly, he became ill and was diagnosed as a diabetic. Insulin was so new that the physician would not prescribe it until Lester's weight dropped to 130 pounds. For the rest of his life we accommodated to the demands of diabetes. Lester continued to work until the Depression. During this time we lived on a farm where Kentucky saddle horses were bred. Lester was happy doing chores, raising a garden, and canning enough food for an army. I learned to ride, and it was fun to help care for newborn colts.

I was able to make only a small salary. At the beginning of my junior year I was offered a student assistantship. From then on I held a part-time appointment in psychology in one capacity or another while I earned A.B., M.A., and Ph.D. degrees. The Depression came just as I was ready to defend my thesis, delaying my Ph.D. until 1937. As I look back now, the Depression may have been a plus in my life. It forced me to develop knowledge in several fields, all people-oriented, which sequentially added to my professional knowledge and furthered new opportunities.

During World War II Lester worked in a bomber plant, and I had his breakfast ready at 3:00 A.M. I had two research assistantships studying the maze learning of white rats and determining whether behaviors of guppy fish were learned or genetically determined. After the Depression Lester sought employment but was unable to find a suitable job. This was very distressing to him, but I included him in the opportunities that were opened to me, and his help enabled me to set and achieve the goals of my career.

Student Health Service, Mental Hygiene Clinic (1937)

I was offered an appointment on the staff of a newly established mental hygiene clinic in the Student Health Service. Although I had no training in mental health, I accepted, delighted to leave my research friends (white rats and guppies) to work under the noted psychiatrist Dr. Theophile Raphael. Thus, I became a clinical psychologist before clinical psychology became a profession. I have done this many times since, that is, went to work to learn a new field. I read the appropriate literature and also arranged to have an internship at the state mental hospital. There, under the guidance of the excellent superintendent, I learned about mental diseases and their management. Raphael also spent time teaching me. There were staff meetings at least weekly. It was a rigorous two-year period of new learning. While the psychiatrists treated severely ill students, I dealt with students who were failing classes due to mental illness, disability, or lack of application. I worked part-time on the mental hygiene staff for ten years. The clinical training and experience expanded my knowledge and gave me professional skills that would be important in the future.

The Institute for Human Adjustment (IHA) (1937–1970)

To understand the institute's role in my life it is helpful to know something of its history and purposes. It was made possible by an endowment from Horace H. Rackham and his wife, Mary, to the university. Horace, born to the family of a Great Lakes sailor, finished high school in rural Michigan and went to Detroit to seek his fortune. While working at menial jobs he read law at night and was admitted to the bar. Henry Ford hired him to draw up incorporation papers for the Ford Motor Company. Ford paid him fifty dollars for the legal service and gave him the opportunity to invest in the company and sit on the board of directors. In 1913 Horace retired to give full time to philanthropy, in which he was joined by his independently wealthy wife.

The Rackhams shared a driving passion to contribute to the "betterment of mankind." The institute fund was to remain flexible, to be used for a variety of purposes or for new needs if they arose. This flexibility led to my spending thirty-one years as a member of the IHA staff—ten with its Psychological Clinic and twenty-one with its Gerontology Program. I report separately on them because for young persons making decisions they illustrate how a new career may be started at any time in life; and, as I found, each new career may prove more interesting than the last.

IHA: Psychological Clinic (1937–1944)

Part of the Rackham gift was used to establish a psychological clinic. Its first director lacked both training and interest in clinical work. To fill that gap he asked me to join the staff, with responsibility for the clinical program. I felt competent to do this because of my training in psychology and my work in the Mental Hygiene Clinic. I accepted with the understanding that I would work part-time in the Mental Hygiene Clinic.

During Stage I of the psychological clinic, in addition to a program of testing schoolchildren, the psychology department began using the clinic as the major field-placement for students in its new master's degree program in clinical psychology. Stage II began with the resignation of the director at the beginning of World War II. I became in charge. There were retrenchment and dwindling as staff and students were called to war. Stage III began post-war, when the university aimed all its resources to help returning veterans. A major increase in the clinic staff was required. I submitted a reorganization plan calling for a Bureau of Psychological Services with four divisions—clinical, testing, research, and counseling. The regents approved the plan and appointed me director. I continued in this role until the late 1940s.

IHA: Gerontology Program (1944–1970)

This program was to begin in 1938 with President Ruthven's appointment of sociologist Clark Tibbitts as the director of the IHA. His first assignment was to develop a plan for a University of Michigan Project for Older People. Tibbitts delivered a proposal to him in 1940. By then the clouds of World War II were absorbing all energies, and Ruthven had no time to even read the proposal. Tibbitts' time was co-opted to direct the University War Board and then the Veterans' Service Bureau. Not until 1944 could he return to his gerontological assignment. With two staff members, Dorothy H. Coons and Woodrow W. Hunter, he conducted a study to learn what older people considered their needs to be. When they were analyzing the results and asked me to help I had my first brush with old age as a field of study.

I had a choice. I could remain with the Psychological Clinic or join the Gerontology Program. I was nearly fifty. I would have to learn another new body of knowledge and its demands.

But here again was a new frontier, something that had lured me all along my path. What assets could I offer? I had taken zoology courses including comparative anatomy and human physiology. I had training in psychology and had experience in clinical psychology. Taking everything together—education, experience, and the attraction of a new field—I decided for the change. Perhaps, at last, I could work for the betterment of mankind on a scale that would have satisfied the Rackhams.

Although I joined the Gerontology Program and gave consultation time to the staff as it began its work, I still worked part-time at both the Student Health Service and the Psychological Clinic. I had a number of commitments in progress. For several years the U.S. Office of Vocational Education and I had collaborated on studies of blindness. We made our findings available through reports (e.g., Donahue, Mechsel, & Meyer, 1951), a conference, and a book (Donahue & Dabelstein, 1950). I tested the first experimental electronic reading device for the blind.

During the years after Tibbitts returned to gerontology, activities were intensive and extensive. We four—Tibbitts, Coons, Hunter, and I—set out to bring older persons to nationwide attention through conferences and books. We stimulated university colleagues to join in our research and service programs. We shared our growing knowledge with the state legislature and agencies. A very successful program was my legacy when I followed Tibbitts as director of the IHA.

In 1951 the regents restructured the Gerontology Program to be organizationally compatible with similar university programs. The name was changed to Division of Gerontology, and I was named director. Now it was necessary for me to devote full-time to its various activities. Lester's health was not good, and I was away from home a great deal, tending to my work. Lester "looked in on" two elderly ladies who lived near us, helped if anything was needed, and provided himself and them companionship.

The mission of the Division of Gerontology included research and demonstration, education and training, and community action and consultation. The annual Michigan conferences continued and, as in the past, were concerned largely with policy, its application, and dissemination to a broad-based national audience. Because these conferences were among the first (if not the first) in the country they attracted a constituency that returned year after year. We tried to make the meetings relevant to the pressing problems of current national affairs.

Through research and demonstration we conducted projects that had significance in the development and application of new theories and technology. It is difficult to choose from the many examples. We established milieu therapy wards for long-hospitalized elderly patients in a mental hospital and proved that environmental treatment, enhanced with good medical care, resulted in many patients recovering their mental health to the point of discharge to live in the community. Another project tested the extent to which financial, personal, and social dependency of aged patients in county hospitals could be reduced by retraining, utilizing vocational and occupational skills, and by enriching social opportunities. The plan involved training patients and staff in hospitals in three communities. The patients improved in health, outlook, and personal and social skills. Each community was inspired to build a new hospital and to provide the kind of care we had demonstrated.

Although the Division of Gerontology did not expect to become deeply involved with academicians, it joined in a project in its category of education and training that involved almost no one except academicians. It began at the 1955 Meeting of the Gerontological Society of America (GSA), when a few members discussed the fact that the need for trained personnel in gerontology was far outstripping the supply and agreed that something must be done. Through the GSA, a recommendation was formulated that called for a training institute in social gerontology to be organized on a cooperative interuniversity basis "for the purpose of furthering the training of more social scientists in the field of aging in order to increase instruction and research in social gerontology." The plan called for establishment of the Institute of Social Gerontology at the University of Michigan. I was named director and had the aid of an executive committee and an interuniversity council, both made up of representatives of the sixteen universities involved in the project. Some of the major accomplishments were (1) the first reference works in social gerontology: *Handbook of Aging and the Individual* (Birren, 1959), *Handbook of Social Gerontology* (Tibbitts, 1960), and *Aging in Western Societies* (Burgess, 1960); (2) syllabuses for five courses; (3) three national surveys; and (4) two month-long summer institutes (in 1958 at the University of Connecticut and in 1959 at the University of California). The institutes provided training for seventy-four faculty members, each from a different college. Many of the trainees introduced gerontology courses into their institutions, and a number of the trainees became national leaders in the field.

Staff members were encouraged to develop their own interests as they related to our overall mission. Hunter became an international authority on preparation for retirement, and Coons established a program in milieu therapy that led to her training of staff in hospitals throughout the country. Coons' book, *Interventions in Dementia*, will be published soon.

On March 9, 1963, his sixty-eighth birthday, Lester died unexpectedly of a heart attack. My partner of forty years was gone, but by then I was able to continue with the career he had helped me plan and develop. His pride in my work was a tremendous stimulus to do ever better, and he never failed the prophetic words of our meeting, "I will help you."

Public Service

Michigan had a succession of excellent governors. Michigan legislators, likewise, were interested in good government and unfailingly gave special attention to older citizens' problems. In this environment it was inevitable that the Division of Gerontology would become involved in state affairs. Governor G. Mennen Williams took the first step in 1948 by appointing a citizen's committee, of which I was a member, to study the problems of older people. The governor implemented a number of our recommendations. Later I was member, then chairman, of the Governor's Interdepartmental Committee on Aging and member of the Legislative Advisory Council on Aging and of the Michigan Commission on Aging. These assignments kept me broadly informed on state matters and enabled me to assist committees and organizations more effectively.

In 1965 the legislature recognized the need for a state-funded agency for research and training in gerontology. The introductory paragraph of Public Act No. 245 reads:

> There may be established at the University of Michigan and Wayne State University, jointly, an institute in gerontology for the purpose of developing new and improved programs for helping older people in this state, for the training of persons skilled in working with the problems of the aged, for research related to the needs of our aging population, and for conducting community service programs in the field of aging. (State of Michigan, 1965, p. 419)

This act was of national importance because Michigan was the first state to have an institute of gerontology as a line item in its budget. I was director of the institute at the University of Michigan and served briefly in that capacity for Wayne State University until the institute could develop its own staff.

During the 1960s I was involved in national public service. President Nixon appointed me for two terms on his Council of Consumer Affairs. President Kennedy asked me to join his Advisory Committee on Taxes, and President Johnson continued that appointment. I attended President Johnson's White House Rose Garden signing of the act that created the Administration on Aging. A week later I was in the Truman Presidential Library in Jefferson City, Missouri, when President Johnson signed the Medicare Act.

The Washington, D.C. Years (1970–1983)

1971 White House Conference on Aging (1970–1973)

The mandatory retirement age at the University of Michigan is seventy. Busy in my office until the last minute, I gave no thought to what I would do after I closed the office door that last night. However, as before, an unexpected opportunity presented itself—an invitation to be on the staff for planning the 1971 White House Conference on Aging. One week I retired, and the next week I went to work in Washington. It was an interesting learning experience, especially working with the Honorable Arthur S. Flemming, chairman of the conference. His skill in dealing with conflicting circumstances calmed the misgivings of the large, powerful organizations on aging. He gave special interest groups an opportunity to present their recommendations. Yet, he made no changes in the original plan that was aimed at increasing knowledge and improving the ability of state and local groups to develop and present their recommendations.

Flemming asked me to stay on to help the post-conference board finish reports and disseminate information about the conference's contributions. I was pleased to do this, but it left no time to decide what to do next. There were possibilities, but each would require that, once again, I engage in new learning.

International Center for Social Gerontology (1973–1983)

Among my resources was a considerable acquaintance with gerontological leaders and programs in Europe. One activity in which I had participated had particular relevance. Dr. J. A. Huet, physician, anthropologist, and former mayor of a Paris suburb, was determined that an international conference be convened to bring as much attention to the social needs of older people as was being given to their health and material needs. He took his concern to the largest union in France and persuaded its president to organize and financially support such a conference, which was then held in Paris in 1968. Clark Tibbitts and I were the U.S. representatives. One result was that the union established a Centre for Social Gerontology with headquarters in Paris. As a member of its board I participated annually in the training conferences in various European countries.

Unexpectedly, the International Center of Social Gerontology (ICSG) was incorporated in New York. But it failed to mature when its founder lost interest. The board, then, asked me to take over. Obviously, this could be useful to me at a time when I was finishing my 1971 White House Conference assignment and had no specific plans for the future. Luck was with me once again. I consulted with my European colleagues. They were enthusiastic about an active ICSG in the United States. To introduce it worldwide we held an international symposium in Washington, D.C., on Housing and Environmental Design for Older Adults. It was planned with the cooperation of the American Institute of Architects and the U.S. departments of Health, Education, and Welfare (HEW), Housing and Urban Development (HUD), and State, and it was convened at the State Department. The symposium was a success in every way. We were urged by the delegates (representing twenty countries from around the world) to develop a program that would integrate our foreign and domestic constituents, and so we did.

The Washington-based ICSG was recognized as a partnership of American and foreign professionals concerned with improving the lives of older people. We quickly launched a busy schedule of activities. A staff of experienced, creative professionals was assembled who took responsibility for various programs. Our agenda included conducting studies and surveys; sponsoring conferences and architectural competitions; preparing and publishing reports; and providing consultation on housing policies, design, and services to governmental and volunteer agencies, city planners, builders, developers, and financial institutions.

A few examples illustrate the scope of activities. We studied congregate housing (shelter with services) in this country and employed a Swiss researcher to examine the same questions in European countries. We held the first national conference in the United States on congregate housing and published the first book on the subject (Donahue, Thompson, & Curren, 1977). This led to the ICSG becoming further involved with Congress and federal agencies in helping develop the concept. We worked with the Department of Agriculture and the Administration on Aging to develop a ten-community project of housing for older rural residents (Beall, Thompson, Godwin, & Donahue, 1981).

One project, repeated in several states, was a Vacation Residential Exchange for older people living in old-age public-housing developments. Two communities would agree to develop the project together and arrange for interested residents to exchange apartments for a ten-day period. Consequently, the entire town often became involved in entertaining the visitors. We developed manuals for communities and organizations to use in planning exchanges. ICSG was especially concerned about deinstitutionalization of elderly mental patients. It convened a National Conference on Housing the Elderly Deinstitutionalized Mental Patient in the Community. The American Psychiatric Association devoted an issue of its *American Psychiatric Quarterly* (1983) to report the conference. Our efforts were too late. By 1982 the political climate had changed radically, and housing special-need populations was no longer a priority.

Going Home to Ann Arbor (1983)

I closed the Washington, D.C. office and opened the Center for Social Gerontology in Ann Arbor, its program being law and aging. Recently retired as president, I remain on the board. Am I retired? If the criterion is, "Do I have a salaried job?" then, "Yes." If the criterion is life-style, "No." I live what I consider a productive life, spending my time in activities I believe will make a difference in the well-being of other persons or of society. I have an office at the Institute of Gerontology at the University, where I am listed as emeritus director because I am credited with being its founder. (I call myself its "icon.") I use my office, as always, for consultation, management of engagements, and especially these days, organizing and preparing materials in my files for the university's Bentley Historical Library. I serve on the boards of various organizations.

Most of my time is spent pondering. Before my so-called retirement I was in the trenches; today I sit behind the line of action and ponder what the consequences of policies or lack of policies are doing to our society. To make sure my pondering is in touch with the times I read. I subscribe to *Time, Newsweek, U.S. News & World Reports,* the *Washington Post,* and my very good local paper. I receive a half-dozen professional journals, some oriented to research, others dealing with action and policy. After I read and ponder I express my opinion by urging the movers and shakers about the way I hope they will proceed. So, in my own way, I have not retired. With the leftover time I manage a small cottage and my wooded yard, which I share with the birds, squirrels, and other furry animals. Although it has been nearly three decades since Lester's death, I cling to continued living in the little cottage where we made our home, because it is filled with memories of the happy times we had together. Thus, I am not lonely. My friends and neighbors keep watch but respect my independent way of life.

References

Beall, G. T., Thompson, M. M., Godwin, F., & Donahue, W. T. (1981). *Housing older persons in rural America.* Washington, D.C.: International Center for Social Gerontology.

Birren, J. E. (Ed.). (1959). *Handbook of aging and the individual.* Chicago: University of Chicago Press.

Burgess, E. W. (Ed.). (1960). *Aging in Western societies.* Chicago: University of Chicago Press.

Coons, D. H. (in press). *Interventions in dementia: Designing and implementing innovative special care units.* Baltimore, MD: Johns Hopkins Press.

Donahue, W. T., & Dabelstein, D. H. (1950). *Psychological diagnosis and counseling for the adult blind.* New York: The American Foundation for the Blind.

Donahue, W. T., Mechsel, S. G., & Meyer, L. (1951). *Research suggestions on psychological problems associated with blindness.* Washington, D.C.: Federal Security Agency.

Donahue, W. T., Thompson, M. M., & Curren, D. J. (Eds.). (1977). *Congregate housing for older people.* Washington, D.C.: United States Government Printing Office.

Special Issue. (1983). *American Psychiatric Quarterly, 55,* 2/3, Summer/Fall.

State of Michigan. (1965). *Public acts.* Lansing: Michigan State Legislature.

Tibbitts, C. (Ed.). (1960). *Handbook of social gerontology.* Chicago: University of Chicago Press.

Chapter 3

The Career of an African-American Woman Artist

Lois Mailou Jones

Introduction to Lois Mailou Jones

According to Edmund Barry Gaither, curator at the Museum of Fine Arts in Boston and director of the Museum of the National Center of Afro-American Artists in Washington, D.C., Lois Mailou Jones is "one of the most distinguished artists of the twentieth century" (Gaither, 1990, p. vii). He adds:

> Not only did she overcome the barriers imposed by racial and gender prejudices and discrimination, she asserted the integrity of her own highly developed artistic gifts and thereby wrote herself into the art history of our century. (p. viii)

Her first solo exhibition was held in the garden of a home on Martha's Vineyard Island, Massachusetts, during the summer of

Lives of Career Women: Approaches to Work, Marriage, Children, edited by Frances M. Carp. Plenum/Insight, New York, 1991.

1923, when she was seventeen. Her most recent (1990) one-woman exhibit, "The World of Lois Mailou Jones," was held over at Meridien House International in Washington, D.C. because of its popularity. Now it is touring the United States for two years. In the intervening years there have been many exhibits of her work, and she has received many honors.

She has lectured and her works have been exhibited not only widely throughout the United States, but also in places such as Paris, Ethiopia, Kenya, Congo-Kimshasa, Nigeria, Ghana, Liberia, Sierra-Leone, Senegal, Haiti, Lagos, Japan, and Brazil. Permanent collections of her paintings are in such prestigious institutions as the Metropolitan Museum of Art in New York, the Boston Museum of Fine Arts, and in Washington, D.C. at the Corcoran Gallery of Art, the Phillips Collection, the Hirshhorn Museum and Sculpture Garden, and the National Museum of American Art.

Lois Mailou Jones was one of ten African-American artists honored by President Jimmy Carter at the White House for Outstanding Achievement in the Arts (1980). In 1981 she received the Honorary Doctor of Humane Letters degree from Suffolk University, Boston. The Massachusetts House of Representatives cited her in recognition of "her contribution, preservation, promotion, and development of the universality of art" (1983). In 1984 "Lois Jones Day" was declared in Washington, D.C. The Women's Caucus for Art at Cooper Union, New York, presented her their Outstanding Award in the Visual Arts (1986). In 1986 the Massachusetts College of Art awarded her an honorary Ph.D. in fine arts, and in 1987 Howard University awarded her an honorary Ph.D. in the humanities. The city of Annapolis, Maryland presented her a Certificate of Honorary Citizenship (1987). The *Washington Post Magazine* commissioned her to paint "We Shall Overcome" for its April 3, 1988 issue.

Widowed since 1982, she maintains a home in Washington, D.C. and studios on Martha's Vineyard Island, Massachusetts and in Haiti, where she continues to work and develop her artistry. Although she suffered two severe heart attacks during the preparation of her chapter, immediately upon its completion she left to paint for the summer on Martha's Vineyard.

Parental Influences

In my early childhood my parents were sensitive to my artistic endeavors, encouraged me to pursue an art career, and provided me with materials that channeled my creativity. Very early they gave me colored crayons, and at seven I had my first set of watercolor paints, still my favorite medium. My mother, especially, took pride in my work. She was my mentor and primary source of inspiration, and she encouraged my development as I began to structure my life and goals as an aspiring artist. Her support gave me the confidence I needed to sustain me through the years ahead, determined to gain recognition in a field where keen competition limited its achievers. She had considerable artistic sensitivity and talent herself. Our home was flooded with colorful, freshly cut flowers all year round. My mother was a talented and enterprising beautician, and as another source of income she created and adorned hats. "My Mother's Hats" is the subject of one of my paintings.

Much of my drive—wanting to be someone, having ambition—surely comes from my father. Both he and my mother were born in Paterson, New Jersey. They lived in the same neighborhood, attended the same school, were childhood sweethearts, and married young. About the turn of the century they moved to Cambridge, Massachusetts. He attended night classes at Suffolk Law School while working as superintendent of a large office building and received his law degree in 1915.

Developmental Milieu and Education

I was born in Boston, a city with a long tradition of art history. With the aid of four annual scholarships I attended the High School of Practical Arts (HSPA), where my foundation in art was established. My talent was doubly strengthened as I was awarded four successive scholarships to attend the high school's vocational drawing class from 2:00–4:00 P.M. after HSPA hours were over and on Saturdays at the Boston Museum of Fine Arts (1919–1923). These sessions at the museum anchored my decision to follow a career in the visual arts. I made the museum my home, drawing from works in it until it closed. During this time I first addressed the concept of heritage. As apprentice to a costume designer and professor at the Rhode Island School of Design I assisted in designing costumes for the Ted Shawn School of Dance and a branch of the Bragiotte School in Boston. I worked Saturdays and after 4:00 P.M. on school days, designing costumes and, especially, masks. I was introduced to Africa through creating these masks.

After graduating from HSPA and the vocational drawing class I was awarded the Susan Minot Lane Scholarship to the School for the Boston Museum of Fine Arts for four years. While a student there I roamed through the museum galleries admiring the works of the old masters. I was particularly inspired by the watercolors of Winslow Homer and the impressionist paintings of John Singer Sargent. Their explorations of nature reinforced my own love of the landscape and the ocean, which had its beginnings on Martha's Vineyard Island, where I spent practically every summer of my childhood.

Our family had a home on the Island, and my mother, as a cosmetologist, had private customers whom she attended. Most of them were wealthy people who would invite me to make watercolors of flowers in their gardens or to see their art books. This exposure had a lot to do with my development as an artist. I recall painting a seascape at Menemsha, one of my favorite spots on the Island. Jonas Lie, president of the National Academy of Design in New York, observed me at work. He offered me constructive criticism followed by high praise for my watercolor technique. It was also at Martha's Vineyard that I met the famed African-American sculptor Meta Warwick Fuller, who had studied in Paris and worked in the studio of Rodin. She told me that if I wanted to be successful in my career, I would have to go abroad. America was not ready to accept us, women and blacks, as artists.

Upon receiving a diploma from the Museum School with honors (1927), I did graduate work on scholarship at the Designer's Art School (1928) and the Boston Normal Art School (now Massachusetts College of Art) (1928). I continued my studies at Harvard University (1929), Columbia University (1934–36), and Howard University, where I received the A.B. in Art Education (1945).

Career Development

I began my career as a freelance designer in Boston and New York with F.A. Foster Company and the Schumaker Company. I would submit about a dozen designs from which two or three would be selected, purchased, reproduced, and sold all over the country. It was exciting to see my designs transformed into patterns for draperies and other fabrics, but as a textile designer for these companies, my name was never known or affiliated with the patterns. It was standard practice for textile designers to be anonymous, but I was determined to become known as an artist of merit and to make a contribution to the history of American art. I realized that for this to happen I would have to become a painter. I decided that becoming a serious painter was my goal and immediately turned to painting.

In 1928 I applied for a position as an assistant at the Boston Museum School, but there was no opening. The director mentioned that I probably should be thinking of going south to help my people. This was rather shocking to me because in Boston we did not know much about the South. We knew about Fisk and the singing groups and a little bit about Tuskegee. We did not think highly of the schools in the South, so I was embarrassed at his idea of sending me there after all of my exposure in Boston. About the same time an outstanding educator lecturing to college youth in Boston emphasized the need for African-American men and women to take their talents to the youth in the South. When I was invited to establish the art department at the Palmer Memorial Institute, one of the first preparatory schools for African-Americans in the nation, in Sedalia, North Carolina, I could no longer ignore the "go south" message. Once there I not only established the art department curriculum, served as chairperson, and taught art classes, I also taught dancing, coached the basketball team, and played piano for Sunday morning services.

After two years I was recruited by the head of the art department at Howard University in Washington, D.C., who had been impressed with the quality of my students' work when he came to lecture at the Palmer Institute. I joined "the family" in 1930 as professor of design and watercolor painting, and I remained there until my retirement in 1977. My work has evolved stylistically over the last five decades. However, the elements of design, structure, and color are basic in my compositions, whether they are renderings of nature, or the human figure, or creative paintings. Environment has also been an important factor in my work.

Environmental Impacts

During the summer of 1934 I enrolled at Columbia University in New York to return to the study of masks of various African groups and to broaden my study to include masks of other non-Western cultures, including American Indian and Eskimo. That summer I met two persons who were to be important in my life. One was the African dancer Assadat DeFora, who directed a troupe of dancers in New York. I designed masks for DeFora's troupe and attended rehearsals in order to coordinate the costumes with the movement of the dancers. The other was Haitian graphic artist and designer Louis Vergniaud Pierre-Noel, who was also a student at Columbia. After summer school was over we corresponded for a time, but lost contact and did not meet again until 1953, when Pierre visited Washington, D.C. Then, after a whirlwind courtship, we were married in Cabris, France.

Paris had attracted me since my formative years in Boston, and I was profoundly affected by the advice from the famed African-American sculptor, and similar advice from a noted musician and composer of Negro spirituals, to the effect that if I wanted to find professional recognition I would have to travel to Paris as they had done.

For my first sabbatical (1937) I chose a year of study at the Academie Julian and was able to do so with the aid of a General Education Board Fellowship. During that period I painted as an impressionist. My studio in Montparnasse and my classes at the Academie were extensions of each other. Unencumbered by the constraints of race for the first time, I felt free to create. A vintage year of oil paintings resulted. The scenes of old Parisian streets, houses, and gardens, and still lifes and landscapes (my favorite subjects) were rendered in misty tones of silvery grays and a low-keyed palette. It was a revelation to have a number of these paintings accepted for inclusion in the exhibitions at the Salon des Artists Francais, the Galerie de Paris, and the Galerie Charpentier, purely on merit.

While painting on the Seine near Pont Marie I had the good fortune to meet Emile Bernard, the "father of French symbolist painting," who greatly encouraged me by predicting that I would go far as a painter. I visited his beautiful studio overlooking Pont Marie and had the thrill of studying his work and his collection of Japanese prints, which had inspired him and his colleagues Van Gogh and Gauguin to introduce the new movement of symbolism into French painting. These were important moments in the development of my career.

I had missed the opportunity to meet the master painter Henry O. Tanner, an African-American who lived in Paris and who died just four months before I arrived. However, it was fortunate that I did meet the African-American painter Albert

Smith, who decided to live in Paris after having served in the United States Army during World War II. He was amazed at the forty-plus works I had completed at the close of my year in Paris. He assisted me with the packing of my paintings and insisted that on my return to the United States I let him know how my work was received. He had returned to New York after painting for several years in Paris, with the hope of marketing his works. However, because of his color, no gallery would accept his works. He went back to Paris, never to return to the States again.

I was more fortunate on my return to the United States, as the Vost Galleries in Boston gave me a one-woman show (1939), which was very successful. However, exhibition of my work was not always easy or guaranteed. In order to have my work shown in major exhibits I would pack my work and ship it to the National Academy of Design or the Philadelphia Academy of the Fine Arts. In this way they never knew that I was black. In one case (1941) I asked a white friend to submit a canvas, "Indian Shops, Gay Head," a scene from Martha's Vineyard, to a Corcoran Gallery of Art show. The work was accepted and was awarded the Robert Woods Bliss Prize, a prestigious honor for oil painting. I felt uneasy about appearing in person to receive the award. Instead, I chose to receive it in the mail.

In the summer of 1938 I traveled throughout Italy, studying the architecture and visiting museums and art galleries. This augmented my reservoir of rich memories to chronicle with paint upon canvas.

My meeting with Dr. Alain Locke, the first black Rhodes Scholar, philosopher, and an early advocate of "negritude" (black consciousness), caused a change in the subject matter I painted. He congratulated me on my Parisian street scenes and informed me of his plan to use one of them in his forthcoming book, *The Negro in Art* (1940). He advised me to introduce the black subject more forthrightly in my paintings, along with the arts of our ancestral heritage. In the book he wrote:

> The Negro artist, doubly sensitive as an artist and as an oppressed personality, has often shied off from his richest pasture at the

slightest suspicion of a Ghetto gate . . . Yet after pardonable and often profitable wanderings afield for experience and freedom's sake, the Negro artist, like all good artists, must and will eventually come home to the materials he sees most and understands best. (p. iii)

He predicted that African art would prove as marked an influence on the contemporary work of black artists as it had on that of the leading modernists: Picasso, Modigliani, Matissse, Epstein, and others. His advice was convincing, and as a result I created works that focused on the black experience. "Dans un Cafe a Paris" in 1938, "Jennie" (a black girl cleaning fish) in 1943, "Mob Victims" (a man about to be lynched) in 1944, and many others were created as a direct result of his challenge and influence. I call the 1940s my "Locke period."

During the 1940s I continued to spend summers at Martha's Vineyard, escaping from city life to the daisies, buttercups, clean air, and ocean waters I had loved since childhood.

Another environmental influence was stimulated by my first trip to Haiti. I went as a guest of the Haitian government to serve as instructor at the Centre d'Art in Port-au-Prince. This memorable visit, along with my marriage to the distinguished Haitian artist, Louis Vergniaud Pierre-Noel in 1953, transformed my life and my art. From 1954 on I made regular trips to Haiti and fell increasingly in love with the place and its people. Haiti is full of art. The color, the light—everything was so different that my whole style changed. The colorful marketplaces, the voodoo rituals, the landscape, the people, and the exotic atmosphere produced highly keyed colors in my compositions. Haiti was a distinct contrast to the misty, gray skies and muted colors of Paris. The resulting works were presented in a one-woman exhibition at the Centre d'Art and the following year at the Pan-American Union in Washington, D.C. The exhibition was in honor of the visit of President and Madame Magloire as guests of President Dwight Eisenhower in 1953. On this occasion I was present to receive the Diplome et Decoration de l'Order National "Honneur et Merite au Grade de Chevalier" from the Haitian government. It was an honor that I treasure to this day. For over thirty years Haiti has been a fertile source of inspiration to my work.

In 1969 I received a grant from Howard University to conduct research in Africa. I traveled to eleven African countries (Sudan, Kenya, Ethiopia, Congo, Nigeria, Ghana, Ivory Coast, Liberia, Sierra Leone, Senegal, and Dahomey), compiling biographical material on African artists, photographing works of art, interviewing artists, and visiting museums. I gave the extensive slide collection and archival material to the university. Probably because of the black art movement underway in the United States the United States Information Service asked me to lecture on African-American art and artists and to act as cultural ambassador in recruiting African artists to come to the United States. This trip greatly influenced my artistic style, proving to be a revelation and a rich experience. It was a thrill to see the ancestral arts in their original settings and in the museums and galleries. Since 1971 my work has reflected the powerful impact of this close association. By combining the motifs from various regions of Africa, I try to explore on canvas a sense of the underlying unity of all of Africa.

Some of my paintings that show a strong African influence were created in my studio in Haiti. For me, Haiti expresses the links, ties, roots of Mother Africa. For me, Africa, black America, and Haiti are one.

Coming Full Circle

In the summer of 1989 I went again to France, to the lovely area around Grasse and Cabris, a return to a milieu that had so liberated and invigorated me long ago, to appease my continuing fascination with nature and the fleeting beauty of place and with some thought of "completing a circle" in my career. Not surprisingly, curators say that the resulting works are reminiscent of the impressionist/post-impressionist style that I abandoned more than thirty years ago.

Looking back at my painting over a period of more than sixty years, I feel that my work has come full circle. Early in my career I had designed masks for the Ted Shawn Dancers and designed fabric patterns. Currently, some of my works involve the themes of African and Caribbean masks and other icons. These works are symbols of the great power, full of mysticism, that I discovered in Africa and Haiti and are aimed to alert Americans to the richness of the cultures and the arts of Africa and Haiti. Usually I use acrylic or sometimes mixed media on canvas for these works of masks and other icons. I use watercolor, still my pet medium, to portray my Martha's Vineyard home and scenes from my travel abroad, especially in France.

Recognition of my career of sixty years is coming late. During its span, events like the retrospective exhibition "Reflective Moments," curated by Barry Gaither, marked the first exhibition by a black artist to be shown at the Boston Museum of Fine Arts in 1973. The second retrospective followed at the Phillips Collection in Washington, D.C. in 1979.

My more recent (1990) retrospective, "The World of Lois Mailou Jones," curated by Professor Tritobia Benjamin, director of the recently named Lois M. Jones and James L. Wells Gallery at the Howard University Galleries of Art, was presented here in Washington at Meridian House International. Its chronological arrangement of over seventy paintings allowed the viewer to walk through the life of the artist. The criticism of the show was indeed gratifying and, I believe, well deserved after sixty years of constant production.

The road has not always been easy. I have based my career on excellence, striving for the highest standards of the art world. My work mirrors the direction and the myriad changes undergone by African-American artists. It is my sincere hope that the accomplishments made throughout my career will be viewed in the broader cultural context of American art.

References

Gaither, E. B. (1990). Introduction. In *The world of Lois Mailu Jones*. Washington, D.C.: Meridien House International.

Locke, A. (Ed.). (1940). *The Negro in art: A pictorial record of the Negro artist and of the Negro theme in art*. New York: Hacker.

Chapter 4

The Political Life

Margaret Collins Schweinhaut

Introduction to Margaret Collins Schweinhaut

Senator Schweinhaut is the longest-serving woman—and, according to many of her constituents, the most admired member—in the Maryland state legislature. She has been a member of the General Assembly for over thirty years and, since 1961, a member in the Senate. For twelve years she has chaired the Executive Nominations Committee, which reviews all gubernatorial appointments. In 1971 she was named to the Legislative Policy Committee that controls the operations of the Senate, served in this important capacity for eleven years, and was reappointed to it in 1986. Currently, she is also on the Judicial Proceedings Committee.

As a member of the Maryland legislature Senator Schweinhaut's achievements reflect the depth and breadth of her concerns. To cite a few examples, she was author of the legislation that created a statewide public defender system; leader of the successful effort to establish a Maryland Commission on Aging and

Lives of Career Women: Approaches to Work, Marriage, Children, edited by Frances M. Carp. Plenum/Insight, New York, 1991.

chairman of that commission for twenty-four years; author of an amendment that significantly broadened educational opportunities for the handicapped and disabled; chief proponent of legislation that outlawed drug paraphernalia; sponsor of legislation that broadens the protection afforded to school teachers who report instances of drug abuse; responsible for the enactment of a nursing home patient bill of rights; co-sponsor of legislation creating an office for a special prosecutor to investigate and prosecute official wrong-doing; and responsible for the enactment of an innovative program of sheltered housing for older citizens, enabling many elderly persons to maintain independent living.

In addition to her broad and intensive legislative efforts, Senator Schweinhaut is a long-time member of the League of Women Voters, a board member of both the National Council of Senior Citizens and the National Council on Aging, and a former consultant to the secretary of the Department of Health, Education, and Welfare. St. Joseph's College awarded her an honorary Doctor of Laws degree. She has been recognized for her outstanding service by such diverse groups as the Montgomery County Association for Retarded Citizens, the Veterans of Foreign Wars, the Knights of Columbus, the Cerebral Palsy Association, and the Bethesda–Chevy Chase Chamber of Commerce.

She is the mother of two daughters and has seven grandchildren. Now widowed, she lives in Kensington, Maryland, with her twin sister Marie McGuire Thompson, and continues to serve with distinction in the state legislature. She is seen as unbeatable in her district. Her strongest challenge came in 1978, but when her opponent suggested she was too old, the tides turned into a landslide for her. In a recent interview for the *Washington Post* Senator Schweinhaut brought up the 1990 elections and said she will probably seek re-election. The only concession she makes to a long-standing visual deficiency is to have a staff member read written materials aloud to her. She dictated her chapter on tape.

I have been a member of the Maryland state legislature, representing Montgomery County, since 1955, serving now in the upper house, the Senate. How did I get there? What did I do? Do I have anything to say that will help young people, especially young women, who wish to enter the political arena?

I will describe some factors in my background and experiences that seem relevant, and point out some opportunities open to young persons now that were not available when I started out.

Early Preparation

It is very important to have a political base in the geographic sense. In that I was fortunate. My family ties to Montgomery County extend without a break back to 1792, when one of my ancestors settled there to work on the C & O Canal. For business reasons, my father moved the family to Georgetown, D.C., but he always felt misplaced. As we were growing up he frequently apologized for the fact that his children were not born in Maryland. Georgetown was once part of Maryland, which made it more acceptable as a birthplace and residence. My father insisted that we children understand we were Marylanders, though we spent only summers there. I became a resident of Maryland in 1929, but my husband and I and two small children moved back into the District of Columbia, where we stayed until 1940, when we moved to Maryland permanently.

It also helps to have a member of your family who is interested in politics and who will instruct and encourage you in carrying on that interest. I was raised in Washington, D.C., where my father was a wholesale grocer, but my twin sister and I spent summers with our grandfather on his farm in Maryland. Grandfather was deeply interested in Maryland in general and Montgomery County in particular. He knew the history and, when we were fairly young, insisted that my sister and I also become familiar with it. Grandfather talked to us about it often. He had a marvelous library and, in addition to encouraging us to use it, he read to us things that he found particularly important.

In addition to a solid historical background, keeping up with latest developments is important. Here again, Grandfather played an important role. He insisted that we learn how and continue every day to read all the newspapers available, from cover to cover if possible. As a result, my sister and I were consistently A students in current affairs. Newspapers are very important—not that you believe everything you read in them—but they bring the world to you in a way that nothing else does. So, with or without a grandfather to insist, you must learn to read newspapers carefully and critically.

Politics has a practical side that must be mastered if one is to succeed. Grandfather's influence played a role here, too. On the Sunday before the Tuesday election every four years he held a political meeting in his home. Men from all nearby farms came to hear what he thought was the best vote. My sister and I were allowed to sit in if we did not move or speak. (Women could not vote at the time.) I was enthralled by what went on in those sessions. Observing them taught me a great deal about how to approach and influence voters.

As in most careers, education is a plus in politics. I attended George Washington University in Washington, D.C., and I studied at the National University School of Law before marriage.

Wife, Mother, and Political Volunteer

My husband was United States district judge for the District of Columbia. He was born and raised in the District of Columbia, where, in those days, people did not have the vote. Probably because of that background, he was not interested in politics and had no political affiliation or connections. My later political interests and activities were the only politics that were ever in our house.

We became the parents of two daughters. During the early years of our marriage, when the children were little, I was involved primarily with the babies, golf, and bridge. That was the pattern of the day. There is nothing wrong with that pattern now. For me it seemed natural. As a young woman I had no ambition to run for public office, though I did have an interest in politics. Because of this interest I evolved into a concerned, hopefully contributing, citizen.

The first step toward what turned out to be my career was taken when my interest in politics stimulated a desire to help elect Franklin Roosevelt when he ran for the presidency for the first time, in the early 1930s. Toward this end I offered to do volunteer work at the Democratic National Headquarters for two or three months. I worked without pay at a desk in the headquarters office. I filled envelopes, looked up voting records, and greeted people who walked in the door. I did anything that came along. Whatever they needed an extra pair of hands or an extra pair of eyes to do I did. In that way I learned who were the important people in the political arena and who was coming to the Democratic National Committee to talk with various people on various topics. I met congressmen, senators, hopeful candidates, and people who wanted appointments to various positions, as well as many interesting people on the staff and among the volunteers. If there is a place where you meet all kinds of interesting men and women, it is in the arena of politics. I found great interest in all of this, and it added excitement to my life.

I was able to do volunteer work because I had full-time, live-in help. I was free to go whenever and wherever I wanted. Just as I could go to play bridge or golf, or do church work, I could volunteer at the Democratic National Headquarters without any problem in regard to home responsibilities. My volunteer work was not a strain on the household because I had someone there who was caring for the children, preparing dinner, and so on.

By the third Roosevelt campaign I had established myself at the Democratic National Committee. In the last six weeks of the campaign the Democratic National Committee moved from Washington, D.C. to New York. I was invited to go along and involve myself with what women were doing in the campaign. (My sister came from Texas to take care of the children.) One of the publicity stunts was to have women go to heavily crowded areas, get up on stepladders, wave American flags, and speak to the crowds through megaphones about why they should vote for Roosevelt for a third term. I was asked to be a stepladder speaker, and I found it very difficult. Simply the thought of it scared me. But I found that New York crowds were no different from any other crowds, and I stood on the stepladder, waved the flag, and spoke through the megaphone, voicing the issues in that campaign.

We had a great time and many funny experiences. One day a fracas began within the crowd that had gathered around, between those who were for Roosevelt and those who were for Wendell Willkie. The police asked us to please move down a block so they could quell the near riot that was starting. There was lots of excitement in that trip, and it proved to be a valuable learning experience for me. On the practical side, because I was still volunteering, I was fortunate just to have my expenses paid.

I was deeply interested in my volunteer work, and I did a good job. During the 1940s a man who had observed my work as a volunteer, and who lived in my county, went to the county officials and said, "Look, you've got something here. She's very good at this game and you ought to pick her up and bring her into the democratic fold." The county officials did not just take his word, but talked with me themselves. However, his suggestion was the reason for their invitation. My opportunity was based directly on the volunteer work and on the fact that someone in the volunteer office knew I could do a good job and, therefore, thought I should get involved at the county level as a political person. I had been perfectly happy with volunteer work, and to run for political office myself had never occurred to me. However, when the door opened, I did not hesitate to walk in.

When I was invited to run for the first time it was a closed system. A group of people completely controlled who could run and who could not. In 1949 or early 1950 they wanted to have a woman on the ticket and asked me to run for office in the house of delegates. Not many women were running for public office then; we were rarities. After I said that I did want to run for office the first question they asked when they interviewed me was, "What organizations do you belong to? First of all, what church do you attend?" I told them. Then, "What other organizations do you belong to?" By that time, in addition to golf and bridge, I had become deeply involved with organizations such as the League of Women Voters. I named them all. "Do the people at these meetings think well of you? Have you held office in these organizations? Have you worked in them?" Fortunately, I had, for example, during the Second World War, handled food stamps for the school my children attended. I listed these activities for the interviewers. They looked over the list and said, "If you were running for office, could you go before these organizations and speak to them about the campaign?" Of course I could.

At last they were satisfied that I had enough breadth of experience and enough contacts through organizations so that the people who I knew felt good about me could be also convinced to support the people with whom I was running. Satisfying them about my organizational background was the first and the largest step on my journey. In addition to volunteer activity in political headquarters, it pays to join appropriate organizations and gain leadership status within them to build a political career.

The second question from my interviewers that first time I ran for office was: "Do you have any way of raising funds to pay some of the expense of the printing, the postage, the signs, the newspaper advertisements, all the things that make a campaign very costly?" I admitted that I did not have too much money but said I thought I could carry my own weight in the matter of funds if they would tell me what they thought my share might be. They gave me a ballpark estimate, and I went home to my husband and said, "If I run for this office it is going to cost us $6000. Can I do it?" My husband thought about it for a long time. Then he said, "I think we can do it if it's no more than that, and I assume there will be some fund-raising activities." I assured him that there would be fund-raisers. He settled it: "OK, if you want to do it, go ahead." I gave this information to the committee.

I had answered, I hoped satisfactorily, all of the interviewers' questions. All I could do was wait. The tension was released by a telephone call during a Fourth of July party at a friend's house. A woman lawyer, very prominent in the county and a member of the local Central Democratic Committee, phoned to say that the selection committee would like me to be on the ticket and wanted me to think about it and let them know. I consulted with my husband and called them back the next day to say that I was indeed interested. Although I had never attended a session of the state legislature and knew very little about it, I was willing to give it a try. The next day I went to the headquarters office and met all the people who wanted to run for office, and we went as a group to sign up to be candidates and pay our fees. (At that time it was twenty-five dollars.)

The First Campaign as a Candidate

I was running for office! I did not know what was going to happen or how, but I was ready to start. One of the things I was given to do, probably because I was "the new kid on the block," was neighborhood canvassing: "Go house to house, starting in your own neighborhood, and talk to people at their doors. Tell them about yourself, and see if any of them would be interested in inviting people in to have coffee and talk with you, to help you." I was scared to death! I had never done anything like this, approaching strangers and such—but it was part of my being tested as to what I could do and how well I could do it. So I had to do it. I had no choice.

Believe me, I was extremely fearful in the first two or three hours as I knocked on doors, and when people answered I am sure that I stammered and was very ineffective. But after a while I overcame the fear and realized that others had done it, and so could I. The people behind the doors were just folks like me. Initially, it was tough, but that phase of fear and ineffectiveness passed quickly, and my confidence increased. That confidence was transferred to the persons to whom I was talking, and they, in turn, listened to me. Yet, at every door I approached I continued to wonder what sort of reception I would get and I tried to be prepared for whatever it might be.

Since my name is a difficult one I was advised to have a calling card made up. You have to see my name in writing before you can remember it. I had cards made up with my name that said I was candidate for the Maryland House of Delegates. I went door to door and rang doorbells, saying, "I am your neighbor. I live down the corner there (or wherever). I want you to know that I am running for office—I want to be a delegate to the state legislature—and I certainly would like to have your vote." I left my card with them and went on to the next house and did the same thing. At some houses people were hospitable, and at others they said, "Not interested," and closed the door. After a while I got used to that. I never became accustomed to the occasional dog that ran out and threatened to do me harm. In every such case I left as quickly as possible and did not try to impress the animal.

Whatever happened, every day I canvassed two or three blocks. When I got home I wrote down my experiences and the names of the people I had talked to, if I was able to get them. The next day I went to another area and canvassed two or three more blocks. Gradually, I began to find out what the people were interested in as far as the state legislature was concerned. Of course, many of them were not interested or did not even know what the state legislature did. In any event, I talked with them about what kinds of things the state legislature did and told them that I wanted to be part of it.

In addition to house-to-house canvassing, I gave public speeches. I remember one early incident in particular: We candidates had to do our speeches in three minutes because everyone wanted a chance to speak. I had worked very hard on my speech and had it down pat. I thought it was pretty good. As I came off the platform down into the audience a woman rushed up and said, "What is your stand on vivisection?" Well, of the many issues I knew about and could talk about, vivisection was not one. I said, "I have no position." Her response was, "Then I cannot vote for you. I am interested in vivisection and how people feel about it, and if you have no feeling about it, then I cannot vote for you." As she left me another woman came up and said, "Young woman, you made a very nice speech. However, when you sat down you crossed your legs, and I thought, 'No lady would cross her legs,' so I just want to tell you that I am not going to vote for you." That was a rather unhappy beginning. I had to learn that this kind of reaction could happen. I tried to profit, for future performances, from useful criticisms people had made and to forget the rest.

During this campaign I was on radio for the first time, along with my fellow candidates. (Today it would be television.)

All during the spring, all during the summer, and up until November in the fall, I worked every day as hard as I had ever worked in my life, and when the votes came in that November ninth, all of our group had lost. I was heartbroken. I thought I would never get over it. I could not believe that you could put that much into a campaign and lose. But I did lose. At the time the loss was very bitter.

It was difficult to accept the fact that all of our funds and all of our effort had gone for nothing. Actually, my share was less than $5000. Friends had sent contributions, and I had sent out a letter asking for contributions from people I knew, so about half of it was paid by contributions. The remainder came out of our family budget.

Looking back, I believe that the most important contribution I made to my political career was losing the campaign in

1950. I learned more during the days preceding that loss than I have learned since. I learned what to do, what not to do, how to approach people, how to receive their support when it is offered, and how to convince them to give you their support when it is not immediately forthcoming. The basis of my political career was the four years which culminated in losing the election. In terms of my personal development in how to conduct a campaign and what politics are all about, these were the richest years of my life.

I had become even more interested in politics, and I decided that if I had another opportunity, I would try again. So, for four years I was a precinct chairman, that is, chairman of a small area in my community. I canvassed again to let everyone know that I was their precinct chairman and that if they had any problem, to please get in touch with me. It was back to the door-to-door operation to organize my precinct until it was a good one. People behind those doors knew who I was, and I knew who they were and what their political interests were. I worked hard to organize my precinct because I was determined to run again and win.

Election and Re-Election to Public Office

It was 1954. Again, the people who were building the ticket— that is, deciding who would best help everyone on the ticket get elected—asked me to run. I filed again, paid my twenty-five dollars again, and started working again. All of my group worked very hard, and this time, all of us won. One difference from four years earlier was that we had become known in the interim. Name recognition is very important in politics. If you keep your name before the public long enough, many people will recognize that name when they come to vote. They may not know why, but they do and, therefore, give you their vote. So for this and probably other reasons, all of us won.

When I was first elected to the state legislature I was forty-nine years old. Both my children were off to college, and at home there was just my husband and me. He was a very encouraging person. He had said that if I wanted to be in politics, he would give me his full support. And he always did. Without genuine understanding of your need to be involved and full support from your husband, if you have one, a political career would be very difficult.

I was in the House of Delegates seven years and in the Senate one year. Then I lost the re-election. By then I had done some work with a nonprofit, social welfare organization, and I continued to volunteer my services to it. I worked for the State of Maryland, free, for four years. Then I was re-elected and have been re-elected ever since. A state legislature is an interesting place to be in. It may not be as prestigious as the Congress and the Senate, but it is important to the people in the state. There is a great sense of making a contribution, in diverse ways. The state legislature touches many issues that are important in people's lives—education, taxes, roads, schools, welfare, everything you could think of that people deal with every day. I have enjoyed every minute of being in the Maryland legislature.

Earning Your Spurs

My advice to any young person who wants to get into politics is that there is no short-cut. Some think that all they have to do is pay the fee to put their names on the ballot and that something mysterious will happen and they will be legislators. Not at all. That approach results only in waste of the filing fee. First, you must understand politics and how it functions, and you must become known to key people.

Despite what you read occasionally, it takes a great deal of hard work and many months or even years before you can run for office with some expectation of success. First, you have to earn your spurs. The course I took, and the one I recommend, is volunteer work. One way is as I have done, to volunteer to a national committee. Every state and every county has a headquarters for the Republican Party and one for the Democratic Party. Another way is to watch for candidates whom you want to support and volunteer at their headquarters. They may be candidates for any office, whether at the national, state, county, or community level. Candidates are eager for people to know where their headquarters are, so you will probably have no trouble finding the headquarters. If you do, call the supervisor of elections in your locality for assistance.

When you have found the headquarters just walk in and say, "I would like to volunteer. I want to help. I will be glad to do anything you have for me to do." They will welcome you with open arms. Then do *anything* they ask you to do. The virtue of this approach is not that you will be given an important job immediately. The virtue of it is that you will learn who the people are who control politics. Who are the movers and the pushers? Who are the persons doing things in politics? You must get to know *them* or you will never be involved personally. If you do a good job as a volunteer in a candidate's office or a headquarters office, not only will you get to know the people who are important in politics, but also they will get to know *you,* which is even more important from your point of view.

However, you must make up your mind that, for quite a long time, you will do drudgery. And there is a lot of it! But gradually people will come to know you. Eventually an occasion will occur when everyone is tied up and no one can keep an appointment with a person or a committment to speak before a group of people. If they think well of you they will ask you to go and represent the office. Your first impulse might be to respond, "Oh, I would not know what to say!" But consider what is involved: the issues in the campaign. By this time you know the issues as well as anyone else in the office. You have been listening to talk about the issues, and you know what your candidate stands for and what your party stands for.

Getting up to speak before a group, especially without much time for preparation, takes a great deal of nerve if you have not done it before. You will feel better if you keep in mind that everyone in the audience is a human being just like you. They do not expect miracles. They do not expect you to be an Einstein. Go in with the feeling, "I am going to speak to them as though I like them, even though I have never met them." That feeling of liking your audience will be transmitted to them.

As to the performance itself, the first thing you do is explain why the person running for office could not be there, and that he or she asked you to come as a personal representative. Explain that the candidate is so concerned about and so interested in this particular group that he or she asked you to bring the candidate's personal greetings, speak on his or her behalf, and try to answer any questions. Right away, you probably have your audience on your side, and you are off to a running start. If they are impressed, one of them will let someone higher up know that you can "speak on your feet." If someone is sufficiently impressed to write in to headquarters to say what a good job you did, that is a great step up the ladder.

You will then return to the headquarters office and report to your superiors. You will tell them how many people were there and who they were (you will, of course, have had a pad of paper with you), what literature you handed out to them, what you told them, and what questions they asked you. Of course you will remember what questions they asked. That is a great help to the candidate. Perhaps you will be able to report directly to the candidate: This is what they were interested in, this is what I told them, and here are the names and addresses of everybody who was there.

Reporting back from contacts with prospective voters is very important. If you do it well, the candidate will realize that you can be very helpful and will not hesitate to send you out to another group. Now you are learning to know people and how to conduct yourself in various situations. But it is difficult in the beginning. Do not think for a moment that it is going to be anything but hard. If you do, you will be fooling yourself.

I suggest that when you speak, even to small groups, you do not use a soft voice, particularly if you are a woman. A small voice does not carry conviction. You must speak with a firm voice as though you are convinced of what you are saying, so that you will convince your listeners. If you are ladylike and speak in a gentle voice, people will think that you do not know what you are talking about or are not convinced about it. Therefore, why should they be persuaded? Use a strong voice. Everybody has one. Just put enough energy into that voice so that people in the audience feel the energy from you. Get voice coaching if necessary. Be prepared when the opportunity to give a speech comes along.

Now that you have some experience, we come to the important matter of why any group should decide that you are capable of running for office and that you will bring strength to the other candidates. This raises such questions as: Whom do you know? How many do you know? To what organizations do you belong? Do these organizations recognize your ability? Can you raise funds? In other words, what can you bring to the ticket?

I was lucky that the selection committee decided I was worthy of running. Today the system is much more open, and there are many programs to help a young person get started in politics that were not available when I started out. In nearly every part of the country there are programs of instruction in how to volunteer (what to volunteer for, how to do it, when to do it), how to canvass, how to speak in public, and so on. For example, the Women's Caucus in the Maryland state legislature holds such seminars. All kinds of activities are going on with the purpose of training young people in the "how to" of politics. The programs are announced in the newspapers. All you have to do is join one of these seminars or caucus groups and follow the suggestions you are given.

Miracles seldom occur. You should expect to work hard for

an extended period of time in order to be prepared when an opportunity for your own personal advancement comes along. However, I found every step of the way to be exciting and rewarding. So, to any young woman who is thinking of a career in politics, Godspeed!

Chapter 5

Washington, D.C.—To the Wild West and Back Again

Marie McGuire Thompson

Introduction to Marie McGuire Thompson

During her long service as the last commissioner of the United States Public Housing Administration and her subsequent years as special advisor to several secretaries of the United States Department of Housing and Urban Development, as well as to several presidents of the United States, Marie made a monumental contribution to both public and private efforts to provide quality shelter for older Americans and had a lasting impact on the quality of the design of all federally funded housing—for families, the handicapped, American Indians—as well. She pioneered the United States government's program to provide decent, safe, and sanitary housing on American Indian reservations.

She helped forge a close working relationship between the forces of urban development and assisted housing by demonstrating the vital role public housing can play as a relocation

Lives of Career Women: Approaches to Work, Marriage, Children, edited by Frances M. Carp. Plenum/Insight, New York, 1991.

resource for low-income persons displaced by public action. By innovating and identifying opportunities for profitable involvement she turned the organized interests of home builders and architects from vigorous opponents of the low-rent housing program to staunch supporters of federally assisted housing. By her sound fiscal stewardship of the Public Housing Program, by the spotlight she turned on the genuine needs of tenants and the importance she attached to the sensitive treatment of them all, and by the procedures and attitudes she generated to insure good design, Commissioner McGuire turned a mostly apathetic and often antagonistic Congress into an informed and involved ally. She elevated the concern of the Public Housing Administration Regional and Central Office personnel to the level they historically had for the brick-and-mortar dimension of the program.

Throughout her career she worked with and supported scores of other truly great American women. Widowed a few years ago, Thompson lives in Kensington, Maryland, with her twin sister, State Senator Margaret Schweinhaut. Marie dealt with the visual decrement she shares with her twin by touch-typing chapter drafts and recruiting a good friend to correct them and to work with her in making later revisions.

My twin sister Margaret and I grew up with our brothers, who were older, in Washington, D.C. Mother was a quiet, dear, deeply religious woman who had come to America from Ireland. Father was imposing and strict but supportive. We had a large and close extended family.

Funds were not available for "the girls" to go to college, so after high-school graduation I immediately got a job as a clerk-typist. After a time I was hired as a secretary by the American Federation of Labor at its Washington, D.C. headquarters. (I took dictation from Samuel Gompers.) Unlike my twin I was shy and retiring. My spare time was devoted to reading literature, which I loved. I used my salary to attend night classes at George Washington University. The subjects that most interested me were English and literature.

After several years of routine office work by day and classes at night I was swept off my feet by a handsome and dashing young Irishman, John Henry McGuire. He was passing through Washington between jobs in South America and western Texas. He proposed, suggesting that we marry as soon as possible and spend our honeymoon traveling by automobile to Texas. My mother was especially taken with the charming young man from Ireland. I accepted and, after a whirlwind courtship, was heading west for a great adventure that held promise of being quite different from the previous five years of secretarial work and study: following my husband west in his search for oil.

The Texas Years

Ten years later I was a bored Houston housewife. My husband was away for long periods of time, and my only "adventures" were bridge games with other housewives.

Back to School

I read in the newspaper that the University of Texas planned to offer in Houston a series of programs on planning and housing. I had always loved the university atmosphere, and when I read that courses were being offered on a subject new to me, my intellectual curiosity was aroused. They were to be held only two blocks from my home, and I had nothing to do with my time, so I snapped at the chance to attend the sessions and find out what planning and housing were all about.

The first lesson intrigued me, and there was no doubt about my continuing. It was late in 1939, and the federal program of public housing was just getting underway, which occasioned provision of the courses. The recently appointed officials of the new Houston Housing Authority were my co-students. We became friendly and often they asked me to join them. Before the end of the series of sessions the executive director asked me if I would like to be the housing manager of a new project that was about to open. Although I knew absolutely nothing about what being housing manager involved, and although all I knew about public housing was what I had learned in the course, I agreed to give it a try.

I had not been looking for a job or even contemplating the possibility of one and therefore had never discussed it with my husband. Also, unlike the classes, the housing facility was at some distance from home. Neither consideration posed a problem. I had a car and was accustomed to driving. My husband's work required that he spend much time away from home, mostly in western Texas, and he was delighted that I had found a new interest.

The First Job in Houston

On the following Monday I reported to the newly constructed 318-apartment complex. The project had been originally planned for very low income families. Although the United States had not yet entered the Second World War, federal regulations directed that one half of the units were for "essential" defense workers who had limited incomes. The project was to be totally leased within a thirty-day period. I was given a staff consisting of an inexperienced young girl, who was to be the bookkeeper, and two maintenance men. Rows of people lined up to apply for apartments. About half were workers in "essential" defense jobs, and about half were very low income citizens living in substandard housing.

At that time we had "home visitors" on the housing authority staff who inspected the living conditions of all applicants except the defense workers, to document that conditions were substandard and would qualify the applicants for public housing. In order to find out what the housing authority meant by "substandard" I made some home visits myself. I was astonished to find human beings living in such squalor.

I was particularly struck by the plight of so many old people. Many lived downtown in dilapidated former office buildings. In at least one instance frail elderly persons had to climb four long flights of stairs to reach their dingy rooms. Usually there was one toilet for the use of all occupants. I was truly horrified. I had been amazed at the number of old people who applied for our new housing, but after seeing the kind of miserable living conditions most had, I understood. They were unable to afford more adequate housing because of very limited incomes, often just small, monthly welfare checks.

Back then, single occupancy was not permitted in public housing. Elderly persons living alone—among the most needy of the elderly—could not be admitted. I had to see to it that only elderly couples were given units. Moreover, when one died, the other must move out within thirty days. While the rule assured maximum use of the premises, one of my most difficult duties was to inform the remaining spouse that in addition to coping with bereavement she or he must vacate the apartment within thirty days. How cruel this was! In the weekly status reports that I began writing for the executive director I made frequent mention of this painful and unfair rule. I was thankful that the regulation was later removed by the federal government.

A Step Up at the Local Level

I had been a manager for only six months when the executive director said that a new 500-unit project at San Felipe would be ready for occupancy within a month, and that I would transfer to it as its manager since I had experience in opening a project. It was an opportunity and a challenge, but I was sorry in some ways. I had started activity programs in our community room for the residents, and I had grown fond of and felt close to them.

The many experiences at my first project stayed with me

throughout my career. I was impressed that our federal government recognized the awful slum conditions in which so many Americans lived, and that it initiated the Public Housing Program to help solve the disgraceful problem. Throughout my public housing experience I attempted to involve social workers with the needs of low-income people residing in public housing. I hoped more effort would be made by social workers in various agencies to tie their activities in with the housing program. The new housing provided an environment that could help solve other serious family problems if other social service programs were better coordinated with it. Unfortunately, this did not happen.

The Move to San Antonio

When the second 500 units at the San Felipe site had been completed my job again was to lease them. Shortly after that was accomplished I received a phone call from the regional office of the United States Public Housing Administration in Fort Worth. The official stated that the Housing Authority of San Antonio was seeking a new executive director. He asked if I would be interested. I was astonished and immediately asked whether a woman would be considered seriously for the top post. The regional official responded with what he knew about the situation. The federal government had only recently taken direct control over the San Antonio Housing Authority due to mismanagement. A new board of directors had been appointed. The chairman of that new board had asked the regional federal officials to find an executive director suitable for the job and capable of meeting the board's approval. The criteria for board approval were unknown to the man who phoned me.

With some inner trepidation I said I was interested. I was invited to San Antonio for an interview with the new chairman of the board. He was not at all disturbed by the idea of a female assuming the position of executive director. So, within one week, I moved to San Antonio, delighted with my new $7500-a-year salary, a significant increase. My husband endorsed the move. The location of his home base made little difference, due to the amount of time he was required to be in the field, living at the site where they were attempting to find oil.

San Antonio badly needed more public housing. Its slums were even worse than those of Houston, though I would not have thought that possible before seeing them. Many families had as many as eleven persons in one room. Called "corral developments," they were the usual residences of the poor Mexicans who flooded into San Antonio. I felt that the city should do something about these horrible and unhealthy conditions. Toward that end I promoted slum tours for the Junior League and other influential civic clubs. The Junior League was very concerned with civic matters. One call from me was all it took to recruit them. As horrified as they were at what they saw—in one instance two ladies fainted—nothing resulted except a request for more federally supported public housing.

When we received approval for 2500 new units the interesting job of seeking proper sites began. The city council had to approve all of this, and the usual battle with private real-estate and home-building lobbies began. Their efforts were in vain because this time there was no requirement for a referendum. Federal funds had been allocated to build the 2500 units. There were just as many low-income seniors as I had found in Houston. I decided to set aside a few hundred dwellings specifically for the elderly.

From local architects and planners I asked for help in finding suitable sites for 2000 family units, explaining that I was holding back 500 of the total number of units for older citizens. Fortunately, we enlisted the support of an especially good architectural firm. Its principal was an architect who was also a planner and had taught planning at the University of Texas. Eventually nine family projects were built.

The First Public Housing Facility for the Elderly

While in Houston I had begun keeping a notebook pertaining to the unique requirements of older folks in regard to their living environments. I recorded the many accidents among the elderly in our units and what caused them. The two dominant causes of injuries were falls resulting from steps or other changes in floor levels and getting in and out of bathtubs. Slippery floors, insufficient illumination, lack of color to provide differentiation, and many other specifics about what should be different in designing housing suitable for old folks came to mind from the notes I had kept in my previous experience.

I consulted with medical personnel and hospital staff about the accident cases they handled with older people, and with anyone else who had an interest in or any idea about their safety needs. Such inconveniences as high shelves that caused the occupant to stand on a stool or chair to reach the top shelf were identified as villains. With the help of many people from diverse disciplines in the city we began to compile what later was called "The Architect's Checklist," which noted the special design considerations of housing older persons.

Until that time most housing built especially for older people was placed in rural or country areas. To me that seemed improper since the elderly often are lonely as well as lacking in opportunities for something to do. I felt from what I had observed and been told that the "birds and bees" concept was wrong. Housing for seniors should be as close to the center of the city as possible. There should be a grocery store within easy walking distance and, if possible, a drug store. It was essential that the site be on a bus route that had a conveniently located waiting station with benches. Within the project there should be a garden space and a safe walking area, as well as a closed-in veranda in which to sit on rainy days or when the south Texas heat was too great for out-of-door exercise.

During the late 1950s lenders and regulators—to say nothing of Congress—would not hear of an eight-story, 185-

unit, subsidized apartment building being totally air-conditioned. We had to settle for air-conditioning on only the first floor, but this did include the community room. Special attention, therefore, was given to orientation of the apartments to take full advantage of the prevailing breeze (when there was a breeze). We designed the roof to provide more sitting-out space, but it was not heavily utilized. It was too hot during much of the year, and the concrete floor added to the heat.

We tried to keep in mind the problems with sight, hearing, and agility among the elderly. We decided that all electrical outlets should be waist-high to avoid the pain caused by stooping to the floor or to baseboard level. We increased the light intensity over what is standard. We determined that there should be color in every apartment. We gave much attention to kitchen safety, including cooking ranges and ovens and any other features that could conceivably cause accidents. We installed emergency bells in bathrooms, where many accidents happen.

When the project was completed, occupied, and dedicated in 1960, it was the first project in this country, as far as I know, designed especially for older people. Victoria Plaza, as we called it, generated much interest. Many persons came from Europe to visit, inspect, and study this new concept. Dozens came from other local public housing authorities and asked if they could borrow our architectural plans. So many made this request that we finally had to charge twenty-five dollars for our plans. Some local housing authorities built exactly what we had. Others designed different types of buildings but retained the details related to safety and other special features for housing the elderly. The concept received broad publicity in professional building and housing journals, as well as in the public media.

Subsequently, the San Antonio Housing Authority, under my direction, built or converted additional housing facilities for low-income persons, some of them especially designed for elderly residents. Though I never experienced serious problems of leadership because I was a woman, there were some interesting incidents. For example, one of the developments showed shoddy workmanship (e.g., cracks began appearing in the foundation shortly after construction). I called a meeting of the planners, architects, contractors, and subcontractors to determine who was responsible and to see that the errors were corrected. I was the only woman at the meeting and was also chairperson. One contractor, known for his loud and often crude language, shouted at me while shaking his finger: "Mrs. McGuire, I wish you wore pants!" I replied, "What makes you think I don't?" The room exploded with laughter, the meeting was adjourned, and the contractor redid the faulty work.

Unfortunately, during this time my husband developed a serious drinking problem, which eventually made him unemployable. During the last years in San Antonio I devoted much attention to caring for him and trying to provide a comfortable home for him. Eventually we separated and divorced.

The Nation's Capital Beckons

One day my phone rang, and when I answered a male voice inquired, "If the president, John F. Kennedy, decided to appoint you the commissioner of the United States Public Housing Administration in Washington, D.C., would you accept the post?" My immediate response was that I was not my idea of what the commissioner should be. He answered, "That is not your decision." I then said that, of course, I would accept if appointed, and that I felt it was a great honor to be asked.

The following day I left for a planning meeting in Virginia. While I was there word came that I had been appointed and that I must appear the next day before a Senate committee for confirmation in Washington, D.C. Fortunately, due to the planning meeting, my trip was from a neighboring state rather than the one in which I normally worked.

I went directly to Washington to appear before the committee. My uneasiness lessened when I saw that three members were women. There were many interesting questions, but the questioning was not beyond my knowledge and experience or antagonistic. The one potentially controversial question was what would I do if Congress passed a law decreeing that there could be no racial discrimination in public housing. (At this time most developments were segregated.) My answer was that I would follow the law. This seemed to satisfy the committee.

And so I came to the nation's capital as head of an independent agency, with responsibilities to which few women were privy in those days. Things continued to move rapidly. The morning after the Senate confirmation I was sworn in by Dr. Robert C. Weaver, who had been appointed by President Kennedy as the administrator of the Housing and Home Finance Agency. Clark Clifford was present and explained that the president had asked him to be the president's personal representative. Staff members and three members of my family were there. After the ceremony I lunched with friends and then made my way to the commissioner's office.

The commissioner's desk and the large conference table were piled high with contracts awaiting the commissioner's signature before they could be activated. The former commissioner's secretary, a very knowledgeable woman, was awaiting me. Initially, I had her read to me all the data and documentation attached to each file jacket that supported the regional office approval of each contract.* After several hours I realized that it would take literally months to hear the substantiating data. Meanwhile, as I well knew, local housing authorities were screaming for approvals so that their building programs could begin. In addition, I knew from personal experience that regional office personnel had carefully reviewed and passed upon every aspect of every case. Therefore, I signed contracts that first day in office until two o'clock the following morning. Jay

---

Editor's note. A person to serve as a reader was requisite, even at that time, to compensate for Marie's visual problem.

stayed with me. All of the contracts were in the mail that morning. What a day it had been.

I knew a few of the headquarters staff, but only a few. It took me a while to find out who was who and how competent each was. A number of directors of the various headquarters sections had resigned due to the election. The heads of the legal department and development division had resigned following the departure of the previous commissioner. The public relations post had been vacated also. I was faced with the job of finding willing and suitable replacements. On my first full day in office phone calls began bringing dozens of suggestions about persons someone thought should be considered for the vacant posts. One of the staff vacancies I found on that first full day in office as commissioner was the key post of assistant commissioner for development. That slot was eventually filled by Thomas B. Thompson, of the American Institute of Architects, the San Antonio architect and planner who had proved so effective in working with the San Antonio Housing Authority.

Also on that first full day in office my staff explained my already packed calendar and began advising me about what should be said at various already-scheduled staff meetings and other meetings and appointments. Once again, my desk was piled high with correspondence, reports, and proposals awaiting my decision. But now I had a large trained and experienced staff and held authority at the highest level. Although it entailed more responsibility and provided quantitatively and qualitatively superior support, in some ways my job was similar to my first position with the Houston Housing Authority not that many years before.

I thoroughly enjoyed the many years of serving as commissioner of the Public Housing Administration. The job was demanding, requiring hard work and long hours, but it was interesting and, in my view, very important to the welfare of the nation's less well-off citizens. I left the position only because the Public Housing Administration was eliminated in the course of a governmental reorganization. I continued to serve the national government and the housing needs of the poor for a number of years as a special advisor to several secretaries of the new Department of Housing and Urban Development (HUD), as did the outstanding architect/planner I had first met in San Antonio while preparing for Victoria Plaza.

Retirement

After both "Tommy" Thompson and I retired from HUD we married and enjoyed many happy years together. We lived in a delightful apartment in Washington, D.C. and were constantly surrounded by old friends and acquaintances. We both remained active and kept ourselves well informed about matters of housing and design.

In Retrospect

Looking back, what most comes to mind is the gratitude I feel for the many opportunities that were presented to me. To be sure, one must be sensitive to recognize and evaluate opportunities when they do appear, and one must be willing to take some chances in accepting them. Meanwhile, it is essential to concentrate on doing your best at whatever your current task may be.

Chapter 6

My Life as a Professional, a Wife, and a Mother

Josephine Rohrs Hilgard, M.D., Ph.D.

Introduction to Josephine Rohrs Hilgard

While Josephine Hilgard was writing this chapter she suffered a
sudden, unexplained coma and died peaceably in her sleep. Her
husband, Ernest R. Hilgard, Ph.D., completed it on the basis of her
notes and what she had told him.

Josephine Hilgard conducted several lines of important research while pioneering with a two-career marriage and children.
Her studies are recognized as significant among behavioral scientists and have won her high praise and honors, of which she was
justifiably proud. However, most of her work time was spent and
her most significant accomplishments were made in therapy sessions. Of them her chapter has little to say. Psychologists, psychiatrists, and psychoanalysts are schooled in confidentiality with
regard to clients or patients. She was all three—first psychologist,

Lives of Career Women: Approaches to Work, Marriage, Children, edited by Frances
M. Carp. Plenum/Insight, New York, 1991.

then psychiatrist, and finally psychoanalyst—which may explain her reticence with regard to this major sector of her life work.

Her chapter was written from jottings she had made through the years with the intention of writing a memoir "just for the family." The children were well aware that she did clinical work, since one of her offices was attached to their home, and she may have felt that they were less well aware of her role as researcher. As a couple, the Hilgards were members of an academic community in which research was the highest goal, and this social context may have influenced her perception of her own accomplishments. At any rate, through the many years of her practice, privately and in affiliation with prestigious psychiatric and psychoanalytic institutions, Josephine Hilgard influenced for the better the lives of countless persons—children and adults. For this outstanding contribution she richly deserves the credit she does not claim for herself.

Because my later career was shaped by my upbringing, education, and prior professional experience, I include some notes on my biography prior to marriage in the expectation that they will explain some of the problems that arose when I attempted to combine a professional career conjointly with that of my husband, while I was also a wife and a mother. I faced, then, the same problems as those who prepared other chapters in this book, but each of us has had unique experiences based on our backgrounds and the circumstances that we later faced.

Family Background

I was born and raised through my high-school years in Napoleon, Ohio, a small town near Toledo that prided itself in being the county seat, with its court house visible from miles around. I was the only child of a physician and surgeon in general practice. He received his M.D. from Jefferson Medical College in

Philadelphia and subsequently spent one and a half years in post-graduate study at the University of Berlin. He spoke German fluently because he was a first-generation American raised in the home of a German-born father, and many of his patients continued to speak German, a language still prevalent in our community. His father had strict patriarchal control over the children, contrasting with the more democratic American model. Father remained up-to-date in his medical practice. He was the first, and for many years the only, physician in the community with equipment for the X-ray examination of broken bones.

My mother attended the Oberlin Conservatory of Music for three years and continued throughout her life to have broad interests in music and art, including a detailed knowledge of oriental rugs, of which she became an ardent collector.

Childhood and High-School Years

Mother took a great interest in my education. Early in my life she did her best to make a musician out of me, but I was not adept at piano, violin, or voice. She finally gave me my choice and permitted me to play the banjo, from which I derived satisfaction throughout my life. A combo met in our home on Saturday nights for many years, even into my retirement.

Accepting the possibility that early discipline has a lasting effect, I have thought back on how discipline was handled in my case. How did my father, who had experienced Grandfather Rohrs' absolute authority, treat me when he became a father? And how did my mother contribute? She did not have a German background and had been raised in a more relaxed atmosphere.

My parents guided me carefully, setting clear limits on what I could or could not do. If I violated the home standards when my father was present, swift punishment by way of a short, sober discussion or a spanking followed. Once, when I was a little girl, my father reminded me at the dinner table that I should *not* dip my fingers in the luscious whipped cream on the strawberries. When I did it again, my father, whose eyes seemed to see everything, led me to the next room and calmly administered a light spanking. After a few minutes we returned to the dining room, and I recall no feelings of ill will. For Father the incident was closed, and I was soon in good spirits. Mother did not spank, but she always supported Father's handling of a situation. Mother and I were apt to compromise. She reported only serious infractions to my father, who, after a brief discussion with me, decided on the punishment. While standards were high and strictly enforced, disciplinary episodes were rare after my very early years.

I had a happy childhood. Lack of siblings was made up in part by the companionship of a girl cousin, slightly older than I, who lived with our common grandparents in Napoleon when I was between the ages of two and eight. Later, she and her younger brother, about my age, frequently spent summers with us.

Although I worked hard to earn it, my class rank in school was always high, and I enjoyed extracurricular activities. In the high-school yearbook ("The Buckeye") in my senior year I listed as my activities four years of participating in the glee club (my musical ability was up to that), each year having a part in the annual operetta, and as a senior playing in the orchestra and becoming a member of the basketball and the debating teams. I served also as business manager of "The Buckeye," soliciting advertisements from local merchants to support the costs of publication. At graduation I received a special award for proficiency in literature, including some prize money. I am slightly embarrassed now by my contribution to the Class Will, reported in "The Buckeye" as: "I, Josephine Rohrs, do will and bequeath my ability in school activities to anyone deficient in them." At least I wanted to share!

College

My mother had heard good things about Smith College and desired that I apply, but I balked at taking the entrance examinations as the graduate of a small high school in competition with girls who had gone to preparatory schools. So, with her permission, I chose Radcliffe for my first two years because I could be accepted there on my high-school record without examination. I enjoyed my years at Radcliffe and profited from all that the Boston area offered, but, true to my mother's wishes, I transferred easily to Smith College for my last two years, majoring in child psychology, and graduated in 1928 with a Phi Beta Kappa key and magna cum laude on my diploma.

It is not easy for me to determine precisely what led to child psychology as a major at Smith, to be followed by child psychology in graduate school. Possibly the problems of having been an only child made me reflective about psychology to begin with. At Radcliffe I took experimental psychology with Boring and social psychology with McDougall. Boring was an interesting lecturer, but the psychology that he preferred did not capture my imagination. McDougall was something of a bore, reading his assigned textbook aloud to us in class. At Smith, where I had the choice between a more conventional psychology and child psychology, I became excited by the child psychology course of Margaret Wooster Curti. Part of our work was observation of children in a nursery school, and this program gripped me. In considering graduate study it was easy for me to turn to Yale, where Arnold Gesell had become prominent. Thus, one's career is shaped not only by the home background but also by the opportunities that appeal along the way.

Graduate School and Marriage

I went to Yale as a graduate student in child psychology to study with Dr. Gesell, a foremost representative of that area. The undergraduate college was still entirely male, but women were accepted as graduate students, and special dormitory arrangements were made for them on a small scale.

I met my future husband, Ernest R. "Jack" Hilgard, soon after I arrived. He was an advanced graduate student and teaching assistant. At the end of the first year I left to gather data for a master's thesis at the Merrill Palmer Institute of Child Development in Detroit, where I was supported by a fellowship. There I gained more experience in working with young children. I returned to Yale to write up the thesis and receive the M.A. in 1930, in the same commencement during which Jack received his Ph.D. He continued at Yale as an instructor in psychology. We were engaged but postponed marriage in agreement with my parents' wishes for me to have a year to demonstrate that I could use my training to earn a living as a professional woman. During that year I served as the only clinical psychologist in the Child Guidance Clinic in Buffalo, New York.

We were married in the fall of 1931 in my home in Napoleon. After a honeymoon in the Robert Yerkes' summer home in New Hampshire we took up residence in New Haven. I continued to study, working as assistant to Dr. Gesell, and earned my Ph.D. in 1933. Along the way I was elected to full membership in Sigma Xi, the scientific honor society. I published both my master's thesis and my doctoral dissertation as J. Hilgard.

The First Two-Career Issue

Early in 1933 came the invitation for Jack to go to Stanford as an assistant professor, and Yale agreed to meet Stanford's offer. Eventually we decided that it would be best to join a faculty not composed of Jack's teachers, although it meant the first of several times when my career was redirected because of his. I had the offer to remain on the staff of the Yale Clinic of Child Development, so this was the first time a two-career issue had to be decided in reference to our intertwined lives. The remainder of this chapter addresses such issues as they affected me.

The decision to go to Stanford was not easy, particularly for me. Jack, although attracted by the offer, was eager to give me equal rights and at first refused the appointment. It was eventually my decision to have him accept the appointment. I was prepared to take chances. We arrived at Stanford in the fall of 1933, Jack with his assistant professorship and I with my newly earned Ph.D. The psychology department chairman, Lewis M. Terman, and his wife, Anna, invited us to live with them until we found a house and until our furniture arrived.

From a professional point of view there was no easy road ahead for me. Private practice of psychology was not in vogue in those years, and the antinepotism rule at Stanford made it difficult for spouses to be appointed in the same department. After investigating and discussing employment prospects I found only one minor position available as a psychologist—to do a limited amount of testing for the psychiatry department of Stanford Medical School, which at that time was in San Francisco.

In the face of these prospects I decided it would be better to find a career of my own that would not confront the "two psychologists" problem. I decided to undertake premedical work and go on to medical school. Before this time I had not thought of studying medicine. I suppose this was part of the stereotype that women did not go in for medicine, although as the only child of a physician, even though a daughter, I must have had some identification with my father. Had I been a son I would have undoubtedly chosen medicine. Jack's father was also a physician, and had he not died in World War I, Jack probably would have been one also. So in some sense there would be fulfillment of the family saga if I did. There was also the practical consideration that psychiatry would make use of my psychological training while giving me independence in choosing the manner in which I exercised my profession.

In those days premedical requirements were more formal than they are now: inorganic chemistry, qualitative analysis, quantitative analysis, physics, comparative anatomy. I, having had none of these, set out to acquire them during my first year as the wife of a faculty member in a new place, with all that that entailed. I managed everything except qualitative analysis and quantitative analysis during the first year and completed those requirements the next summer at Bowling Green State University in Ohio, near enough to Napoleon for me to commute while Jack worked at my parents' home on what was to be *Conditioning and Learning* (E. R. Hilgard and Marquis, 1940).

Medical School and Motherhood

I was accepted by Stanford Medical School, although in the thirties there were only one or two women in a class. The two preclinical years were at the main campus in Palo Alto, so I could live at home. I continued to live at home and commuted by train after my classes were in San Francisco, until I became pregnant.

I dropped out of medical school for a year, the pregnancy being difficult for me—not because of any difficulty directly associated with the pregnancy, but because of being lonesome at home while my husband continued his busy schedule, including many evening obligations that had not had that effect on me while I was busy at medical school and commuting. It was a period of conflict for us both. Clearly, he did not mean to neglect me, but I resented the fact that he did not alter his plans as I had had to alter mine. But, it was satisfying to have a son born in 1936, and, with my mother's visit to assist me, the long period of lonesome waiting ended.

We soon moved to an apartment in San Francisco so I could go on with my medical training, and Jack did the commuting to Palo Alto. By good fortune we were able to have live-in help. We both sought ways to augment Jack's depression salary. We accepted whatever moonlighting tasks each of us could find, such as teaching psychology in nursing schools in various hospitals in San Francisco. I graduated in 1940 after one year of residency and was elected to the medical honor society Alpha Omega Alpha.

Chicago and Washington, D.C. (1940–1944)

My choice of additional residency training was limited by an offer Jack received to spend his first sabbatical year on a project at the University of Chicago, which supplemented the half-salary of the sabbatical. I arose to the occasion as best I could and obtained a Rockefeller fellowship that paid for a training psychoanalysis in Chicago while I gained further experience at the Institute for Juvenile Research, where I was a fellow during that year and a staff member the next year. At the University of Illinois Medical School I became well acquainted with Franz Alexander and Thomas M. French, leading psychoanalysists and young professionals. Our son, Henry, was old enough to enjoy the nursery school connected with the university. As I look back I realize that the decisions I was forced to make, although conflictual at the time, usually turned out to make me better qualified for subsequent professional activities.

I have mentioned a second year at Chicago, although Jack's appointment was for a single year. He returned alone to Stanford for the autumn quarter, but then war was declared and he was soon in Washington, D.C., in connection with the war effort, hoping that I would join him there when my obligations were over in Chicago. We had never been separated that long. I managed without him in Chicago because of having live-in help that permitted me to give my young son the attention he needed and to carry on with my professional obligations and training.

When it came time to join Jack in Washington what was I to do professionally? I took advantage of the opportunity to continue my psychoanalytic training in the Washington-Baltimore Psychoanalytic Institute, which led to my certification as a psychoanalyst in 1946. I served also on the staff of the Chestnut Lodge Sanitarium in Rockville, Maryland. There I had rare opportunities of working with psychotic patients while under the guidance of Harry Stack Sullivan and Frieda Fromm-Reichmann, both known for their innovative work. I have reflected on that experience in a chapter in a recently published book (J. R. Hilgard, 1989). Although this move to Washington was not on my own initiative, it proved, like the move to Chicago, to enrich my experience enormously.

As I write about these moves they seem to follow so naturally that one forgets the amount of negotiation in the face of uncertainties that they required and the incidental problems of living arrangements and care of children. As the war was winding down in 1944 we gave thought to completing our family by adopting a daughter, if it could be arranged. I was about to have my thirty-eighth birthday and Jack was approaching forty, so it seemed desirable not to wait much longer to provide a sister for Henry, who was seven. Because of my ties in Washington I was able to make arrangements with a thoughtful adoption agency, and by good fortune a baby born in January, whose parental background was similar to ours, proved to be up for adoption. We were happy to complete our family with a son and a daughter. Our Elizabeth (whom we call Lisby) has been a joy to us from the start.

In subsequent years it was flattering to both Lisby and me that many people, unfamiliar with the history, remarked on how much our daughter looked like her mother. It could not have worked out better, and Lisby fits completely into the family tradition. Informed early of the fact of her adoption, she seems always to have had deep feelings toward me as her very own mother and toward Jack as her very own father, and we feel that she is our very own daughter.

Career Development

We returned to Stanford, where Jack had been selected to head the psychology department. He had to prepare for the influx of veterans from the war who would become students under the GI Bill. I received a half-time appointment as director of the Child Guidance Clinic of Children's Hospital in San Francisco, 1945–1948, which was an enriching experience despite the long commute. In 1947 I began what was to be my long service with the Department of Psychiatry at the Stanford Medical School, which had moved to Palo Alto. I was associate clinical professor and later clinical professor until I became clinical professor emerita in 1971. In the meantime, I maintained a private office in Palo Alto, where I practiced psychoanalysis and psychiatry while doing my research through grants from funding agencies such as the National Institute of Mental Health, the Ford Foundation, the Wheeler Foundation, and the National Cancer Institute.

My research often entailed several scientific reports in closely related areas. Both my master's thesis (J. R. Hilgard, 1932) and my doctoral dissertation (J. R. Hilgard, 1933) in psychology were concerned with the interaction between intrinsic growth factors (maturation) and skill learning in young children. During the early years beyond the M.D., when I was in advanced professional training (1933–1945), I had little opportunity for research, although I published two collaborative papers from the Institute of Juvenile Research in Chicago.

My next research direction was a study of sibling rivalry and what I called social heredity, because the rivalries between siblings often took a form traceable to rivalries in the childhoods of the parental generation. There followed a series of nine data-based reports on what I termed "anniversary reactions," in which the psychopathology demonstrated in one generation— including late-appearing psychotic symptoms—represents reproductions of events in the parental generation. The specific "target dates" for appearance of the symptoms support the concept of "anniversaries" in a broad sense, not implying that these target dates appeared annually. These studies were published between 1953 and 1969. A later paper includes a summary of that work (J. R. Hilgard, 1989).

Another program was undertaken on affiliative therapy. Well-adjusted adolescents joined with disturbed ones in activities that involved supervised interaction. The youngsters were not identified as "normal" or "disturbed" except as they were known individually to the professionals. The experience proved therapeutic for the disturbed adolescents and profitable to the others. Three studies were reported in 1969.

Toward the end of my active career I joined Jack's program in hypnosis research and published books and articles on this subject, such as *Personality and Hypnosis* (1970, revised 1979) and, with Jack, *Hypnosis in the Relief of Pain* (1975, revised 1983). Finally, through a grant of my own from the National Cancer Institute, I co-authored *Hypnotherapy of Pain in Children with Cancer* with a junior colleague (J. R. Hilgard and LeBaron, 1984). For my contributions to the scientific study of hypnosis, the International Society of Hypnosis awarded me its Franklin Gold Medal at its International Congress in 1985.

In the same year, fourteen years after I entered emerita status, I had the satisfaction that the book on hypnotherapy of pain in children was given an award as the "best book on hypnosis published in 1984" by the Society for Clinical and Experimental Hypnosis. A third event in 1985 was a symposium at the annual meeting of the American Psychological Association sponsored by three of its divisions—Psychological Hypnosis, Clinical Psychology, and Psychotherapy—and entitled

"Intertwining Clinical and Experimental Research: Symposium Honoring Josephine Hilgard."

Another event that happened in 1988 was a source of satisfaction. Stanford University dedicated a new cluster of residences for 776 single graduate students, naming them the Rains Houses after a donor who made them possible. These are eighteen three-story houses, twelve two-story houses, and eight community buildings arranged in five groups called courts. The courts and four community lounges within the courts are named, as the dedication program announced, "for distinguished past faculty members." It was a pleasure to find one of the courts named Hilgard Court after my husband and me. I was honored for my long service in psychiatry in the education of graduate students in the School of Medicine, and my husband was named for his career in the psychology department and as dean of the graduate division. Despite my failing health I was able to attend and enjoy the outdoor dedication ceremony.

Home and Family

I fear that in recounting so much of the satisfaction I received through my professional work and research I may have appeared to show a lack of interest in my home and family. It would be a mistake were I to leave that impression, for my family and I spent much time together and had much fun from day to day, as well as on trips and vacations. For a number of years we had a year-round beach house on the Pacific Coast, which we shared with our extended family. It provided an opportunity for recreation not only within the family but for frequent beach picnics with our professional associates and other friends.

Summers and quarters off permitted travel. Occasional summer teaching by Jack at other universities, with the family along for all or part of the time, provided opportunities for experiences in Seattle or Portland, Oregon; or Provo, Utah; or Los Angeles; or Hawaii. Family trips to Europe (in part for gatherings of our European relatives) and to Mexico and Central America were managed also. We made cross-country trips by car and visited Yosemite and other national parks.

During the years we had our own groups of special friends in addition to our colleagues in psychology and psychiatry, including a small bridge club, a interdepartmental husband–wife discussion group that met monthly for a meal and social gathering in one of our homes, and a wives' group, in which I took some leadership, which met for daiquiris, a luncheon, and bridge. Clearly, my life was not all professional.

I was sometimes worried that I may not have been as good a mother as I should have been, but both of our children have turned out well. Our son, with a Harvard B.A., a Stanford M.D., and a Minnesota Ph.D., is a professor of biology at the University of California in Santa Cruz. He is married to a marine biologist, and he and his wife have three daughters, all now university graduates, two from Stanford and one from the University of California. The eldest was married in 1989, and I was pleased to be able to attend her garden wedding in Santa Cruz. Our daughter studied along with her husband at Chico State University. After they moved to San Luis Obispo he earned an M.A. degree in economics from California Polytechnic University. He is a member of a firm of real estate appraisers. Their daughter has entered college, and their son is in junior high school. The children, their spouses, and the grandchildren all are sources of satisfaction to my husband and me.

Retirement Life-Style

In 1981 Jack and I moved to a retirement residence in Palo Alto, where all of our needs are taken care of in the midst of a number of old friends and colleagues as well as delightful new acquaintances. We soon took an active part in the organization of residents. My role as chairperson of the Continuum of Care Committee permitted me to make use of my professional background to insist, with the help of my committee members, upon improved equipment for the in-house infirmary and care facility and to deal with other problems associated with the well-being of those throughout the house. Jack was soon elected president of the Residents' Council, and during his term gave active leadership. All along we have taken part in community organizations such as the Family Service Association and the Palo Alto Cooperative Society; and Jack, in recent years, has served on the Board of Senior Adults Legal Assistance.

General Remarks on Intertwined Careers

Recent recognition that the sexes have not been given equal treatment in the past is on the right track. I feel that my adjustments were more difficult than my husband's because of the standards of the time. We both early adopted an ideal of mutuality in which each would have the full opportunity to develop as an individual with the support of the other. We preferred the kind of cooperation in which neither partner is subordinate to the other. Then, whatever the two can achieve by living and working as a unit becomes a bonus if the pair can arrive at something above what the two individuals could have achieved independently of each other.

That was an ideal we shared, but society made it easier for my husband than for me. One prevailing notion was that a husband was being "kind" to permit his wife to carry on her professional career, unless she had outstanding talent as an instrumental musician, opera singer, or actress. Otherwise, she was expected to be, first of all, a good wife and mother. If she could do that as well as the wife who had no profession of her own, then working outside the home was tolerable.

We met little of that view among our friends. The problems lay at another level. It was Jack who had the job offers and got the rapid promotions, even though our academic records were comparable and we had begun with equivalent Ph.D.'s. My later M.D. gave me career independence, but only after a struggle to meet additional requirements. Because of that independence and the associated career flexibility, it was usually I who had to make the adjustments when favorable opportunities presented themselves to Jack.

The management of the home continued to be my responsibility. Jack was always willing to help, but he did not take the initiative in planning the meals or in doing much of the shopping. He took care of the yard and the garden, but the gardener did a larger share of that than my help did in planning the meals, inviting guests to be entertained, and looking after the housekeeping in general. I do not blame Jack, for I believe he did more than most husbands; but the general expectations were that the wife was the manager at home. (The era of the house-husband had not arrived.)

On the whole, my health was good until recently. Without a strong constitution I could not have done what I did. Would I do it again? Of course I would! But maybe my husband and I would have worked out a somewhat different division of labor. As an octogenarian, without being immodest, I believe that I can reflect upon a reasonably well-rounded life.

References

Hilgard, E. R., & Hilgard, J. R. (1981). *Hypnosis in the relief of pain* (rev. ed.). Los Altos, CA: William Kaufmann.

Hilgard, E. R., & Marquis, D. G. (1940). *Conditioning and learning*. New York: Appleton-Century.

Hilgard, J. R. (1932). Learning and maturation in preschool children. *Journal of Genetic Psychology, 41,* 36–56.

Hilgard, J. R. (1933). The effect of early and delayed practice on memory and motor performances studied by the method of co-twin control. *Genetic Psychology Monographs, 14,* 493–565.

A Professional, a Wife, and a Mother   **101**

Hilgard, J. R. (1979). *Personality and hypnosis.* (2nd ed.). Chicago: University of Chicago Press.

Hilgard, J. R. (1989). The anniversary syndrome as related to late-appearing mental illnesses in hospitalized patients. In A.-L. S. Silver (Ed.), *Psychoanalysis and psychosis.* Madison, CT: International Universities Press.

Hilgard, J. R., & LeBaron, S. (1984). *Hypnotherapy of pain in children with cancer.* Los Altos, CA: William Kaufmann.

Chapter 7

The Other Journey

Shirley F. Woods

Introduction to Shirley F. Woods

In a gentle but firm manner "Mother Woods" has nurtured and guided hundreds of individuals, enabling them to see their potential and reach their goals. The Very Reverend Shirley F. Woods did this in two concurrent roles: associate rector of an Episcopal church and dean of the School for Deacons in the Episcopal Diocese of California. The title "Reverend" is because she is an ordained priest; the "very" is for being dean of an Episcopal institution of higher education. She narrowly missed adding "Dr.," almost completing a Ph.D. in Greek. She does not pay much attention to her titles, unless she is "writing to an uppity male."

When she retired as dean in 1990, the graduating class arranged with the bishop and board of trustees for her to receive the first "Doctorate of the Diaconate" ever given and established a tuition assistance fund in her name. The Right Reverend William E. Swing, bishop of the Episcopal Diocese of California, unable to be present, sent a video tape:

Lives of Career Women: Approaches to Work, Marriage, Children, edited by Frances M. Carp. Plenum/Insight, New York, 1991.

Shirley, you and I have worked together in California. We've trecked together in the Judean desert. This is just the first time they've 'beamed me up' to be with you in the East Bay. First of all, I congratulate you on receiving that honorary doctorate today. I can't think of anybody who deserves this honor more.

I well remember, about a decade ago, when you and I talked about the possibility of a school for deacons. It hadn't been done in this diocese and hardly in the nation. In my wildest expectations— and I have some pretty wild expectations—I never would have believed that this institution would grow as broad and deep and be as competent as it is now. And that is, as everyone knows, due to the Holy Spirit's great work through you.

The people who are in this building today with you, and the people in the Diocese of California, and your bishop not only applaud you, we have great affection for you and profound appreciation for what you have done. This is a venerable diocese— we've been around for over 140 years—and I think there's no more venerable person in it than Shirley Woods. If you're venerable, you should be called that, and the way you get to be called that is by being made an archdeacon by the bishop. You are going to be the first woman archdeacon in the Diocese of California. I can't wait to install you and call you "the Venerable." It'll be fun to put you in your place!

As soon as a new dean was selected, Shirley and her husband, Bob, spent a week in Moscow and then cruised down the Volga.

The headings in her chapter are selections from *The Book of Psalms,* and the concluding poem is her own.

Spiritual autobiographies have been written in many ways by authors from Augustine of Hippo to Thomas Merton. I view mine as the history of myself as I relate to God. What is Spirit? What is Soul? Is there a piece of mind that detaches itself and floats free so that after death some of "you" is left? Is the Spirit a piece of God that comes to inhabit your body, making friends with your soul? There is a romantic idea. Facts suggest that the functioning of mind is a physiological process. Neural psychology removes the old-fashioned soul to an electrochemical complex, the brain. Genetics suggests that much of the cast of mind and action results from chromosomal patterns. Sociologists make the environment responsible for the rest.

I Have Been Sustained by You Ever Since I Was Born; From My Mother's Womb You Have Been My Strength

I was born in 1917 in Spokane, Washington. My brother was three years younger. Mother said, "Two is enough. Have your babies in the hospital and see that they cost a lot. Then you won't have many." We were sickly; we "cost a lot." When I was five I had "heart trouble" and spent months in the hospital. George had diphtheria and mastoiditis. Father had to sell his business and the house. Put a five-year-old alone in a hospital room and she will discover "the other world," to which I still retreat. I also discovered a worldly truth; a sick child bravely singing "Jesus Loves Me" garners attention. I had angel cake for my birthday because I was "a little angel." This is my memory of how the three tracks of my life began: The cake typifies my life in the family; the child singing for attention represents my career life; and the retreat into fantasy is the seed of my spiritual life.

I started school and began my career as a person. By 1928 my father could buy a house in an area of Protestant, lower middle-class, white, working people. Streets were not paved. Milk and ice were delivered from horse-drawn carts. In summer the water wagon sprinkled the streets to keep down the dust, and we all went barefoot. In winter, ice formed on mud puddles. Every other corner had a mom-and-pop store where one charged it until the end of the month. We bought one or two eggs at a time, a quarter of a pound of hamburger, one pickle. A chocolate was a penny; if you bit into a pink center you got one free. Children wore good clothes to school and changed to overalls afterward.

I liked school. When I started third grade my second-grade teacher said, "If you would study and pay attention you could be on the honor roll." It had never occurred to me that I had anything to do with it. Honor rolls were for little girls who were rich and popular. But after my teacher said that to me I was always on the honor roll. When I learned about a plaque for the "Best English Student" graduating from the eighth grade, I determined to get it. I did.

I had a love affair with language. Fascinated with foreign words, I read *Our Little French Cousin, The Belgian Twins,* and similar books. At nine, I copied foreign words and their meanings into notebooks. I begged Mother for a Spanish grammar, which I put under my pillow when I slept. My English teacher asked what I was going to do with "all that." I was going to learn all languages, even Latin and Greek. She snorted, "No one learns Greek."

There were the family's cultural patterns and values. My mother was of Mennonite heritage, but the family had drifted away. I never thought of her as religious, yet she had a lively interest in church and taught me what each sect was about: "Don't join those Methodists, Shirley; they're southern Methodists, not the real thing"; "We'll not go to church today; there's communion" (whatever that was); "Not the Catholics! How could you dream of such a thing?" "When Carol joined the Episcopal church, the first thing they asked for was her pledge"; "Your grandma's church lets people faint away on the floor. They speak in tongues and go crazy babbling"; "When Sister Aimie came to the Tabernacle she was so pretty, but she left them a beauty-parlor bill of fifty dollars."

My brother and I were not baptized as infants; we could make our own decisions regarding religion. I do not remember my parents going to church. My brother and I attended where we pleased. Somehow we were imbued with a conservative fundamentalist pietism: The Bible was true. Christ came to save sinners. It was sinful to smoke, drink, dance, gamble, or go to movies on Sunday. Chastity was required. Obedience came close behind. We did not have to work at poverty. We disliked Catholics, Jews, Negroes, and Greeks.

At the Methodist Sunday school they gave a two-by-three Bible picture for memorizing a Bible verse. One could trade ten of these pictures for a four-by-six. I went to Sunday school for pictures. When one was eleven one could join Epworth League. After prayers the chaperones left, and we played kissing games. The boys walked the girls home and there were long good-night kisses. I became so obsessed with guilt that I stopped being a Methodist and went to the Christian church, where the chaperones were more eagle of eye.

My father was a descendent of German immigrants. Reared a Lutheran, he joined a group that abhorred ritualism and fancy dress and adhered to a vegetarian diet, a strict exercise program, and literal interpretation of the Bible. During my growing years Father, a policeman, was much affected by the immorality of the Prohibition era. He believed in the law and struggled to uphold it. I remember him as frustrated and overwhelmed but still an idealist. We theologically disagreed on small points, so we never got around to large ones.

At fourteen I entered a school in which John Dewey had been discovered. If you enrolled in Spanish you were switched mid-semester to Latin—and I have taught Latin for forty years! I was editor of the paper, which won the national gold medal. What greater glory could there be? Then I went to a school with little creativity. I took the classical course: four years of Latin and English literature and two years of French; a little math; no science, world history, art, music. To satisfy Mother I also pursued the commercial course: business practice, economics, bookkeeping, typing, shorthand. It has served me well.

For You Are My Hope, O Lord God, My Confidence Since I Was Young

My earliest spiritual stirrings came at this time; their source was the Latin language. *Aeneid VI* had a powerful influence on me. At seventeen I translated the first six books of *The Aenied* into dactylic hexameters. I went through the Harvard Five-Foot

Shelf. I read Thomas a Kempis' *Imitation of Christ* during a required football assembly. I was exposed to Darwin and convinced of the validity of evolution, and so I began a life-long controversy with Father.

My friends went to Christian Endeavor. To join you had to be a Presbyterian. To be a Presbyterian you had to be baptized. To have friends you have to make concessions. The elders asked, "Do you acknowledge the Bible to be the truth and Jesus Christ to be your Savior?" It seemed politic to answer in the affirmative. The baptismal water rolled down my new hairdo and wet my new jacket. On Christmas Eve a girlfriend and I went to midnight mass at Our Lady of Lourdes Cathedral. The pageantry and solemnity were beyond my experience and dreams. I fell to my knees when everyone else did, and so for the first time found the prayer position. Walking home we paused to see the Spokane Falls with the moon shining on the spray. I almost discovered Christmas.

The life I have described is a child's life. A child *is* for a moment, but the thrust of a child's life is *becoming*. When my sons were youngsters they played "animals." "Let's be dogs," and there was enormous growling and barking and shaking of toys with the teeth. "Let's be lions": The roaring was tremendous and the room shuddered with activity. "Let's pretend we're people." That is what childhood is about: playing people, becoming people. My childhood was a struggle to hurry the process of becoming a person. My fantasies became dreams of being an adult and controlling my own life. I do not remember enjoying childhood but trying to escape from it. My parents were loving, concerned, and protective, but my goal was to put myself out of their reach.

We spent summers at Neuman Lake. One day I joined a crowd at the beach. A naked woman lay on a blood-covered blanket, her body ripped open from ankle to shoulder, hit by a speed boat. I observed the nakedness of the body, the quivering muscle, the pearly whiteness of bone. "That is what we are like inside," I thought. The woman died and was covered. "That is what it is to die—to be covered, to be out of sight." That evening my parents talked together about the terrible accident. When they saw me they were silent. And I was silent. I began to protect my parents. As for me, the fairy world was blown away, and I began to contemplate the nature of reality.

Oh God, You Have Taught Me Since I Was Young, and to This Day I Tell of Your Wonderful Works

I started college at the University of Pennsylvania in 1936. Edward VIII was renouncing a throne for Mrs. Simpson. We were denouncing the Krupp industrial complex and supporting the anti-Falangists. Barcelona fell to the Fifth Column at the same time Hannibal crossed the Ebro in Latin class. By my junior year Jewish refugees from Czechoslovakia were joining the faculty. At the beginning of my senior year Warsaw was taken. I majored in Greek and Latin, waited tables for my supper, and was initiated into Phi Beta Kappa.

I attended a Lutheran church with my roommate. Church was about the only excuse for getting out of the dorm at night, so we did not miss Maundy Thursday services. I had not been confirmed, so I could not take communion, but when the holy elements were raised at the consecration, the cup seemed ablaze with light. My soul stirred and said, "This is it! This is what religion is about. *This is my body; this is my blood.*" The revelation was instantaneous. I could hardly wait to discover how to participate in the glorious mystery. On Pentecost I was confirmed. I have never fallen away from the truth of that first revelation.

My conversion changed my studies. I dabbled in ancient history, began to study philosophy, and took such Bible courses as the college offered. I sought closeness to God and felt that I ought to pray, but discovered I did not know how. Suddenly, I realized that the only thing I was preparing for was to be a minister. My pastor was troubled: "When I am dressed in my cassock and surrounded by my pulpit I have no sex, but I see no future in the ministry for you."

Our Steps Are Directed by the Lord. He Strengthens Those in Whose Way He Delights

After a year at the University of Pennsylvania, taking a master's degree in general linguistics, I was accepted for a course at Deaconess House in Fort Wayne, Indiana and was alternate for a fellowship at the University of Pennsylvania; but the world was at war, and I enrolled at the University of Washington for the credits necessary to teach high school. During the next summer there was a whirlwind romance. Robert Woods and I were married in 1942 just before he was called into the Marine Corps. Everyone was doing it. I left my classroom Friday afternoon and was back in it teaching Monday morning.

In April I enlisted in the Army. While at Nacogdoches I attended the Episcopal church. At Walnut Ridge I taught Sunday school, played the chapel organ, and sang solo soprano in *The Messiah*. Transfer to a course for physical therapists at the University of Wisconsin Medical School was one of the better things that ever happened to me. It put me in a life of service to humanity and introduced me to scientific thought. Physiology, human anatomy, and physics were most rewarding. The studies were easy because of my foundation in Latin and Greek.

There was a polio epidemic and we trainees spent twelve-hour shifts doing kenny packs. I awoke to the fact that there was purpose to life. My final Army year was at McCaw Army General Hospital. The patients were paraplegics. Though they were turned every two hours in their Striker frames, they developed bed sores. One of my college professors who was

visiting the wounded came to me white as a ghost: "Is that bone
I see?" I nodded in assent. My favorite patient smiled weakly,
took my hand, and then died. Every day here I was ten years old
again, back at Newman Lake. There are questions that fire like
machine guns, and no place to hide. The inside of the body is
just as real as the outside. The difference between living and
dying may be an instant of time. Poetry and philosophy do not
explain it; physiology and pathology do not comprehend it. The
seed of understanding waits deep within to be engendered.

When the war was over I was Shirley Frese Woods, A.B.,
A.M., R.P.T., 2nd Lt., and married. Shortly, my husband
returned from the South Pacific. I had found the Army exhilarating and educational. He had been through Tarawa, Saipan, a
kamikaze attack, and Nagasaki three days after its destruction.
His educational plans were in shambles, and he had no training
for anything except artillery. We did not know each other. Had
it been 1986 instead of 1946 we probably would have said, "Nice
knowing you," and gone our own ways; but in our background
marriage was for life.

We enrolled at the University of Washington on our military educational benefits, he to finish his B.A., I to start on a
Ph.D. We cashed our war bonds and bought a house. Between
1946 and 1953 we had four children, bought and sold three
houses, went through at least six automobiles, and earned
hundreds of hours of college credits. I taught Latin, English,
and history in two high schools; became a physical therapist in
charge of cerebral palsy patients; and acquired my own physical
therapy clinic. Bob began a high-stress career in sales and
brokerage. Our religion was powdered skim milk, wheat germ,
and black-strap molasses.

During those years I first thought of what it means to be a
woman. My mother knew, but she taught me that the Nine-
teenth Amendment changed all that. My teachers (all female)
must have been flaming suffragettes. They imbued us with the
idea that girls (first) and boys (next) were equal. It never
dawned on me as a child that there was anything I could not do

because of my gender. Gender was a grammatical concept. In retrospect I see that as young ladies we lived very constricted lives. We had to be in our dorm by 7:30 P.M. We could not smoke on campus. In scholarly circles I had never felt unaccepted, and I had been an officer in the Army. But that has nothing to do with being a woman.

In the war years I began to experience a longing. I wanted a child. When I heard of anyone having a child I was consumed with envy. I would wake at night and think I must be pregnant, only to feel my flat stomach and small breasts and realize it was not so. Why did so many of us have all those babies? The earth was groaning to replace her dead. There is no orgasm like that of childbirth, no fulfillment greater than nursing a baby. Our grandmothers knew this, but our daughters try to deny it.

The creativity required to produce and nurture a child subverts all other creativity. Would you compose music? A lullaby will suffice. Would you be an artist? Try finger paints. Would you study or write? A child will tug at your skirts, and you will be happy for it. The children were tow-headed and pink and full of cute sayings. They clamored to be fed and rocked and bathed and dressed. Through it all I taught school, graded papers, canned fruit, and even raised chickens. In 1954 asthma caught me, and I lay on my bed while the children climbed over me. Was that Spirit I sought a feminine Spirit?

Spirituality requires a whole life. The years in Seattle did more than produce children and work. There were times of joy and play—picking oysters on the beaches, ferry trips to British Columbia, visits to hot springs in the Olympic Rain Forest. There were times of despair—looking down into the black waters of the lake from a bridge and wondering how cold the water would be when I plunged in.

In 1954 my husband and I declared bankruptcy and moved with all our belongings, children, cats, and dogs to California. My asthma became worse; I was driven to desensitization shots, though we had no money for this. I concluded that I suffered more from medications than from asthma. No more epinephrine, just breathing exercises. Remove the rugs, curtains, and kapok-filled pillows. Read more books on the nature of the mind. What worked was undoubtedly a combination of shots, removing offending substances, getting off the drugs, and moving to Livermore, where the radiation laboratory had jobs. We moved into a new house surrounded by clay mud. There were no fences or trees, and the wind whistled unhindered. On my fortieth birthday, hanging up laundry in the wind, I thought, "This is how it is going to be."

While in the Army I had felt a lump, no bigger than a pea but excruciatingly painful if touched. It began to grow. Now that we had a medical plan I saw a doctor. It was cancer of the parotid gland. Awaking from surgery, I found that I could see. I was desperately thirsty. The nurses tried to get me to drink from a straw. I could not. A facial nerve had been severed.

My speech was blurred. I had signed a contract to teach, so I practiced. The prayer book was the only one at hand: "Blessed is the man who walketh not in the counsel of the ungodly . . . but his delight is in the law of the Lord . . ." The *b*'s and *w*'s were hard; the *s*'s impossible. The doctor said, "Of course he will love you in spite of your face." He said, "Here is a new hat." It had a wide brim and a scarf that hid most of my face. After one day of school it was all right. Though everyone else could see my face, I could not; so I forgot about it. It proved to be a blessing. Before I had looked bland and anonymous. Now people recognized me.

People talked to me of healing and faith: "You need only the faith of a mustard seed." The size of the seed is not the measure of faith; the shape produces the parallel. A mustard seed is round. You think you see it from all sides because you think all sides are alike; but you can see it only one hemisphere at a time. And there is the inside. To bite into a mustard seed provides a surprise; faith is not easy to know. My faith is that God is faithful, not capricious. God will not break His laws, not even for me. A nerve was cut. Cries, beating the breast, fasting will not grow it together. God says, "Bite into the mustard seed;

you will find the surprise." Begging God for healing is not faith. It is saying, "Prove that you are God by giving me the impossible healing." God does not accept challenges. Faith accepts life as it is given. My faith was strengthened.

The Lord Cares for the Lives of the Godly; and Their Inheritance Shall Last Forever

My oldest child was in eighth grade, my youngest in first. Teaching is an almost ideal job for a mother with school-age children, but I was not always home on time to pass out milk and cookies. My teaching career began in Moclips, Washington, where I taught Latin to the Indians on the reservation. Students are easily motivated if the learning excites them. Teenagers and young adults are easily stimulated by the spiritual and seek out the mystery of life with longing to know it. The teacher's reward is the education she receives.

Reading is an important rung of the spiritual ladder. Reading for pleasure is only indulgence, no better for you than the box of chocolates that often accompanies it. Reading for information is only little better than digging a hole. Schools mistakenly reward students who read the most books, as if quantity had merit. Advocates of speed-reading reward the one who can wet his finger fastest. Those who profit from reading know that it opens the gates of the universe. One lives far beyond the boundaries of one's own small world. The reader stretches his soul to accommodate the worlds without and the world within. The soul is the principle of life by which one lives, and reading gives breadth to the experiences from which it is made. The interior world opened up in childhood now becomes the place where the spirit dwells and fosters insight for living. By reading Dante I learned Italian. I studied Hebrew and am rewarded by comprehending the Old Testament in its original language.

Reading and writing are soul mates. When you read enough you will complete the act by writing. The work of the soul is creativity. Writing became my habit with those early notebooks of foreign words. In high school I enjoyed journalism and accumulated my own poems. In college I collected the thoughts of great persons. Later I kept journals of my own thinking.

They Shall Not Be Ashamed in Bad Times, and in Days of Famine They Shall Have Enough

After years of misunderstanding, my husband and I divorced. The judge only asked me if I could support the children. My daughter was a freshman in college, two sons were entering high school, and the youngest was eleven. It was 1967, the Summer of Love. I taught summer school at the University of Kansas and took one son, Jamie, with me because, I reasoned, the boys get along better when one is gone. I notified their father to take care of the other two boys. They promptly ran away to join their sister. The boy in Kansas felt he was missing all the fun.

On the way home, in the middle of the Mojave Desert, the car lost its brakes, turned over three times, and left my child and me hanging upside down. We crawled out of the windows and painfully made our way to a lonely service station. A state trooper looked in on us, decided we were whole, and left. The local bus refused to stop. Finally, we got a ride in the back of a service van. The temperature was 118. Jamie had filled our thermos jug with ice that morning. That jug of water saved our lives. That night he said, "We were supposed to die." My ex-husband came and took us home.

The dark night had come. There were marijuana, long hair, beads, rock music, and LSD. For none of them had my life prepared me, and in short time I met them all. The oldest boy spent two weeks in "juvie" because he refused to have a hair cut. Jamie, who had taken a journalism course that summer in Kansas, took his older brother to the newspaper to have him photographed wearing the beads that got him suspended from school. The youngest was expelled from school for selling a Lifesaver laced with LSD. From model mother I quickly dropped to the worst mother in town. The church objected to acolytes with long hair. I who had not known how to pray began to pray.

My daughter graduated from college, married, and went to New Orleans. My two oldest sons graduated from high school and went their separate ways to college. When I was alone with the youngest I recognized a pattern I had seen in three generations: It was not just pot; he truly was detached from reality and saw the world through different eyes.

I Waited Patiently upon the Lord; He Stooped to Me and Heard My Cry. He Lifted Me Out of the Desolate Pit, Out of the Mire and Clay, He Set My Feet upon a High Cliff and Made My Footing Sure

I often strolled to a church in the evening and sat in the garden to meditate. One evening, in the stillness and calmness, I heard a voice quietly but distinctly say, "You will be a deacon." I looked around. No one was there, yet I had heard the voice very clearly. Whether it came from inside me or outside I do not know. In my life story there are two epiphanies. The first was an experience of light (the chalice); it was as though I was nudged to turn in a direction I would not have taken otherwise. The second was this experience of calm, of the still, small voice. Both remain very real to me. I make no attempt to explain either.

I did not know what a deacon was. I found a tract, "You are Never Too Old to Become a Deaconess," and consulted the rector, who said, "The diocese is just starting classes on Saturdays." I enrolled, the only woman. Still, it got me away from home on Saturdays. In May they gave the deacon's examinations. I passed them all. The Diocesan Standing Committee asked my expectations. I replied, "To be a deaconess." They looked at me suspiciously and asked if it was not really ordination I had in mind. "I want to be a deaconess," I reiterated. The standing committee warned, "Then don't come back and ask to be ordained."

I was too naïve in church history and polity to understand. St. Paul recognized the work of women in the new Church. They are "deaconesses," *servers*, in his Epistles. In the early Church deaconesses brought word and sacraments to women, especially those in purdah. Mid-nineteenth century Protestant churches again recognized women workers as deaconesses. Unlike their male counterparts, deacons, the women were "ordered" not "ordained." Ordination requires the consent of the standing committees of Episcopal dioceses; ordering does not. I learned this later.

That summer I decided I must escape. I borrowed money for a trip to Greece. One day I was trying to avoid the rock music at home, and the next I was dining on a rooftop of a hotel in Athens listening to the bouzoukis and gazing at the lighted Parthenon on the Acropolis. It was a wonderful summer— Athens, Delphi, Olympia, Maecenae, Crete, sailing to Rhodes and to Cyprus, then to Ephesus, Smyrna, Ankara, and Stamboul. I steered a small boat through the Bosphoros like Jason sailing the Argo.

Upon return I was greeted with, "The standing committee will see you at 4:00." Elated with my adventures, I walked in and said, "I have flown from Constantinople to see you." Their response was more dramatic: "You have been admitted to ordination as a deacon." During my absence the Episcopal Church had voted that all women who had been ordered as deaconesses with prayers and the laying on of hands were deacons. In 1970 I was ordained to the diaconate. Thus I became a deacon without asking for it.

My ordination was an out-of-place incident; life went on as usual. There were still difficulties with my sons, who were trying to adjust themselves on the threshold of manhood. On Washington's Birthday, 1972, I was trying to calm myself by painting kitchen cupboards. The middle son phoned to pour forth his troubles. He mentioned suicide. We talked and he agreed to go to the university infirmary. At midnight my parish priest knocked at the door crying, "Jamie's hanged himself." Washington's Birthday, 1972, was the end and the beginning. Ten days later I was back in the classroom. I taught W. H. Auden's poem on the death of Yeats. When summer came I went to Italy to mourn. The sun shone warm as I climbed to Francis' Hermitage atop Mt. Subaccio.

For Your Arrows Have Already Pierced Me, and Your Hand Presses Me Hard

Facing death: This was the lesson it was now my task to learn. It was bitter. Still, I am grateful for the lesson that became bittersweet. We can console only when we have allowed ourselves to be consoled; we cease to fear death when we have seen our dearest ones go into death. He said "We should have died" that day when we were in the desert together. Instead, he separated himself from me and I began to live.

My oldest requested funds for another attempt at college— his fourth. It was that or the Marines. I thought the Marines would be fine. By December he had finished boot camp, and I went to graduation. His father sat down beside me. Bob was in the midst of his second divorce. We all had dinner together. I spent Christmas alone in Anza Borrego Desert to think. Later I wrote to suggest that Bob come home. He came, and with him the hope that the old days would return. However, we do not live backward. Bob and I are different people now, with different goals. Sometimes they coincide; often they do not. Sometimes we go together; sometimes not. We can depend upon each other in an emergency.

Understanding love was more difficult than learning to pray. I have "been in love"; I have experienced "mother love"; I believe I have "been loved." But being loved by parents or husband or children or friends is varied. I even believe that I have experienced "the love of God," but whether that is subjective or objective I hesitate to say. Love must be important; of all the commands of religion, the greatest is to love. "Not to love" must be the most desolate of states, "not to be loved" the most comparable to nonexistence.

Love is "passionate concern." The Latin verb for concern, *cerno,* means *see,* with the mind's eye, to understand. *Passionate* comes from a word related to suffering. So "passionate concern" is a caring that brings one to the point of suffering. If I love my children, this may cause me pain. If I am "in love," I am so concerned with the object of my love that I put this concern above all others. Passionate concern for the hungry, sick, or imprisoned is identification with them so that the lover is hungry, experiences pain, or lacks freedom. "Love for humanity" is taking on the sufferings of mankind. We say of God's love: "He loved us so . . . that he suffered and died."

Shortly after my ordination I was asked to teach theology in the diocesan training program. When the Diocesan School for Ministries was formed in 1976 I was on the faculty. The years from 1970, when I became a deacon, to 1977, when I was ordained to the priesthood, were a heady time for women in the Episcopal Church, which had been very conservative on women's issues. Ten years before recognition of the female diaconate, women could not vote in the councils of the church or be seminarians. I was the third woman in California ordained to the diaconate. Within two years there were two more. We met for support and to discuss the issues of priesthood. By 1976 we were about eight. Women were graduating from seminaries with theological degrees.

I had not thought that women's ordination as priests would be accepted soon, but it happened in 1976. My earlier request to take the General Ordination Examinations was denied because "there is no reason for you to take them." Soon I took and passed the examinations. I was ordained to the priesthood on St. Bede's Day, 1977. The Venerable Bede is a favorite of mine. I had classes read the beginning of his history in Latin as a conclusion to Caesar's wars. I stood at his resting place in Durham Cathedral and felt a certain familiarity. The day after learning my ordination date, reaching for a book on a top shelf, I jiggled the bookcase. A book shook loose and hit me on the head. It was Bede's *Ecclesiastical History*. I acknowledged our relationship.

I believe I have been a good priest. I have never doubted that I am a priest. My first priestly act was hearing confession and granting absolution to a man just out of the penitentiary. This signified to me that my past was forgiven. It had been forty years since my first vision of the meaning of the Eucharist. Now I lift the chalice and paten, thankful for that vision, and present it as a vision to others.

Priesthood puts a public character on one's life. For many this is unexpected and unwelcome. A person who has cultivated a devotional life may find that ordination gnaws into the privacy of the love affair with God. At first the diaconal role took me away from private prayers. I made accommodation to that. Then priesthood required a new accommodation. As a priest one is praying with and for everyone, with no time for private thoughts. The reward is that contemplation must be done at times other than Sunday morning, and stronger habits of prayer and study must be developed on other days of the week. Emergency becomes the rule, and the priest's time is everybody's time, so flexibility must be part of priestly character. The trade-off is that the life of a priest is never boring and can be highly exciting.

It dawned on me that an old way of life had gone and a new way had come. I was more and more involved with the Diocesan School. By 1979 I was thinking of being its director. I was nominated for the California Teachers' Association Teacher of the Year Gold Award. I had been suggested as bishop of a new diocese. I knew I would not be nominated for the post of bishop but decided to apply for it and the gold award. The gold plaque now hangs on my wall. What I wanted was to be director of the school.

At Grace Cathedral in San Francisco I was instituted as dean of the School for Deacons with glorious hoopla. At my desk I discovered that the faculty had not been paid for the previous spring semester. We ran the school on $17,000 that year, including the previous year's faculty pay. The budget now is over $100,000 a year, and we have never been in debt. The school is qualified as a degree-granting institution. The last ten years have been the best. The scholar can bloom; the writer and editor has a forum; the teacher has eager students; the traveler finds the world open; the priest celebrates and prays.

I Shall Pour Out My Spirit on All Mankind; Your Sons and Daughters Will Prophesy, Your Old Men Will Dream Dreams, and Your Young Men See Visions

When does dream become vision? I want to express my life in terms of the dreams I had. Dreams are flimsy things, part sunlight, part shadow. Flesh and blood existence gets in the way of dreams and casts its shadow, obscuring the sunlight. But flesh and blood existence is a necessary structure upon which to hang a shadow. The shadow hangs there like a coat on a hook; it needs flesh and blood to fill out its substance. Only in mythology does substance exist without its shadow, without reflection in the mirror. Whoever has lost the dream life lives precariously with no past and no future. Dream lives start early, in fantasy. The substantial life impinges upon the fantasy and tames it; for a life lived in fantasy is psychotic. The tamed dream takes its shape from what we call reality and extends reality from what *is* to what *could be*. Thus the dream becomes vision.

Vision takes the world as it is and extends it into a world as it could be. The next step is to process the "could be" world into the "is" world.

Prayer has been called an investigation of one's own mind. In this search may come discovery of "the Other." The ego senses that there is something, someone else. The shadow life is not alone; there are other shadows. Sometimes light shines through, and the visionary becomes aware that it is possible to communicate with the Other. Nebulous nothing becomes numinous nothing. Shadows disappear when they play in the sunlight. When the ego begins to communicate with the Other, shadows disappear into the sunlight and reappear as visions touched with glory.

For a visionary who has begun to emerge from "could be" into "is," there is a sense of the revelation of truth, a "knowing" that the dreamer has from communication with the Other. This "knowing" does not bring power but humility. Without humility, dreams are dangerous. One should not seek to know the mind of God, for that is impossible. In prayer, one accepts insights that come as light through the cloud cover. Visions are for the young who can fulfill them. Old age turns us back into dreamers who know there is not world or time enough. But there is time to play in the dreams and review what a lifetime has taught. The only way we can seek meaning is to reassess the past. The future unrolls in the mind of God.

> I seem to be one of the God-struck.
> Does God single out an individual?
> Or are all people "God-struck"?
> Do some hide it better than others?
> Do some ignore it?
> Are some incapable of response to it?
> Does God strike this man down? – Saul.
> Does God lift this one up? – David.
> Is it in our genes, predestined?
> Or are we masters of our own fate?
>   Or perhaps there is no God
>   And we are tangled in a net of consequences

Over which we have no control.
Bertrand Russell said, "The pain is in the mind."
If so, can we change our minds?
Re-thinking is our last prayer;
Now we lie in the hand of God.
Outside of time, with no boundaries.

Chapter 8

Disorder or Congruence?

Frances Merchant Carp, Ph.D.

Introduction to Frances Merchant Carp *

In the chronicle of her life Frances Carp portrays by allusion and inference some qualities that explain the scholarly achievements of her life. Let the record show that the book from the Texas period she quietly mentions is one of the classic works in gerontology (Carp, 1966). In this book she performed an incredibly demanding feat of combining an ethnography of the people and their milieu with hard-nosed research data analysis. Having seen her report in manuscript form, I urged her to split it into two reports, on the theory that those interested in people would not read her statistics and those interested in facts would prefer to ignore people. I was wrong. Her touch with people, facts, and words was exactly right to produce this highly readable book, which still stands as a model for evaluation research, enlightened by the best knowledge in both clinical and theoretical psychology. This incident has the elements

---

*By M. Powell Lawton, Ph.D., Philadelphia Geriatric Center, Philadelphia, Pennsylvania.

Lives of Career Women: Approaches to Work, Marriage, Children, edited by Frances M. Carp. Plenum/Insight, New York, 1991.

of the lifetime theme and variations of Carp's work that belie any thought of "disorderliness" of career.

First and foremost, the theme in her work has remained that of people *and* facts. I know of no work she has done that has not begun with the needs, capabilities, or problems of human beings. All along the way, every bit of her research addressed ways of improving the well-being of persons. Her research on the BART (Bay Area Rapid Transit) system remains fifteen years later *the* exemplary attempt to probe the human experiences associated with a vast socioenvironmental system like public transit.

The early book displayed Carp's ability to discern and use the best in research methodology. I first learned the statistical method multiple regression analysis from the effective way this technique was applied in this book. Subsequently, a whole series of applications of once-esoteric analytic methods to different meat-and-potatoes problems have put readers far ahead in their knowledge of social research.

The end of this chapter alludes almost in passing to the theoretical contributions Carp has made, especially in operationalizing person–environment congruence. In many different settings her work has demonstrated that outcomes for a person are better if the person's needs and abilities are matched to what the environment can provide.

Without presuming to contribute to the substance of this book, I can still point out one way in which women did not always come in second: Were I writing about my own career I could document that virtually every major step in it was taken with scientific stimulation and personal motivation provided in one way or another by something Carp did first.

Although I feel it most important to document her scientific contributions, it should be noted that the warmth and vivaciousness that come through so clearly in this chapter are very much in evidence "in person." She has challenged and inspired colleagues, and has nurtured many young scholars, having been totally generous in encouraging their own development.

The pattern of my work—mostly unplanned, with unexpected turnings and surprising components—suggests a "disorderly career," one of the least successful patterns (Wilensky,

1961). Subjectively, however, it was satisfying. I think that is because the work I did was a good match with my needs and abilities, and that it fit well with personal aspects of my life. This suggests that congruence (Carp & Carp, 1984) is a better explanatory concept.

Growing Up in a Rural Slum

An unincorporated town among citrus and walnut groves (now near Disneyland) was a delightful place in which to grow up. There was no policeman, and no doors were locked. The fire department was volunteer. When the siren blew, everyone went along to watch. We had a post office, a bank, a grocery store, a butcher shop, and two churches. Beaches were close and the mountains not far. Country children were bused to school. The rest walked the few blocks.

Grandparents were important in my life. My mother's parents were said to follow the typical immigrant pattern in emphasizing education. All of their girls were teachers. Dad's parents' families were in this country before the American Revolution, but they paid equal attention to education. Their daughters were trained to be self-supporting, though in a variety of ways (hat making, nursing, commercial art) to fit individual inclinations.

We were relatively affluent in the community—the only family in which both parents held paying jobs. My mother was the only married teacher. Her mother and two youngest siblings lived with us. During the Depression, other relatives moved in. At school we used both sides of the paper, then practiced penmanship on it sideways and on both diagonals. I was unusual having private lessons in piano, cello, and ballet. My mother taught me to follow the rules and put everything I had into whatever I did. Dad taught me to think for myself.

A club was meeting at school in March 1933 when the

earthquake hit. As we ran out the door the facade above it fell. The girl beside me was killed. And newspapers reported that I was. Unconscious, I missed the uproar. A blow to the lower spine fused a section. The doctor taught me that injury and pain are not excuses for avoiding or missing out on anything.

My high school had fewer than 400 students. The boys' coach taught the first two years of math: We filled in workbooks, and he read the newspaper. I was editor of the school paper and annual for two years, which excused me from English. Of course, I had planned on going to college, but in my junior year the science teacher pointed out that I would not be eligible for a four-year college because, like the other girls, I had not been enrolled in sufficient math and science classes. That summer he tutored me in chemistry and algebra II, and in senior year I took physics, solid geometry, and trigonometry with the boys. I was vice president of the senior class and of the student body. Because I received a B−in an art course I did not take−I was salutatorian. Girls were never first.

Stanford University

I applied to Stanford and to a prestigious girls' college in Southern California. Upon receipt of a full scholarship to the latter, my mother and I went to visit. The students seated at lunch did not disguise their disdain for the students who served them to earn their own meals. I declined the scholarship. Stanford did not accept me because my high-school transcript had not arrived. So Dad went to the high school, and shortly after he beckoned me from a class to hand me a letter from Stanford. I was accepted, though I would live in what was normally a trunk room.

The last two years of high-school math were so enjoyable that there was no question about a major. However, the instructor of my first and only college math course was strongly aversive to female persons. He would not respond to our raised hands or talk to us outside class. I was assigned to an "advanced standing" section in history of Western civilization. After one assignment I was in a regular section. The senior sponsor of my wing of the dorm literally wept over me as finals approached because I did not study. What a shock to see all C's except one B.

My English instructor said I should "learn more about human nature" in order to improve my writing, and I had to fulfill a social-science requirement, so I enrolled in introductory psychology. I enjoyed it as I had enjoyed the summer and final year of high-school math and science. The professor suggested I consider psychology as a major. One day I received an anonymous letter: "I hope you are satisfied!"—enclosing a newspaper clipping. My high-school boyfriend, for whom I had found little time on term break, had dived into shallow water and had broken his neck. I did not date for two years but focused on courses and modern dance under a student of Martha Grahams'.

As a sophomore the introductory philosophy professor allowed me to take his seminar in St. Thomas Aquinas' *Summa Theologica* with two graduate students, one of whom had left a Jesuit seminary because he was permitted to read only portions of the *Summa*. The books were taken from the rare books library to a locked room in the philosophy department, to which only the instructor and we three students had keys. It was an exciting experience. Probably I would have been satisfied with my B and might have majored in philosophy had the professor not told me that my grade was not an A only because I was an undergraduate.

By junior year I was a committed psychology major, on scholarship and grading papers for professors. I graduated with Greatest Distinction, a member of Phi Beta Kappa and Sigma Xi. At graduation, a professor informed my parents that the department expected me back for graduate work in the fall. (I had not told them.) My mother said I must be practical and get a teaching certificate. Dad pointed out that I could be self-supporting at graduate school (with a fellowship and assistant-ships) and should make the decision. I minored in education on condition that I do all of that work on independent study.

In one project I kept coming across the statement that high-school students have unrealistic occupational goals, but could locate no study to support it; so I did one. Boys' "want-to-be" goals were unrealistic, their "expect-to-be" goals realistic. A girl typically "wanted" to be a nurse, a teacher, and the like, but "expected" to be "just a housewife." The professor suggested I submit the results to a journal. It published the findings on males but judged those on females "not of general interest."

World War II

In October I met a transfer student. On December 7 we both were at a party when the news of Pearl Harbor came. Our first date was December 18. On December 22 I told a young man who expected to go home with me for Christmas that he could not. In January the department said my credentials would be stronger if I took the Ph.D. from another university and suggested where to apply. I had a tough decision. I had found the man I wanted to marry. He had earned the A.B. degree from Massachusetts State College and the M.A. degree from the University of Oregon, and he had completed most Ph.D. requirements at Stanford, so he would return to Stanford after the war. Continuing in school while the men were in the service seemed frivolous. My Ph.D. could wait. In March Al was sworn into the Navy, which gave him one day's leave in June. We were married in the garden of one of our professors by her husband. As we drove down the coast to Al's station in Los Angeles, I was awarded the M.A. *in absentia.*

As a uniformed civilian with the Army Air Corps I taught military correspondence—100 men, 200 field boots, 100 type-writers, from 6:00 A.M. to 3:00 P.M. Al and I agreed that this was no time to bring a child into the world, but I found my hands making baby clothes. "For friends," I said, but soon my head caught up with my hands. It was not that simple. Two miscarriages later, Al was sent to Harvard University in preparation for the South Pacific. If pregnant I should not risk the trip. If not I would join him. The rabbit said, "No." I took the first train. The rabbit was wrong. Alone in the hospital, except for visits from our perfect newborn son, Bert, I truly celebrated Christmas.

That summer Bert and I lived in a cabin in the Sierra Nevada. Transportation was a baby carriage. We had no phone, and I fetched our water and wood for the stove. Protection from bears who snuffed our garbage each night was my toothbrush through a hasp. When Al returned we decided sagely that introduction to his almost year-old son should be when the child was awake and happy. So we drove 250 miles and plucked Bert out of bed at 2:00 A.M.

Back to Stanford

We returned to the university for Al to complete the Ph.D. Mine, from another institution, would come later. I worked for the registrar—telling veterans not to bring their wives! For full pay, I went to the office mornings, while Al was at home, and brought work home to do in the afternoons. The head secretary in the administrative offices called me in to tell me I was turning in too much work. In late summer the professor in whose garden we were married came to me offering a fellowship. I said that I could not leave the registrar just before registration, that we needed the money, and that the department had recommended another university for my Ph.D. The registrar said that the university could survive without me in the office, that I would get more money from the fellowship, that Stanford's prestige was excellent, and "Go back to school!"

Many male graduate students had wives working in jobs such as I had held, but my husband and I had been unique in having a child. Now we were doubly so in working on two doctorates. I scheduled work after noon, when a neighbor or student came to sit with Bert. In clinical case conferences it was often suggested that a mother's job contributed to a child's problems. I matched clinic children with well-adjusted school children on age, sex, I.Q., and social status; gave their mothers a standard vocational interest test; and asked whether they worked outside the home. I found that the mother's work status was not related to her child's adjustment. The fit of that status with her profile on the vocational interest test was: both mothers with strong occupational interests and who were not working, and mothers with "housewife" profiles who were working, were more likely to have children with psychological problems. Journals found this, too, "not of general interest."

Al brought home a stray puppy. Bert named him Thesis because "everyone else around here has one." What were we doing to our precious child? On the afternoon of my French exam, the babysitter did not come, so Bert went with me. The French professor was charming with him while I did the written work, and Bert napped during the oral section. After two years Al had completed all requirements for the Ph.D. and I all but the orals, despite another miscarriage. One orals date remained. A male student had a job *if* he had the Ph.D. The faculty left it to us. He took the orals.

A Doctor and an "All But"

We drove to Madison, where Al had a position at the University of Wisconsin in September. For a while we lived off the garden of a friend. I found a job as clinical psychologist at the County Mental Health Service. The director of the service was the wife of the chairman of the psychology department, which sent its clinical students to the service for practicum training. Al was in charge of the clinical program. Two "Camerons" confused the students sufficiently, so I was asked to use my maiden name. The service shared a building with the Service for Unwed

Mothers. As I, "Miss Merchant," became noticeably pregnant I came in for much ribbing. Pregnancy further delayed my Ph.D., but I wanted another child. Bert attended an excellent morning pre-school, and at noon I took him home where there was a neighbor or a college student.

Al enjoyed all of college teaching except teaching and found an opening as chief clinical psychologist at a Veterans Administration hospital in Michigan. I found one at a college in Kalamazoo for the fall. On the third day of Richard's life we headed for Michigan via California for a visit with my family. In Kalamazoo I hired a woman who was wonderful with both boys and who was a trained housekeeper and cook. We reveled in this find until her husband was told to leave town or go to jail. I then found a woman who did well with the children, and returned to cooking. Mornings, Bert went to work with me to attend the college pre-school, and Richard napped. We three had lunch at home together. I was usually home again by the time both children woke up from their afternoon naps.

The college offered the B.A. in psychology but had had no mainline psychologist for two years, and many students lacked courses required for graduation. Therefore, I taught a heavy load of large classes in experimental psychology, beginning and advanced statistics, abnormal psychology, and history of psychology. The college gave me one day off to take my orals. I flew to California at night, took the orals, flew back the next night, taught the next day, and drove to Grand Rapids to teach an evening extension course for the University of Michigan. The president of my college was shocked at my request to apply for the chairmanship of the department that the college intended to open and was glad to accept my resignation. I found a position at Michigan State College (now University) for the fall.

A "Pair o' Docs"

The Ph.D. diploma was handed to me by the registrar who had encouraged me to go for it. We moved to a small town, from which Al drove forty-five miles to the VA hospital and I drove thirty-five miles in the opposite direction to East Lansing. A grandmotherly woman lived with us during work-weeks. One icy evening, after both cars had skidded, we decided to find jobs in a balmier climate. Al found one with the United States Air Force (USAF) Personnel Research Center at Lackland Air Force Base (AFB), Texas. I completed my teaching contract and followed him with the children. Soon I was a research psychologist in the USAF Combat Crew Laboratory at Randolph AFB, on the opposite side of San Antonio. The Navy wanted to recall Al for Korean War duty. We held our breaths until the Air Force classified his civilian work "essential." My laboratory studied the phenomenon of "crewness" and devised measures of it which, along with measures of relevant skills, predicted bombing success of B 29s. A nice young woman, mother of two girls, was at home watching my boys while I was away.

I was hired with the understanding of short days, but the USAF had no appropriate mechanism. Each pay period my record showed x hours paid leave and y hours unpaid leave, and the accounting office complained about the work I created. My job was interesting, and co-workers were capable and congenial, but one day they "locked down" the base. For national security reasons I could not even phone home or Bert's school. When the all-clear sounded, I drove much too fast and found a sad little boy sitting on the school steps. I resigned from the job.

Fortunately I had the credentials to establish a clinical practice. One summer I taught at a Catholic college and the next at Trinity University. The dean called me in. The university wanted to establish a solid psychology department in the School of Arts and Sciences, removing psychology from the School of Education. With embarrassment, this southern gentleman asked, "Do you plan to have more children?" We did not. Then, "As chairman, can you fire the entire psychology faculty and recruit more appropriate persons within one academic year?" I could.

Al had a job he liked. I had a challenge. Roads were never

icy, everything was air-conditioned, and, best of all, we liked the people. We bought an acre, built a home, and joined a church. A group of us with children about the same ages bought several lots and built a swimming pool and a basic club house within walking distance of our home. The YMCA was three blocks in the other direction. We grew into a strong circle of friends, among whom I was the only working wife. They considered us an anomaly and introduced us to newcomers as "our pair o' docs." Grandparents came often, and the boys enjoyed going to them while Al and I attended scientific/ professional meetings here and abroad. Major holidays were four- and then three-generation celebrations.

The department was restaffed, developed a solid curriculum, and later qualified to offer the master's degree. The numbers of faculty and major students grew. The physical facilities were greatly expanded and improved. I did some private clinical work and unpaid evaluations for community agencies. The University of Texas invited Al, a Catholic nun with a Ph.D. in sociology, and me to design a study of the impact of rehousing upon the elderly poor. The rules of Sister's order made it necessary for her to withdraw. Al did also because of time spent at the Pentagon. I completed a longitudinal research protocol and received funding.

I drove the boys to their schools on the way to mine and picked them up in the afternoon. The same woman still came to clean when her daughters went to school, and left when we got home. When her third daughter was born, we adjusted for the time being and were glad to have her back. After her youngest had open-heart surgery she brought the child along with her for several months. She did our ironing and had her own "ironing lady." Somehow we managed both households. My four sisters-in-law gave me a hard time about not staying at home. On the final occasion Al's mother sat us down, questioned us, and then pointed out that I spent more time with my children than any of my sisters-in-law did with theirs.

I received a federal grant for my salary and secretarial

support to write a book on the first phase of the "old-person–new-environment" study (Carp, 1966). The department had settled into routine, and I was glad to step out as chairperson. When I returned to the university it was a relief to exchange committee for research time. I was familiar with lower back pain and ignored it except for using a heating pad and aspirin. While making Bert's birthday cake I collapsed and was hospitalized with a "rubber" leg and a "dropped" foot, in traction with a "doughnut" pillow at the base of my spine to protect severe burns from a heating pad. Groggy with morphine, I phoned the dean. Without hesitation he said that my only task was to get well. My check arrived each of the eight months I was away from the university. It was good to go back.

Within months, Al phoned from Washington, very excited. His next step in a USAF career meant assignment to the Pentagon, and he had been invited to be director of selection for the Peace Corps. Through the years we each had had job "feelers," and we had explored appointments for us both at the University of Michigan and the Menninger Clinic, but we had not seriously considered moving. Now Bert was in college, but Richard was just beginning his sophomore year in high school. My relationship with the university and personal friendships had deepened during the months of hospital stay, bedrest, confinement to a wheelchair, and learning to walk. We had arranged to build a cottage on the Gulf Coast. On the other hand, Al needed to switch from armed services to peace; my university position held little challenge, and Washington, D.C. should have interesting job opportunities for me; and we were not delighted with Richard's school. Al went to the Peace Corps. Richard mourned while I fulfilled my university contract, transferred clients to other therapists, and sold the house. I was offered a job in Washington, D.C., nominally as a psychologist but to do administrative work, and turned it down. I arranged for others to take over some ongoing research. I did not want to give up the old-person–new-environment study, but the University of Texas could not fund out-of-state-projects. I packed the data and hoped. I had had federal support to write the book. We bought a house in Bethesda to be near a good high school. After a few weeks Richard was delighted with life. Earlier I had given a paper at a National Institutes of Health (NIH) workshop. When an institute director learned that I had literally moved into the neighborhood he offered me a position with the bonus of intramural funds for my research. My first assignment was to edit the book in which that paper would appear. While working at NIH I met many fascinating people and learned a great deal. My research progressed despite having to clear every instrument through the Office of Management and Budget (OMB). Being a bureaucrat was fun for a few years, which was all we planned. Professional persons went to the Peace Corps knowing they could *not* remain more than five years, which meant that most left after two or three. During the Washington years we marched together for civil rights.

When Richard graduated from high school Al and I went to a research institute in California, he to take the helm of a large, ongoing study and I to establish a program to embrace my research and that of others. Al became disillusioned with the study. He found a position in Berkeley, we moved to San Francisco, and I transferred my grants to the University of California (UC) Medical School in that city. During these years Al and I marched against the Vietnam War and took food and clothes to sitting-in students, Richard among them.

Two years later I was invited by the Institute of Urban and Regional Development at UC Berkeley to head the behavioral science components of two multidisciplinary studies of BART (Bay Area Rapid Transit) Impact with the understanding that, when time permitted, I would continue my own research from that base. The sexism was a surprise. Only recently had the men's and women's faculty clubs combined—largely due to financial straits. Not long before no female was allowed in the men's dining room. My high salary was cited in reports to the federal government, which had an eye on UC Berkeley's equal opportunity record at that time, but as an institute employee I had no voice or vote in university affairs. Women who had long and eminent careers at Berkeley were in its institutes. When I completed an application to continue research I had started before coming to Berkeley the institute director informed me that a male *landscape architect* would be principal investigator (PI). He knew nothing about the proposed study, and the funding agency knew nothing about him. I asked the director why this man was to be PI. He had been approved to submit applications through the university, and I had not. Why not? The director had not requested it. Why not? I might not "pass." On what basis? Few women did, and the director did not want to "look bad." I could face the possibility of not "passing" but could not accept being barred from trying.

With the application in hand I walked a few blocks to an institution established by a professor who had resigned from UC over the loyalty oath controversy during the McCarthy years. The application was retyped and mailed. In due time it was funded. Other projects followed. Al became interested, and we designed and conducted two studies together. One dealt solely with women. The National Institute for Mental Health (NIMH), which funded the study, did not question the selection of subjects, and several journals published articles reporting the results. It was a pleasant change of pace to serve on several doctoral committees for the psychology department at UC Berkeley.

Al is delighted to "act retired," but I maintain an affiliation with the Wright Institute and enjoy completing reports for which there was no time during data collection and processing, and I co-direct research funded through the Center for Environmental Design Research at UC Berkeley. We travel much and enjoy out-of-the-way places (the "Silk Road," rafting down the Colorado River through the Grand Canyon, watching the gray whales from a rubber raft and exploring the desert islands off

Baja California, and driving without itinerary through England or the western states).

Taking Stock with Hindsight

Looking back, was my pattern disorderly or congruent? Some of my university mentors have said that my career did not live up to their expectations, which argues for the Wilensky (1961) interpretation. Without question, it appears "disorderly." For example, it is difficult even to enumerate my jobs. However, underlying the disorder is a theme of consistency: In each I was a psychologist. Throughout I enjoyed the freedom the field gives to perform different tasks simultaneously and at various times (clinician, professor, administrator, federal bureaucrat, researcher) and to fit work with current personal considerations. My choice of field and my work career have fit well with my needs at any one time and as they have changed over time.

Similarly, my personal life may appear disorderly. For example, I count twenty-seven homes. However, I shared them all with the same man. No one thought our precipitous, wartime marriage had a chance of surviving. It is the central consistent and dependable cable in my life. Hindsight's messages are that this was and is the man for me, and that when we married I had a limited idea of what I now understand love to be.

Over the years Al's attitude toward my work shifted. Return to graduate school was all right if it did not interfere with his progress. His first job took precedence over my nearly-completed Ph.D. Increasingly, decisions were based on considerations for us both. When my first book was published Al had a piece of jewelry made to commemorate the occasion. Coming into a research field in which I had worked he expected to be co-PI. Several years ago he assumed responsibility for dinners every other month.

Had our later attitudes been our attitudes earlier we might have acted differently. Would we have moved less? It looks as if our moves were due to Al's job changes. The intra-Michigan move was due entirely to mine—Al stayed at the same job, and we moved to be closer to my new one. The predominant pattern, him going to a new job and me following, was due largely to the fact that a month's notice was appropriate to his work but not to mine when I was at a university. I either had a position when we made the decision or was willing to run the risk of finding one in the new location. The most difficult move for me was from San Antonio. Had we remained I would be professor emerita. I would not trade that for the professional experiences and personal adventures that followed the move, and we are in touch with Texas friends.

Having children involved career disorder. When they were young I wanted work hours that left me time with them, which restricted employment opportunities. College teaching, even with clinical practice and research added, fit with motherhood because my schedule was flexible. Lectures could be planned at any time. Appointments and research tasks were at my convenience. I felt that as long as the kitchen floor was clean the boys' well-being did not depend upon my being the scrubber. I would probably have been a worse mother if I had stayed at home. Both sons say I might have smothered them had I not had compelling career interests into which to channel some energy. To me, the validation of my working while they were growing up is that both are happy, successful men and fathers who chose to share their adult lives with career-oriented women. I would not trade them for the most eminent career in the world.

In the eyes of the beholder disorder may have won the day. In my view congruence wins. First, consider only me: Concentration on career to the exclusion of husband and children might or might not have benefited my career but surely would have left other strong needs unmet and left me unhappy and unfulfilled as a person. Confinement to housewifery would have left strong achievement needs unmet, with similar negative personal results and consequently lessened efficacy as wife and mother. Turning now to Al's and my lack of careful planning and follow-through to achieve consistent careers: By chance, two nonplanners met, and the congruence between us in value systems and life goals resulted in an enduring marriage, work we enjoyed, wonderful family years, pleasant retirement—lives good to us that seem to have had no ill effects on others.

Congruence, in my view, determines the outcomes of the decision to marry or not and the selection of a mate (if any), decisions about children, and the selection of a career field (if any). I believe that the goodness of life does not depend upon which pattern you follow—housewife, career woman; single, married; mother, not; nor whether the pattern is orderly or disorderly as it unfolds. What matters is the fit of your own characteristics with the pattern you follow and the degree of order involved. With benefit of hindsight I would say to young persons: At each choice point, first consider your own characteristics that are relevant to the decision; then look at each option in terms of its resources to meet your needs and fulfill your goals, and your abilities to meet its demands with invigoration and enjoyment.

References

Carp, F. M. (1966). *A future for the aged.* Austin: University of Texas Press.
Carp, F. M., & Carp, A. (1984). A complementary/congruence model of well-being or mental health. In I. Altman, J. Wohlwill, & M. P. Lawton (Eds.), *Elderly people and the environment: Human behavior and environment* (pp. 279–336). New York: Plenum Press.
Wilensky, H. (1961). Orderly careers and social participation. *American Sociological Review, 26,* 521–539.

Chapter 9

A Woman in Academe
Adventure, Fulfillment, Disillusion

Ruth B. Weg, Ph.D.

Introduction to Ruth B. Weg

Biologists of national and international stature (almost all men) respect and admire Ruth Weg for several reasons. She is one of the very few women to win the uphill battle to be an eminent biologist and, having won that battle, to fight on to become a spokesperson for the field. One world-famous male biologist commented regretfully about her struggles: "Our field seems to have an especially heavy tradition of sexual prejudice." Leading biologists regret only that she gave up a career in the wet lab (basic science) to take a path that led to much administrative work. In their view, biological knowledge was the loser because of her talent for basic research, though they realize that sexism was a strong factor in determining this turn in her path.

Weg is one of few biologists of either sex who can bridge the span between biology and the social sciences. In this respect, other biologists consider her one of "a rare and endangered species." She

Lives of Career Women: Approaches to Work, Marriage, Children, edited by Frances M. Carp. Plenum/Insight, New York, 1991.

can craft biological concepts for nonbiologists and distill biological impacts for social scientists. As a result of this unusual breadth of understanding and interpretive ability, she is highly respected by social scientists as well as by peers in her own field.

In addition, Weg is one of the rare humanists in biology. She is in touch with the entirety of the human condition, from the cell level to the humanities, from biological functioning to considerations of ethics and morality. Her artistic sensitivity and talent are apparent in the poems that convey New Year's greetings to friends each year and in those in her chapter.

Through her successful uphill struggle in a field in which power was in the hands of men, with persistence but without compromising her femininity, Weg made the way somewhat easier for women coming after her. Her students, as well as her peers, are aware of this. Her enthusiasm makes biology come alive in the classroom—an ability her colleagues envy and attempt to emulate. Students find her a strong sponsor, ready to support them in whatever they seek to undertake rather than forcing them into any mold. Her wide knowledge in biology, the social sciences, the humanities, and the arts enables her to function creatively with the wide range of students in the multidisciplinary situation in which she works.

A colleague says of her: "Ruth Weg is a gifted intellectual with creativity and determination. She weaves a tapestry of beauty, strength, and possibilities—for all of us to admire and which inspires each of us to weave our own."

Introduction

> Representation of the world, like the world itself, is the work of men; they describe it from their own point of view, which they confuse with the absolute truth. Woman herself recognizes that the world is masculine on the whole; those who fashioned it, ruled it, and still dominate it today are men. (de Beauvoir, 1952, p. 563)

The natural history of career and life—childhood socialization in a family, social and historical backdrops, trials and successes, barriers and opportunities, planned decisions, serendipity—is a continuing search for one's whole self. It remains an ongoing travel of multiple crossroads and turns. Along the way there are many kinds of loves—siblings, parents, mates, children, self, friends; performing as dancer, singer; accumulating knowledge, values, and goals. These interactive variables relate to any individual moving through life. However, the details and outcomes for woman and for man are marked by significant differences.

By the time I was eight I had committed to a career in medicine. At fifteen it won over a deep involvement with ballet. Four years in a small liberal arts college were spent in exploring ideas and seeking to satisfy an insatiable curiosity about physical and human worlds. The excitement of learning supported the earlier decision. After graduation, the long-held choice was reluctantly put aside. Discriminatory quotas against women, and religion and poverty, became shocking parts of my reality.

Unable to become a candidate for medical school in a reasonable time, I made a traditional choice and married the boyfriend of my teen years. In conversations with him, marriage and children were not to eliminate my formal learning toward a career. Interruptions in work-life for women was the norm, as was a direct, unhindered path for men. The nesting and mothering period had a special loving wonder and concern in watching and nurturing two growing individuals. Community needs were attractive parts of my life and provided the balance necessary to days and nights in a nuclear family. When our son and daughter were in kindergarten and nursery school, though, it was time to continue my education.

Medical school was my choice, but a husband's priority for my responsibilities to him, our home, and our children presented another perspective and loomed as an obstacle. Attending classes, even part-time and/or evenings, necessitated some at-home support, particularly child care. It seemed fair and reasonable to reconsider my options and what compromises I could accept to enhance rather than burden family life. To stop endless review of what I had thought were past understandings between my husband and me, medical school was out and graduate status in biology/physiology was my objective. My husband and I hoped the greater degree of freedom in my schedule could keep our relationship growing in a healthy direction. For a number of years during my reacclimation to schooling and work, most of the marriage and family life was fairly happy and loving for us all.

Back to School: Juggling Studies, Family, and Sexism

It was the early 1950s, and I had been looking forward to the day of registration with great anticipation. Conversation with a faculty member of the biology department was memorable. Questions put to me such as, "Are you married?" and "Do you have children?" were answered in the affirmative. The already charged atmosphere was exacerbated by, "Then why are you interested in going to school?" My quick response was, "It's none of your business." Undergraduate education at a women's school did not prepare me for the blatant, intrusive, and irrelevant sexism. I signed up for two courses in biology and one in education. I thought of working briefly as a public school teacher to get a taste of the work world and to see if biology was to be the graduate field of study.

After completing a secondary teaching credential, with biology as the substantive major, I spent two years teaching mathematics, science, and English. Immersion in a large public education system revealed the distorted regard to student needs, faculty talents, rational curricula, and administrative organization. More than ever, I felt more urgently the need to return to doctoral studies. Another year of discontinuity was the leave of absence necessitated by my husband's incapacitating car accident. My concerns were for his welfare and complete recovery, expediting some of his work at home and keeping the family on an even keel.

My enthusiasm in returning to graduate studies was diluted—this time by the requirement (for women only) that a master's research project and thesis be completed before candidacy for the doctorate would be evaluated, despite the excellence of my graduate record. Grapevine wisdom was that most women never finished because female students had to fulfill more requirements and meet tougher standards than male students. Such information was not in print anywhere, but was transmitted during interviews with, "You need the research experience before you can tackle doctoral work." This unofficial requirement added time and cost. However, the stimulation of research, while being a teaching assistant in biology, opened doors into the challenging potential of a scientific milieu. Other doors, less open, exposed second-class citizenship for women students and faculty. More tarnish was added to my early image of collegial activities pledged to truth seeking, equal opportunity, equity, and honest exchanges.

Emotions were wide-ranging. A sense of confidence, the joy of achievement, and the pleasure of integrating the scientific part of myself were almost overwhelming. But there was a down side. In the final year and a half, it was almost impossible to maintain a stable family life. Functioning on four to five hours of sleep, giving up fun and play time with children and husband on weekends, and rushing all home functions became usual rather than occasional. I convinced myself that once the pressure of student performance was over, our lives would soon again return to normal. More damage had been done than I was willing to admit.

At Work: Exciting Unknowns and Rude Awakenings

Upon graduation the biology department appointed me to head a smog research project and to teach two to three courses a year—not on a tenure track. The research responsibilities and the interaction with students and colleagues were stimulating and productive. Three articles from the master's thesis and dissertation were published, many presentations were made at professional meetings, and countless reports went to the smog research agency. An almost typical academic sequence was in place, but the fit was uneasy.

Within one year of my Ph.D. the disintegration of my marriage became clear with the decision to divorce. In retrospect, the process had begun earlier and accelerated when my permanent committment to work was a daily part of our lives. Divorce traumatized us all. I was witness only to the pain of the children and myself. It was difficult to analyze objectively how we had arrived at this unacceptable state. My work was an incredible cushion in landing on my feet, looking forward, and regaining a hold on the responsibilities of mothering. The professional identity that was being forged strengthened me as I began rebuilding myself as a person. I continued with the biology department and found teaching, research, and collegial activities satisfying and challenging.

In 1962 I remarried, and in 1965 my husband and I became the happy parents of a baby girl. The pattern of work, marriage, and children was a variation of the first motherhood and wife phase. I was a working woman when this second marriage was undertaken, and plans for parenthood were crystallized. About four weeks elapsed from my daughter's birth to my return to work. I resigned the research task and kept the teaching, student guidance, and faculty committees at a reduced salary. To spend needed and desired time at home with the baby and my new family, I took leave without pay for the following semester. The decisions worked well. The family was in order, and I returned to the university refreshed and energetic. My husband made a genuine attempt to share in child care and home chores. The attempt to share child care was an eminent success, the home chores less so. Because my career involved conferences and travel, my husband played a major role in parenting. All our holidays, generally mixtures of scientific paper presentations and family vacations, were spent as a threesome. My youngest's growing-up years seem to have been well spent. The joy and playfulness of having a baby in my middle years and as a working professional were reflected in my poem for our New Year's greeting card that year:

> To babes, to birds and bees
> to peace and trees
> To tinkers, to trains and toys
> to peace and joys
> To dolls, to dawn and dove
> to peace with love.

When an administrative and teaching position on the tenure track was offered by the Gerontology Institute on campus I accepted. Liaison with my "home" department remained through membership on faculty committees and teaching one or two courses. The institute position was half-time, but getting a new, low-status program off the ground demanded time and a half: grant writing, chairing the Faculty Preceptor Committee (the student admission and policy-making group), interaction with other departments and graduate student advisors, teaching, chairing and organizing summer institutes, and so forth. I was thoroughly absorbed with the new academic field as a member of a pioneering effort. This kind of challenge suited my talents and personality. I set about educating myself to be the most knowledgeable gerontologist I could, in what I called the newest academic "multidiscipline."

The 1960s were full of productive efforts on my part: scholarly works in education for gerontology, changing images of aging, biology and physiology of age, nutrition and the lifespan, health promotion/disease prevention, sexuality in middle and later years. A special focus was women: their changing roles, their health, their participation in work outside the home. I discussed these areas at professional meetings and in consultation with other programs and institutions. I developed courses to elaborate on these areas. Activity in professional organizations increased. Executive boards, offices, and committee memberships were rewarding. These activities provided opportunities to contribute to critical thinking and to have exchanges with colleagues everywhere.

What began as a research institute evolved into a Center of Research, Education, and Practice with a strong multidisciplinary base. The center, like the field itself, was and is changing and growing from an alien fledgling to a maturing area of inquiry, education, and application that is finding acceptance in the mainstream of academia. After many years of administrative work beyond other faculty roles, I was asked to develop a curriculum and structure a school for a degree program in gerontology. With the assistance of two superior graduate students, all was in place within the year. As I was relieved of administration, there was time for greater focus on teaching, advising, nationwide consulting, and scholarly production in books and journals.

Academic Title, Promotion, and Salary Trail

Promotion to associate professor came rapidly. Remuneration and promotion to full professor were on a slow train. I was naïve to start at a low half-time salary. Increments appeared to be based on that, though evaluations ranged from very good to excellent. Equity eluded me. In its stead, verbal and written appreciations of my work were proffered readily. Activities of the faculty senate—issues of university governance and policies; faculty rights and privileges; and equity across departments, schools, race, and gender—exercised a strong pull for my energy and time. I continued as an equal, responsible, and active person in the center's meetings and committees, frequently as a dissenting voice, at other times with wide collegial support.

The years before full professorship was finally conferred were hard-working and increasingly demanding, at times by my own choice and at others by administrative fiat. Exciting challenge continued, but reasons that kept full professorship from realization continually shifted. Many days, giving up looked good. But colleagues and the American Association of University Professors advised, "Hang in there." They were right, not just for me but for the increased awareness among faculty and administrators required to face and resolve the issue.

When Juggling Shows: At What Cost

Concentration on work had negative consequences in time and quality for significant individuals, groups, and areas of my life. Work and my need to prove myself overwhelmed days, evenings, and weekends. Family, friends, community, and my own personal development were put aside. The balanced life I so respected and wanted was not within my reach. I felt cheated and angry that I missed being with my family more, and that I minimized the roles of music, the arts, and the outdoors to attain what I perceived as my essential academic achievement.

Was my experience with sexism—in a worksite where I had expected everyone to know better—unique to me? Unfortunately, no. Has there been progress in attitude and action toward equity for women (and minorities)? Yes, but woefully inadequate. Has some ground been lost? Yes. The history of higher learning clearly sets the stage for what exists today.

Uphill to the Sanctuary

In the Beginning

There was excellent higher education in law, philosophy, and rhetoric, at the feet of Socrates, Plato, and others. But in antiquity, there were no universities as we know them, with faculties, courses, examinations, graduations, and degrees (Haskins, 1957). These features are owed to the universities of the twelfth century in Paris and Bologna. The "wisdom" of the ancients was recovered between 1100 and 1200 A.D., a twelfth century resurgence of learning brought into western Europe largely by Spain's Arab scholars.

Hidden by the Arab scholars during the Dark Ages were the works of Aristotle, Euclid, Ptolemy, the Greek physicians; new arithmetics; and texts of Roman law. This suddenly available knowledge defused the constraints of monastery schools and created the academic guilds, societies of masters and scholars (Haskins, 1957). The medieval law school at Bologna, with no catalogs, no student organizations, no journalism, no dramatics or athletics, was the origin of modern universities. It offered degrees—Master of Arts and Doctor of Laws—and the first license to teach. Theology, arts, and medicine were soon added. Bologna was an inspiration for the developing universities in Spain, Italy, and southern France (Haskins, 1957).

Significant to understanding the status of women in American colleges and universities is the fact that these ancestral vehicles were "built of men." Soon student societies, all male, organized and exerted a strong voice for the "how" and "what" of the nascent ivory towers. Professional guilds, also male, and the student groups have "worn the robes" in what has persisted as a patriarchal institution (Adams, 1983). Women were not persons to be educated formally.

Women Enter: Against the Odds

The path has been slow and arduous since 1678, when the first woman doctorate graduated from the University of Padua. Elena Lucrezia Coronaro Piscopia was a Benedictine oblate at an early age. Her petition to take her advanced degree in theology was denied by the Bishop of Padua, who reportedly said,

"Woman is made for motherhood, not learning." When finally allowed to study, she had to take the examination in philosophy, not theology (*Academe 69*, 1983). In 1840 Honoré de Balzac wrote:

> A woman who is guided by the head and not the heart is a social pestilence: she has all the defects of a passionate and affectionate woman, with none of her compensations: she is without pity, without love, without virtue, without sex." (Oltman, 1983, p. 73)

Institutions of higher learning began in the United States in 1636 with the founding of Harvard College. Colleges, then, were vocational, training male students for professions in law, ministry, medicine, teaching, and statesmanship (Newcomer, 1959). Women had been assigned to the home, and education of women for the professions was given no consideration. Oberlin College first admitted female undergraduates about 150 years ago. In 1870, when the University of Michigan opened its doors to women students, allowing them to learn was still perceived as "a very dangerous experiment . . . certain to be ruinous to the young ladies who should avail themselves of it . . . and disastrous to the institution" (Oltman, 1983, p. 73). About 100 years ago a woman's college, Bryn Mawr, opened its doors.

Ambivalence in male educational circles about the intellectual capacities of women has a long legacy. In *The Republic* Plato said that all "gifts of nature" are found in both men and women, and that their pursuits are the same, but that in every instance a woman's performance is inferior to a man's" (Jowett, 1982). Only eighteen years ago female applicants to colleges and universities were required to have higher scores on the Scholastic Aptitude Test than males in order to be admitted (Fields, 1982). There were no athletic scholarships for women. The widely used Strong Vocational Interest Test employed separate scoring systems for males and females, including pink tests for girls, which related to "female" occupations, and blue tests for boys, marking the "male" concentrations in science and medicine.

Title IX's ban on sex bias in admissions has helped to change the most flagrant biases in academe (Fields, 1982). Title VII of the Civil Rights Act was amended in 1974 and became the legislative basis for academic sex discrimination suits. The penalty for violation—withholding federal funds unless institutions complied with federal affirmative action programs—became an important tool for progress in employment for women. In 1987 Education Secretary Bell initiated a policy of conciliation and nonconfrontation that put the gain at risk, judging institutions in compliance if they promised to correct violations. President Gray of the Massachusetts Institute of Technology (MIT) cautioned that with the ". . . apparent retreat from a committment to affirmative action" of the federal government, institutions of higher learning will need to depend on their own greater efforts in equalizing opportunities for members of all minority groups and women" (McCain, 1984, p. 3).

In many documented situations, women have been "nominally absorbed, admitted, affirmatively acted upon and have consciously acquiesced to the men's club" (Adams, 1983, p. 139). Many women have been socialized to model their lives and scholarship in as male-like an image as possible; their survival often depended on their being considered "honorary men." Nevertheless, most college and university women still look forward to first class, equal citizenship with men in academe. Today there are realists and advocates among male colleagues. Gray of MIT noted that institutions of higher learning "have traditionally been white and male in composition and outlook," and called for involvement in the struggle to change that fact (McCain, 1984, p. 3).

Sex discrimination in positions and salaries is alive and well. Among persons who completed doctorates at least twenty years earlier, 87% of the men and 64% of the women became full professors; of those who received their Ph.D.'s ten to nineteen years earlier, men with the same qualifications as women were 50% more likely to become full professors (Norman, 1981). Women doctoral graduates during 1970–1974 were doing less well than male colleagues: A third of the women and half of the men had become senior faculty. Another study found similar differences in salaries and rank and Hansen (1983) not only found women more heavily concentrated at lower ranks but also found that, at each rank, salaries for men were higher. The report emphasized the persistent constraint of opportunities to develop mentor and collaborative relationships with established male faculty, which may contribute to lower research productivity and slower professional advancement for women.

Fields that welcome females are few and in lower levels. Fewer women are in prestigious schools or departments, and they earn less than male counterparts (*Academe 72*, 1986; Etaugh, 1984). Moreover, the rate of increase was higher for men than for women between 1972 and 1981 (17% to 13.4%) (*Academe 72*, 1986). Women administrators generally are in low-status "women's fields," such as nursing and home economics, or are in care-taking jobs such as admissions officer, registrar, or bookstore manager. Fewer women receive tenure (47% of female faculty, 69% of male) (*Academe 72*, 1986).

Women are the "new majority" of undergraduates (Hall, 1982). They enter higher education with enthusiasm and talent. By the time they graduate, they are less confident about achieving in graduate school, fewer plan to study in traditionally "masculine" fields, and there are measureable drops in academic and career goals. In 1988, although women earned 52% of master's degrees, only 35% were among new Ph.D.'s (Shavlik, 1990).

Progress has been made. More women students, administrators, and faculty are in the system; laws are on the books, and there appear to be policies and practices that allow women easier access to academe. Some realities remain fixed in an earlier time. Since many of them have been part of the society for so long, they appear to be "normal" and often go unrecognized by women as well as men. Subtleties of women's treatment in the academic milieu, the less obvious ways of discriminating, convey the message of second-class citizenship. The consequences are serious, interfering with the education of women students, setting unspoken limits to women faculty and administrator productivity and advancement, and "preventing institutions from being the best they can be" (Sandler, 1986, p. 2).

Assessment

My higher education and academic worklife have been similar to and different from the patterns that research data suggest. Breakthroughs and discrimination continue in my environment. Significant achievements, personal and professional, are real— but so are the lost opportunities, lost income, and lost time. The rewards in career building have been great, contributing emotionally and psychologically to the fullness of my being.

Are there women in academe who have reached their goals, fulfilled their potential, and received deserved support and recognition? Yes, of course. Are they many as compared to those who could? No, not even close. Ours is ". . . a workplace culture that acknowledges the existence of age and sex discrimination, stands ready to regulate against them, and practices both under a variety of circumstances" (Radeheaver, 1990).

Looking back I can see situations in which I might have behaved differently. I could have persisted for medicine and somehow overcome the discrimination, financial difficulties, and my mate's direction. Why was I not satisfied to rejoice in the growth of my intellect, dismissing the academic inequities as a student and then as a member of a faculty? Possibly I could have used contentious and legal tactics to establish equity. But my goal of always moving toward developing all that I could be as a whole person left little room for such one-sided tactics.

What would I suggest to the young woman, student or faculty member? Fulfill your own agenda. Be flexible, but do not be sidetracked. Wherever you are, learn as much as you can, not only about a particular educational interest, but about institutional structure and values, about administrators as well as faculty. Make time for fun, friends, other talents, and a family (if there is one). Enjoy! The academic door must not be shut again. Developing permeability into the historically male sanctuary will engage all of us who see sexism, racism, and ageism as pathology.

I believe that as more women engage academe, universities will look and sound different. There will be greater potential for the kind of excellence that develops beyond so-called objectivity of scholarship to include values. If institutions of higher learning choose dynamic growth and excellence, not only in a male image, changes in attitudes and behavior are inevitable. All women and men have a stake in that change, for now and for the future. Maximize your competence, confidence, collegiality, and assertiveness. The ultimate defeat will be if each of us stands alone and unequal.

> Nurture self reliance in community.
> Refuse neglect in the name of independence.
> No pride at the cost of being.
> Commit human-ness to each other.
> Muster reason, vigor, laughter for the
>   common struggle —
> To bolster your today, to insure
>   a meaningful tomorrow.

References

Adams, H. F. (1983). Work in the interstices: Women in academe. *Women's Studies International Forum, 6* (2), 135–141.

The annual report on the economic status of the profession, 1885–86. (1986). *Academe 72,* 2, 10.

de Beauvoir, S. (1952). *The second sex* (H. M. Parshley, Trans.). New York: Knox.

Etaugh, C. (Fall, 1984). Women, faculty and administrators in higher education: Changes in their status since 1972. *Journal of the National Association for Women Deans, Administrators and Counselors,* pp. 21–25.

Fields, C. (1982). Title IX at X. *Chronicle of Higher Education, 24* (17), 1–12.

Hall, R. M. (1982). *The classroom climate: A chilly one for women?* Project on the Status and Education of Women, Association of American Colleges.

Hansen, W. L. (1986). A blip on the screen: The Annual Report on Economic Status of the Profession, 1982–83. *Academe, 60* (4), 2–21.

Haskins, C. H. (1957). *The rise of universities.* Ithaca: Cornell University Press.

Inside cover depiction and copy. (1983). *Academe 69,* 5.

Jowett, B. (Trans.). (1982). *The dialogues of Plato* (Vol. 3, 3rd ed.). Oxford: Clarendon Press.

McCain, N. (1984). Affirmative action begins "at home." *Chronicle of Higher Education, XXVII* (10), 3.

Newcomer, M. (1959). *A century of higher education for American women.* New York: Harper and Brothers.

Norman, C. (1981). News/report. *Science, 19,* 890.

Oltman, R. (1983). Women in higher education: Up the down staircase. *Phi Delta Gamma Journal, 45,* (1), 10–15.

Radeheaver, D. (1990). Labor market progeiva. *Generations, XIV, 3,* pp. 1, 42.

Sandler, B. R. (1986). *The campus climate revisited: Chilly for women faculty, administrators, and graduate students.* Washington, D.C.: Association of American Colleges.

Shavlik, D. (1990). Direct communication concerning data for a Fall 1990 book. In *Fact Book in Higher Education.* American Council on Education.

Chapter 10

A Professor's Story

Vivian Wood, Ph.D.

Introduction to Vivian Wood

Dr. Wood is viewed by her mentors, collaborators in research, colleagues, and students in remarkably consistent and positive fashion. She decided on a career in social work somewhat late, but with intelligence, persistence, and unusually good ability to organize, she carved out her life as she wanted it to be. In so doing, she was never jealous of others, but encouraged them to succeed. Once she made up her mind to become a college professor, she made a fine faculty member, teaching huge classes of students, conducting research, and publishing papers. Vivian has sparkle without fireworks. To controversy she brings a nice sense of humor that defuses tension. She is definite in her opinions but makes her impression in ladylike fashion—quietly, sincerely, prudently—and effectively.

Unmarried and childless, she has always loved to have visitors and to visit others, and her life today makes clear the collection of acquaintances and friends she has accumulated

Lives of Career Women: Approaches to Work, Marriage, Children, edited by Frances M. Carp. Plenum/Insight, New York, 1991.

during her life. She keeps in touch with university and even high-school classmates. Recently she was invited to the fiftieth wedding anniversary celebration of her role model in graduate school. She trades visits with her collaborator on Ph.D. dissertations and the collaborator's husband and children. Her home in a retirement community in Arizona—across the country from the University of Wisconsin, where she developed her career—is a gathering place for ex-students, particularly women for whom she was advisor and role model. Ex-students in early stages of career development often turn to her for advice, in person or by phone or mail.

She continues to work for the betterment of conditions for women through organizations as well as through generous provision of personal advice and assistance. She is an active member of the Association of University Women (AAUW) and of the National Organization for Women (NOW). In retirement she fulfills her needs to teach and to serve her community by tutoring in a program to teach English to speakers of other languages.

Colleagues and ex-students frequently comment with a chuckle something to the effect of "take Vivian, take her cats." Even those not fond of felines think that being in Vivian's home is worth the nuisance. Travel is no problem for her; among her local friends there are and always have been cat lovers glad to provide hers a temporary home.

In 1928, when I started school, the odds against a girl in my circumstances getting a Ph.D. degree were overwhelming. Not only were Ph.D.'s extremely rare for women at that time, but also I came from a family in which no one had even finished high school. My father was orphaned, and his education was cut short at the fifth grade. My mother dropped out of high school in her freshman year to work because her family lacked money for appropriate clothes. My father was just getting started at farming in Ohio when the Great Depression, which was particularly hard on farmers, began. I started school one year before the Big Crash on Wall Street.

By the time I graduated from a small rural high school in 1939, things had not improved much on the farm. Not one girl,

and only one or two boys, in my class went directly to college. I was sixteen, and a state law prohibited regular employment until age eighteen. Anyway, my mother was seriously ill and, as the oldest of four children, my help was needed at home. After I became eighteen I worked part-time on the local weekly newspaper. My mother died during the next year, and I continued to keep house for my father and three younger siblings until my father remarried. By this time World War II had started.

So how did a poor farm girl from Ohio end up with a Ph.D. and a career as professor at one of the top ten universities in this country? In trying to understand how oneself and one's life came to be, self-deception is a pitfall of which to be wary. As Heilbrun (1988) said, until recently at least, women were "unable to write exemplary lives: they do not dare to offer themselves as models, but only as exceptions chosen by destiny or chance" (p. 25). I have generally attributed my success to chance. However, I was able, whether purposefully or accidentally, to take advantage of chances that came my way. For example, though I thought realistically that I would never have the opportunity to go to college, I dreamed of going (perhaps Jo of Louisa May Alcott's *Little Women* was my role model) and took a partial college-preparatory course in high school.

Rural Childhood

In retrospect I think both my parents were intelligent. My mother was an avid reader, and so was I, though reading material was limited. The library in the county seat eight miles away seemed very distant in those days of Model T and Model A Ford travel over gravel roads. In any event we did not see the library as open to country folks. Fortunately, a summer traveling library was instituted, and once a week a van with books came to our door. Both my mother and I selected as many books as the rules allowed. By midweek they all were read, and we eagerly awaited the return of the book van.

My mother had a potent influence on my life. She encouraged me to look beyond the limits of the small backwater where I grew up, but she was handicapped by her lack of experience. (She never got out of the state in which she was born; indeed, she seldom went beyond the boundaries of the county.) In hindsight I suspect she was dismayed by my marriage prospects in that small community, yet I doubt that she could envision an alternative to marriage for me. She subtly discouraged young men she thought unsuitable and encouraged more stable types. But I was bored by the young men I knew. I suppose I would have drifted into marriage, but war in Europe loomed, and local young men enlisted or were drafted. My mother's death and father's remarriage gave me the freedom to leave home, and the war gave me the idea of how to do so.

Family Ties

Heilbrun (1988) points out that successful independent heroines in novels generally have no family ties, particularly no mothers. A mother's mission, she says, was to prepare the daughter to marry, to bear children, and to encourage her husband to succeed in the world. Women could but dream of taking control of their lives "without the intrusion of a mother's patriarchal wishes for her daughter, without the danger of injuring the much loved and pitied mother." Women writers expressed these dreams through their heroines.

Had my mother lived, I am not sure that I could have left home. I like to think that I could have, that my mother would have encouraged me to have the independence she never had. I would have liked my mother to share that world out there and my success in it. My mother was young, not quite eighteen when I was born, and I was eighteen when she died. In

comparison to my friends' mothers she seemed young, outgoing, and "with it." I was proud of her, and we had a close
relationship. I am not sure what were all the effects of the pain
and grief of my mother's untimely death on my life. I know that
after my father remarried I felt free to leave. With the wisdom of
age I suspect that my father remarried partly in order to free me
to lead my own life, but at the time I resented his getting a
replacement for my mother.

This resentment steeled my resolve to leave. Since my three
younger siblings were too young to go, my mother's death and
subsequently having a stepmother probably were more difficult
for them than for me. Although I was timid and fearful about
going out on my own, I was determined to do so. It was
fortuitous for me that recruitment for women in the armed
services had begun. Since I was not yet twenty-one I had to get
my father's permission to enlist. I got it after some cajoling.

Military Service

I served in the Marine Corps Women's Reserve from August
1943 to December 1945. You cannot imagine a more naïve and
inexperienced woman (the term "girl" in use then seems more
appropriate) than I was when I entrained for Washington, D.C.,
where I was to meet other recruits and be taken to Camp
Lejeuene, North Carolina for boot training. When the training
was over I was assigned to a base in San Diego. Later, I was
moved up the coast to another base at Oceanside, where I
served until the end of the war. Most of my time was spent in
the women's battalion personnel office, where I kept records
and worked with the classification officer in assigning women to
jobs on the base. I became battalion personnel sergeant-major,
second to the top enlisted woman in the battalion.

Among the positive outcomes of my military experience: (1)
My horizons were widened considerably, not only geographi-

cally but also in getting to know a wide variety of people from many social strata; (2) I learned job skills and developed confidence in my ability to perform, to take responsibility, and to move up to higher levels; and (3) I earned the right to higher education through the GI Bill. Also, I met women who had traveled widely and who had college educations. By the end of the war, college seemed a feasible venture for me.

The most unpleasant part of my military experience was my first conscious encounter with discrimination and prejudice against women. The military had long been an exclusively male domain. From the War Department (now the Department of Defense) to the generals and on down the line there was resistance to accepting women and antagonism toward them once they were admitted. A severe manpower shortage forced those in command to see the need for women in the military services, but acceptance was slow in coming. "In 1943 (the year I joined the Marines), a campaign of slander descended upon the U.S. military women that was of unexpected viciousness and scope . . . Dirty jokes, snide remarks, obscenities, and cartoons became commonplace. It was a humiliating and demoralizing experience for the thousands of women who had responded to what they had perceived as their patriotic duty" (Holm, 1982, pp. 51–52).

Most women marines were aged twenty to twenty-five, "on their own" for the first time and eager to date. San Diego with all its military bases contained plenty of young men—lonely, away from home for the first time, eager to experience everything they could before going overseas to fight and perhaps die. Unfortunately, many of them accepted the attitudes prevalent in the military and the press and considered servicewomen fair game. Some thought military women to be on a par with prostitutes.

Most women dated. Some met men they later married. Most, after experience with insulting attitudes and fighting off advances, gradually gave up dating except occasionally when men from "back home" were in town. Also, a great deal of emphasis was placed on "being true to the guy from back home." Some women never dated but spent their time writing regularly to boyfriends overseas whom they planned to marry when the war was over. Friendship circles developed among women marines. Going to the races, browsing through the shops, or having dinner at a good restaurant seemed preferable to the hazards of dating. These friendship circles served as women's support groups long before the women's movement made us aware of them. The prejudice and insults caused pain and anger at the time, but they toughened me and I learned not to let them bother me unduly.

Post-War Decisions

When the war ended I was eligible for discharge almost immediately. My newspaper job in Ohio was awaiting me, and I returned to work. Most of my friends were getting married. Small-town life no longer appealed to me. The GI Education Bill was announced, and by this time I was ready to try college. I applied to the University of Chicago, but it was swamped with returning veterans. At the invitation of a Marine Corps friend, I went to Philadelphia, took a secretarial course, and got a job at a magazine publishing company. Several of the single men and women with whom I worked took university night courses, and I joined them. Weekly conversations over dinner on class nights whetted my appetite to advance in the publishing field. Eventually I became discouraged with the slow pace of night school and reapplied to the University of Chicago. This time I was admitted.

For the next five years I went to school almost continuously, working part-time to supplement the GI Bill stipend. It was ten years since high school, and studying was difficult. However, learning was exhilarating, and I was content as a student. When I earned my B.A. the publishing company where I had worked in Philadelphia offered me a job on the editorial staff, but their letter got lost in the mail, and I did not learn about this offer until over a year later. Meanwhile, I had become interested in sociology and was working toward a master's degree. After five years I still had a thesis to complete for that degree, but I was tired of school. I signed up with a traveling recruiter for a high-school teaching job in California. I made this decision without much thought for my career, attracted by the opportunity to return to California and by the idea of living in the mountains. I had developed a love of mountains in my childhood in flat Ohio without ever having seen one.

The school in which I taught was small, and I did everything from teaching girls' physical education to being advisor for the school newspaper. After two years I transferred to a larger high school. After another two years I decided that high-school teaching was not for me. Ever since leaving Chicago the thought of that unfinished master's thesis hung over my head. While investigating job possibilities in teaching overseas and in publishing, I worked on the thesis and went back to the university to have it accepted and to graduate.

Going for a Ph.D.

In Chicago I stayed with friends who were working for their doctorate degrees. There were subtle suggestions that I should consider getting a Ph.D. When a mutual friend came back from Sweden with several popular magazines on aging, suggestions became more specific: Studying aging would fit in with my interest in publishing. Academia had regained some of its allure, so it was not hard to convince me. One of the part-time jobs I had had earlier was assisting faculty doing research on aging; I knew the Committee on Human Development was where I should study if I wanted to learn about aging.

I figured that when my savings were used up I could earn money by substitute teaching. However, when I went to register I discovered that the Committee on Human Development had just received National Institute of Mental Health fellowships to encourage graduate students to study aging. I applied for and received one of them, which supported me for three years. The woman who was co-director of the training program became my major professor, mentor, and role model. After I completed my major course work, a fellow student and I worked with her to secure a research grant to study middle-aged women. Data from the study were used for our dissertations research. By now I had dropped publishing as a career and accepted the traditional idea that persons with Ph.D.'s went into university teaching and research.

In the 1960s universities were expanding, so jobs in academia were not hard to find, especially if one's mentor was one of the leading lights in gerontology. These jobs were not necessarily on the tenure track, however, and new graduates knew little about the tenure system and the politics of universities. I took a position with the University of Wisconsin Extension School in Milwaukee with the understanding (nothing on paper) that this would evolve into a tenure-track faculty position.

Empire building was common for ambitious male professors. Within a year or so, two who headed departments in the university competed in offering me positions, mainly because of my expertise in gerontology, a field in which federal training and research funds were becoming available in increasing amounts. My position in the all-male unit in which I was working did not provide a good match of my expertise and interests with the needs of the program. Besides, it was the first time I had worked with males only, and I missed having women with whom to talk. Of the two positions offered to me I chose the one in the School of Social Work on the Madison campus because the prospects for developing a gerontology program seemed better.

An Academic Career

Over the next twenty-one years I taught courses on aging and helped establish a campus-wide gerontology center. It was an exciting time during which aging changed from an area students avoided to one that was a comparatively popular specialty in many disciplines. At the time I went to the Madison campus, women faculty were in the early stages of organizing a campus-wide, and later state-wide, association of women. Sexist attitudes were prevalent in what had been a largely male domain for centuries. The women faculty organizations exposed male/female salary differentials, biases against women getting tenure, and other unfair practices against women students as well as faculty.

In my early years on the Madison campus I struggled to establish myself and get tenure. The fact that I succeeded is due, in part, to the women faculty organizations. As I had more time, I became more involved in them. Working with other women to correct the inequities of the university was satisfying. The organizations and committees became support groups. Women consoled each other in failures and celebrated achievements together. Those were heady years, despite the frustrations, as women tried to change the system.

I made tenure after four years and a full professorship four years later. I worked hard for several years to help coalesce support from faculty members and departments throughout the university for a multidisciplinary center on aging. When the Institute on Aging was established I headed a multidisciplinary training program in aging for graduate students. I often became a mentor to women trainees who had male major professors in their home departments. When a women's studies program was formed I served on its faculty until I retired. I combined my interests in aging and women in a graduate course on older women, which attracted many mature women who were struggling with issues with which the course dealt. Counselors often sent mature women to me to help them think through their educational plans.

I became a kind of role model and mentor for women, particularly for those past the traditional student age. In the 1970s and 1980s there was an increasing number of such women as a result of such influences as the rising aspirations of women, changing job expectations, and more divorces among older women. Although I never felt much expertise as a role model, I did feel a sense of responsibility. Having someone listen to them talk through their dilemmas and suggest new dimensions that may not have occurred to them seemed helpful to many.

Female Role Models

In looking back over my life, the factual obstacles to my developing a career are fairly clear. A less obvious psychological barrier was my low expectations of life. When I became aware of this attitude I attributed it to circumstances. I had accomplished much more than anyone had expected of a poor farm girl. Why should I aspire to more? Related to low expectations was lack of self-confidence. Too often I was passive when I should have been aggressive. (I realize, too, that aggressive women were often knocked out of competition before the women's movement made this more difficult to do.) In later years, as I became aware of feminist writings, I came to know that most women of my generation had rather low expectations of themselves and lacked self-confidence. I am pleased that younger women seem to have more self-confidence and higher aspirations.

Whenever I try to ascertain the factors in my life that enabled me to make of it what I did, the outstanding element is always having strong women in my life. My parents seem to me to have shared decisions, but I was always aware that my mother was the stronger of the two. I was used to farmwives who worked as hard as their husbands in running the farms. I do not know if I was conscious of this at the time, but most farm couples seemed to have fairly equalitarian relationships.

A couple owned the weekly newspaper where I got my first job. Again the wife was strong, and she was the one with whom I dealt. She was a versatile woman who did all kinds of jobs around the newspaper office. In addition, she often "filled in" managing the pool hall that she and her husband owned next door. Sometimes I had to go there to consult her when a problem came up at the newspaper office. I enjoyed seeing the camaraderie she had with the men who frequented the pool hall (women did not go into this establishment of small-town life) and admired her behavior, which seemed unconventional compared to that of most women I knew who were full-time homemakers. When I decided to go into the Marine Corps she encouraged me even though, due to the manpower shortage, it was not to the newspaper's advantage to lose an employee. I believe she knew that if she had been in my shoes, she would have enlisted in the armed forces.

In the Marine Corps I worked almost exclusively with and for women. Because I was in the women's battalion office I had a fairly close working relationship with women officers. As one of the criteria for being an officer was a college degree, all these women were college-educated. Except for my teachers, I had not known college-educated women before, and I had not worked with any until this time. Two or three women officers who handled the administration of the battalion (over 2,000 women) were especially admired by enlisted women. They were not exactly role models, because most enlisted women neither expected nor aspired to be officers. Nevertheless, this experience added to my growing awareness that women could and did do important jobs.

When I worked at the magazine publishing company in Philadelphia many of the editorial positions to which I aspired were filled by women. This was largely because the publication was a farm magazine with a large section directed to farmers' wives. I started as a secretary but was soon promoted to editorial assistant. The personnel director, a woman a few years older than I, became a kind of mentor and encouraged me not to give up the idea of college. When she and I and several other single staff members took evening classes I saw an editorship as a possible career but knew I needed a college degree. It soon became apparent that evening school would take too long. When I began to think about reapplying to the University of Chicago I had the support of the personnel director.

During undergraduate years I had mostly male instructors, but there were several women. After an anthropology course from a colorful woman professor I wanted to be an anthropologist for several months. When I got my B.A. and decided to go on for graduate study I investigated several social sciences and settled on sociology largely because it seemed to deal with more practical problems. All my instructors were men. Although I was not fully aware of it at the time, I learned later that some of the instructors had a strong bias against women students. Perhaps because of the lack of women models, I did not aspire to a Ph.D. degree and a career as a sociology professor. Instead I took education courses and taught high school for four years.

When I returned to the University of Chicago for a Ph.D. it was not with the idea of university teaching as a career. That came still later. The Committee on Human Development had several women professors, and one of them was my major professor and mentor. Having her as a role model enabled me to envision myself as a university professor. She was a model not only for *being* a professor but also for the *kind* of professor I would be.

There were elements of luck in achieving what I did, and I do not hesitate to acknowledge that many people inspired and encouraged me, but my achievements were due largely to my own efforts. I worked hard for what I got. I can truly say that I enjoyed my work and have wasted no time in regretting opportunities missed or things I might have done differently. Being a university professor was a satisfying life for me.

But I was single. A few women of my generation managed both a full career and a family, but for the most part women thought they had to choose between the two. Today many women are trying to have both, but most are vastly overworked. I admire their efforts and believe they are pioneers in a new life-style for women. By doing what formerly seemed impossible, they are forcing society to make adjustments to make it easier for women to have both careers and families.

Retirement

I retired from the university in 1987 and, blessed with no health problems as yet, find retirement one of the most satisfying periods of my life. Freedom marks this new phase of living—freedom from work and from a confining schedule, freedom to set one's own agenda and to do what one wants to do. There is also the freedom that comes with age. As Heilbrun (1988) said, "Age above all . . . is the time when there is very little 'they' can do for you, very little reason to fear, or hide, or not attempt brave and important things" (p. 123).

With age and experience also come a broader perspective and a realization that the struggles for women's equality have been going on for a very long time and will likely continue for a very long time. I intend to continue the struggle. Citing again from Heilbrun (1988): "I do not believe that death should be allowed to find us seated comfortably in our tenured positions" (p. 131).

References

Heilbrun, C. C. (1988). *Writing a woman's life*. New York: Ballantine Books.
Holm, J. (1982). *Women in the military: An unfinished revolution*. Novato, CA: Presidio Press.

Chapter 11

Not a Career
A Life

Lisa Redfield Peattie, Ph.D.

Introduction to Lisa Redfield Peattie

Trained as an anthropologist, Lisa Peattie became a community
planner more by accident than by design. Her most formative
experience was as a resident anthropologist in a squatter community on the margins of the "planned" industrial city in Venezuela,
Ciudad Guana, with her first husband and their four children. In
planning circles, she is especially well known for her writings on
community advocacy. These, as indeed all of her writings, are
grounded in first-hand observation; they are iconoclastic, critical,
and compassionate.

During her distinguished career at the Massachusetts Institute
of Technology, she has also been distinguished professor at the
University of California at Los Angeles; visiting professor at the
Centre for Urban Studies and Urban Planning, University of Hong
Kong; United Nations expert in Bangkok, Nairobi, Lima, Bogota,
and Mexico City; consultant to the World Bank on the urban poor

Lives of Career Women: Approaches to Work, Marriage, Children, edited by Frances
M. Carp. Plenum/Insight, New York, 1991.

173

in Cartagena, integration of marginal areas in Colombia, and squatter upgrading in El Salvador; consultant on design of housing in Egypt; consultant to US-AID on metropolitan planning for Quito; consultant on planning for Bogota; lecturer at Instituto Brasiliero de Administracao Municipal in Rio de Janeiro and at Beijing and Kunming for the Chinese Academy of Social Sciences; and chairman of the Forum on Social and Physical Environment at the 1970 White House Conference on Children.

A long-time advocate of the peace movement, she has been arrested several times and has tried, unsuccessfully, to defend herself in court. Now professor emeritus and senior lecturer in the Department of Urban Studies and Planning at the Massachusetts Institute of Technology, she continues as a peace activist and is working on a book about social movements, dividing her time between Cambridge and a cottage in Vermont.

Recently, in presenting an award to a colleague on behalf of a professional organization, Peattie acknowledged her own debt to feminism and commitment to the struggle for women's equality. She praised the recipient's work in pointing out the disadvantaged position of women in professions, and in asserting that their "complicating and demanding domestic lives" provide a distinctive women's perspective on the nature of work, and commented on the recipient's "woman's skill" of parenthetically slipping in a "crack" about how little male colleagues know about working life, "just as a woman who is simultaneously cooking and discussing the aldermanic election may still see the cat sneaking up on the butter dish and give it a smack." For Peattie, women have a unique and valuable contribution to make: "I hope that as women move toward equality in the profession we do not lose that special sharp eye. Let's not become another set of 'the boys.' "

Although I have been exceedingly well treated by the university in which I have worked for twenty years, I have never felt at home there. I have felt like an outsider. It can be argued that my department, urban studies and planning, has such a mixture (a couple of economists, an historian, architects, besides persons with degrees in planning and public policy) that there is no mainstream and that it is easy for *anyone* to feel marginal. Some male colleagues complain that they feel this way, but I am convinced that my sense of marginality, of being a resident outsider, is, in a complex way, related to being a woman.

My sense of isolation is not of the sort to be alleviated by the remedy usually proposed: more women. When I meet young women trying to make careers in academia I feel as far from their condition as from that of male colleagues. By the time feminism reached the university I was so entrenched in peculiarity, so fiercely attached to autonomy, that I experienced feminists not as being supportive but as exerting pressure to reshape my intellectual agenda in a way that limited my freedom.

I have never thought of myself as having a career or making career choices but rather as conducting a life in which a leading component is a strong intellectual drive to learn and to express my understanding in words. Thinking and writing are intensely *personal* activities, not currency to pay one's way in a professional career. Nor have I seen the world in terms of choices but as paths to explore. Although three of my four children were deliberately conceived, even here I do not think "choice" is the right word. I cannot remember discussing whether, only when, and I have a special feeling for my fourth because she was unplanned—what theologians call "a grace."

Upbringing

My father was the son of a Chicago lawyer, sometime politician, and the beautiful daughter of the Danish consul. He had one sister a couple of years younger than he, Aunt Twinkle, a writer with astonishing blue eyes and a tendency to be nervous and have insomnia. My father was a sickly child. He remembered his mother and two Danish aunts sitting around his bed and crying because they thought he was going to die. The family lived on inherited land outside Chicago, where I and my siblings grew up. There were great hedged gardens and lawns and a large woodland of oaks and cottonwood sloughs, full of violets in the spring. Until my father was twelve he was thought too frail to go to school. He spent much of his childhood in bed, surrounded by books; out of bed he rode a pony, kept phonograph records of bird calls, looked at pond creatures through a microscope, and was painted in a velvet suit with lace collar modelled on little Lord Fauntleroy. In high school and college he wrote poetry.

My mother was a different sort, passionate and physical; as a friend said at her funeral, "warm to the touch." Her father was a journalist and wide-ranging intellectual who, during her childhood, became a sociologist via a German degree in social philosophy. Her mother was an artist, red-haired, impulsive, a feminist, totally personalistic, and inclined to pick up waifs and strays. My mother was the third of four children and in many ways her father's favorite; he thought of her as his intellectual heir. In college she majored in Russian and modern Greek with the idea of helping her father with studies of immigrant newspapers.

My parents' marriage was a love match hard to imagine in these more cynical times. They became engaged reading aloud *The Crock of Gold* (Stephens, 1914). When they married (after a year's wait, enforced by my father's parents who thought my mother too impulsive by half), they took a six-month honeymoon walking in the Rockies. My mother adored my father. She rescued him from the cocoon of his childhood and found him his intellectual career. He had gone to law school and entered his father's law office, but he hated it. His new father-in-law persuaded him to go into anthropology; and when he did field research for his dissertation in a village in Mexico his wife's mother went along to take care of the two babies.

I was the oldest of four, ranging down to a brother twelve years younger, a seven-year-old in shorts when I married. Closest to me was Tito, two years younger, a high-strung and magnetic boy who was killed in a sledding accident when he was twelve. I thought my mother would never get over it. For me, besides a deep sense of loss, there was something else. Years later, when I read about the survivors of Hiroshima (Lifton, 1982), it was with a shock of recognition. My brother's death had focused and intensified experiences that in early childhood had given me the feeling of being marked for and contaminated by death.

The family felt special, separate, different from other people. My father's upbringing made him less than gregarious. My maternal grandmother's wide-ranging enthusiasms for all sorts of people determined my mother to give *her* family a central place. Although during school years we lived near the University of Chicago, we spent long summers isolated in the country. We also went on fieldwork trips to Yucatan or Guatemala, where we were even more isolated. In the field or back at home there was the central ritual of family life. While other children (at least as I had imagined) roamed the neighborhood, my father read aloud to us all while my mother mended.

My mentor was my father. He read me poetry and took me for walks in the woods in which he had roamed as a boy. When we were out of the country he provided books of history to read. I, too, wrote poetry and thought, as he had, that I might become a biologist. I was a woman who identified with her father, a daughter of a woman who identified with *her* father. But the gender-typing within which I made my identifications was in some respects the reverse of the conventional. My father made flower arrangements and gave us poetry books. My mother sloshed around the vegetable garden in muddy gumboots and at Christmas gave us Swiss army knives.

In other ways the structure of the family was traditional. My mother's love for and deep intellectual appreciation of my father helped define a pattern in which the father was the star around which the planets revolved. Both parents collaborated in setting the self-directed, self-justifying, and self-gratifying intellectual life as a central theme of my upbringing. It could be shared in love and friendship, as in reading aloud; but to commercialize the intellectual life as one does, for example, in speaking of "an academic career," had somewhat the same flavor as commercializing love.

There were subthemes—less visible inconsistencies. My father, who considered academic life a calling rather than a career, had been thinking of quitting as a failure when he became Dean of Social Sciences, and he was pleased to be regarded eventually as a most distinguished anthropologist. In these inconsistencies I followed my father. Put up for tenure, I stacked the cards against myself by growing my hair down to my waist and asking nobody for support; yet when I became one of four tenured women at the Massachusetts Institute of Technology (MIT) I felt very pleased. Toward the end of my mother's life I came to understand that she, who had put my father and their family first, had always been jealous of me for having a career. With all the stress on knowledge "for its own sake," there was an unacknowledged interest in career success.

If elementary school was "not very interesting" (a phrase I hear in my mother's voice), high school was a dead loss. After my brother's death we fled to the all-year-round place in the country, and I commuted by bus to a large, modern, suburban high school. I was stunned by the size, the noise, the level of affluence—girls with stockings, boys with cars. I missed most of my sophomore year due to being in Guatemala. In my senior year, besides another Guatemalan field trip, I got diphtheria and did not attend school even one day. On the basis of exams, I graduated in a class of 600, in which I knew not a single person. I had missed socialization into the role of a teenage girl.

College

I went to college a loner and a reader, with the feeling of carrying death as a kind of personal pollution, as intimate as wood smoke in the hair and skin (Lifton, 1982). I picked

Swarthmore because it was Quaker, intellectual, in the country. It gave me all that and more. The introductory biology course was wonderful, and the microscopic drawing was an exercise in clear seeing and rendering. I gave up the idea of a biology major at once when I found that it would leave me one elective in four years. In my introduction to philosophy course I talked so much that the teacher took me aside and told me not to say anything more for the rest of the term (though he talked to me in his office). The great Gestalt psychologist Kohler gave an introductory course in psychology, to which I ran like one in love. I became interested in theoretical economics and on the final exam astonished the instructors with my grasp of theories of the business cycle. I did three years of German in two.

There were other important educational experiences. I saw Martha Graham dance and was stunned to understand that the body has its own speech, deeper than words. I began to dance. I took part in my first social survey (of families living in trailer camps in Delaware County, booming with wartime expansion of the shipyard). I helped the CIO pass out leaflets at the shipyard gate and heard an organizer talk in the barest of union halls. A little group of us set out to get Swarthmore to admit Negroes. Another student and I had dinner with the head of the board of managers. He told us of all his family had done for the underground railway—and of what a terrible idea it would be to admit Negroes to Swarthmore. We went to a NAACP youth conference at Hampton Institute, the only whites there. The students were endlessly kind, and I had my first glimpse of the threadbare world of aspiring blacks. (The next year the college admitted a coffee-colored young woman with a Polish surname. It seems a long time ago!)

The country was beautiful; I would take a pillow sack and roam the farms collecting windfall apples. I was still a loner, a reader, contaminated by death. At the end of my second year I married and went to work in Washington, D.C. It was my way of escaping the cocoon of my childhood.

Marriage, Work, and Graduate School

Pete, the man I married, came from the same corner of WASP academic culture that I did, but there was an important difference. Pete's relationship to other people, inclusive and egalitarian, was central to him. A relationship in high school with a leftist rabbi's family introduced him to the politics of democratic communitarian socialism. As my father had been my mentor in my relationship to myself, Pete became my mentor in my relationship to the rest of the human world.

In Washington we set up wartime housekeeping, cooking on a hot plate in an apartment without running water, a mile and a half from the end of the street-car line. We had a day to get my trunk from the railroad station and buy a table; then Pete went back to eighty-hour weeks at the Army Map Service. Two days later I started my first job as editorial assistant at the *Bulletin* of the Pan American Union. After a couple of months translating messages from friendly dictators south of the border for a journal that seemed to have no redeeming social value, I quit. I spent a couple of months reading, largely from college-level social-science reading lists, at the Library of Congress. Then, the solitary days "got to me," and I took a job at a grocery store.

In the work group I was the youngest, not trusted at the checkout but used as bagger, floor mopper, and stacker of crates. My co-workers were the wartime bottom-of-the-labor-market, women from the Georgetown slums. They moved matter-of-factly through disasters and risks that appalled me. Even I knew more about contraception than they. Sometimes a man from across the street brought over gin for all of us to drink in the back room on our lunch hour; sometimes truck drivers came in to get us to "feel them up." The physical work, the companionship, the very strangeness of it all saved me from what had felt like a spin toward weightlessness. I learned to take, as serious interpretations of real experience, ideas I had thought of as ignorance or prejudice. But the work was too hard. Washing spinach in the icy back room gave me a bad case of bronchitis. After a couple of weeks in bed reading *Jean Christophe* (Rolland, 1913) I set out job hunting.

A contact with one of my father's anthropological colleagues took me to the War Relocation Authority, which had charge of Japanese-Americans whom the Army had moved from the West Coast into what were essentially concentration camps. I worked in the Washington Reports Division, first as typist, then as ghostwriter. I loved the job. My co-workers and I thought of ourselves as fighting the good fight to defend Japanese-Americans in the arena of public opinion, and at twenty I saw myself doing an adult job very well.

As the war ended, so did my job. The Army lifted the exclusion orders keeping the Japanese-Americans from their homes and closed the barracks centers. My boss found me a job running an anti-VD campaign in New Orleans, but I was considering spending my payroll savings on a year to think about public opinion and to try to make sense of what I had been doing. I had only myself to consult with, as Pete, having volunteered as an ambulance driver, was in Hyderabad with the Indian Army. With very little ambivalence I opted for the year thinking.

I went to the University of Chicago because I was familiar with it through my father's being a member of the faculty and because their sociology department had a good deal of work on public opinion. At registration, the sociology department had a long line, while the nearby anthropology table had few customers. It seemed an ingenious strategy to register in anthropology and change to sociology later. However, I learned that the sociology department's work on public opinion centered on opinion polling, which was not what I wanted. I did not know where to find what I did want, which was something more political about the differential representation of interest groups. The anthropology department seemed a livelier place, and I was having fun at the university and in my thirty-dollar-a-month basement apartment.

What began as a year's sabbatical stretched to a decade. Within it I got a master's degree in anthropology, and Pete, having reached the dissertation stage in the Department of Education, switched to architecture and took a degree in that. We also had three children. Looking back, it is hard to understand what I thought I was doing in that decade. I did not think of myself as becoming an anthropologist. I cannot remember events in chronological order; they constitute, instead, elements of a period of life. In memory, a lively and talkative social life, conducted largely in basements, seems at least as important as does academic life.

Although at times the need for income drove me to the eccentric ill humor of Mrs. Greenspan's luncheonette, most of my jobs were fascinating. I was staff for a committee headed by sociologist Louis Wirth, which was supposed to reform the Chicago public schools, and found a long-term interest in schools as institutions. I ghostwrote a review of the literature on economic development. I spent a year working on a book on decision making in the War Relocation Authority with political scientist Morton Grodzins. When he got cancer and could not finish the work, I abandoned it without regret; I had learned from the writing and had no lust to press on to publication. One summer, in a small industrial city in northern Michigan, Pete and I ran a Quaker work camp for teenagers, an emotionally intense and fulfilling experience. I spent another summer with five fellow students at the Fox Indian reservation in Iowa, learning to be an anthropologist and getting a sense of what it means to be an Indian in twentieth-century America.

One job that later shaped my approach to university work was as staff person for a study of research and education in the behavioral sciences at the University of Chicago. Brought up in the idealistic conception of teaching and research as a "calling," I was unprepared for the real university of grantsmanship and academic log-rolling that I found in the study. That year's pregnancy was the only one during which I was nauseated *all* the time, and the nausea ceased abruptly when I went on vacation. The job left a legacy of cynicism about universities and a desire to stay clear of career building within one.

Shortly after I got a master's degree I conceived what I thought an interesting idea for a dissertation and considered going on to a Ph.D. My husband reported this to my father, who was a professor in the department where I was studying. My father's response to my husband: "I think if you were clearer about what you want to do, she wouldn't have such an idea." This was true; and when the comment was reported back I felt that I had done something dreadful, which reflected on my husband's competence and clarity of purpose and caused him shame. I went back to the student life with no goal.

Bearing children did not seem to have marked a new stage but fitted in with the rest of the sociable, intellectual life. I woke up in the hospital the morning after my first child was born, realizing with relief that something had not happened which I had not known I had been fearing: I had not become a new sort of person, a mother, but was the same old me. Pete worked full-time that year at Bruno Bettelheim's school for disturbed children, so for the only year since I was nineteen I did not have a job. It was a rather lonely year, since Bettelheim's school was an intense little world that kept Pete within it; but in my bubble of isolation I adored communing with the baby, this powerful, changing, wordless being. However, true to myself, I intellec-tualized and verbalized that, too: I read Schachtel's (1959) essay, "On Memory and Childhood Amnesia," and thought, through my baby, of what it was to become human.

Fitting children into student life was not effortless, espe-cially when it meant working. We never were able to afford full-scale baby tending. The first time I taught a class I had a buggy with a sleeping infant parked under the window of the classroom. Once when I had two children eighteen months apart, I went off to work after I had been up nine times in a seven-hour night. There was no separation between work and family; they were one. In the long run that unity worked. It enabled me to synthesize elements from many sources. It disciplined me to use everything I had learned and to look freshly at ordinary experience.

I was able to concentrate on writing my master's thesis on the meaning of being an American Indian. We were on vacation outside Taos, New Mexico, in a loaned adobe house. There, every day, while Pete and his nine-month-old son solemnly conversed in a drugstore in town, I laid out my notes on the clay floor.

When Pete finished his architecture course we decided to move to New York. We packed our household goods in orange crates and sent them by freight; we and the children travelled in an old Chevy that we had stripped and fitted with a mattress. Both my husband and I needed jobs. I was pregnant with a fourth child. Everything worked out extremely well. We had the best living arrangement: a joint household with two friends and their child. During the summer the women and children kept house and picked daisies at Pete's family's Vermont farm while the two men went job hunting.

In due course, both men went to work in the same architectural firm. The four of us rented a big, run-down apartment on the West Side. I lucked into an interesting study of schools at Bank Street College. We women took care of the children, consoled and counselled each other, and cooked on alternate weeks. Each of us had a baby that year and was able to leave the household in charge of the other. An arrangement many people told us would never work had only one serious defect: It was so painful when time came for the other family to go back to France.

When our joint family dissolved, matters became more complicated. We could not manage New York rent on our own. We decided to buy a house, covering the cost by renting part of it. We found a beautiful 1839 four-story brick house for $18,000 on a "bad street" in Brooklyn. Then we had the multiple stresses of remodelling plus day-to-day management of a four-child household, without the help of friends. When I got a job teaching nights at Queens College I found myself with two jobs, four children, and the laundry to do. Pete was having trouble becoming an architect. The modest, problem-solving temperament I found so attractive was exactly wrong for the most egoistic of professions. Thus we both were ready for an escape. Pete looked for an architectural job somewhere in the Third World. As for me, a bit of passivity looked appealing, and I thought that being in a Third World city, a place of rapid change, would be a way of developing a different kind of anthropological theorizing, one less focused on why things remain the same and more focused on change.

City Planning in Venezuela

Plans developed otherwise. While I was home with a sick child someone phoned, "We're planning a new city in Venezuela and need an anthropologist right away." "Maybe," I said, "but I'm not just one person, I'm part of a family." Two weeks later Pete and I were on a plane, both hired by the project, giggling about the idea of anyone needing an anthropologist "right away." We stayed for two and a half years—rather, the children and I did. Pete died eleven months later, the day after Christmas, in an automobile accident, as I drove us all to the coast by night.

The job was a deeply radicalizing experience that became the center of my understanding of the nature of economic development, of the state, of the possibilities of social action. Even studies I did on small enterprises like street vending and shoemaking came from Venezuela (Peattie, 1975, 1979, 1981, 1987 a, b). This work was, in one sense, simple application to economic issues of fieldwork methods central to both my anthropological background and to "Chicago school sociology." But the passions that drove it came from my discovery in Venezuela of how the state could favor large corporate firms and rationalize its policy via the conceptual structure of economic planning.

I have written about the project itself (e.g., Peattie, 1968a, b, 1987a). We lived at the site of the new city, a rapidly growing frontier town full of bars, entrepreneurs, aspirations. We bought a squatter house, whitewashed earth-plaster over bamboo lath, with a thin sheet of aluminum roof, from which we looked out over a broad beach to the wide Orinoco River. The planners lived and worked in Caracas, contemplating statistical projections and magic-marker proposals for "the form of the new city." The view from the site and the view from Caracas became progressively more divergent. What Pete and I first experienced as a lack of information leading to failure to take into account the needs of residents we came to understand as an essential feature of a process intended to reorganize the environment for large corporations. We came to live in a state of passionate indignation.

The situation affected each of us differently. Designers' demands for a "big concept" and lack of interest in mundane details of the existing city put Pete in a situation he experienced as a heightened version of the professional inadequacy he had felt in New York. He became deeply depressed. For me, the indignation was a way of organizing and integrating the flood of experience and was intensely energizing.

The Single Years

All the powerful feelings that came with Pete's death in a strange way also helped to empower me (remember the young girl contaminated by death). I was coming to understand important things. I was finding my voice, I was part of historic processes, and the use of my voice to interpret those processes was acting in history. I was steadied by the children. For the next decade we made our little world together. They were my tribe. When the time came to go home, we drove up the Pan American highway with our parrot, hammocks, and special, "found" objects. For years after I had a dream in which I imaged time using the metaphor of automobile travel. I called such dreams the "up life's highway dreams." The long drive northward with my children had become a central metaphor for conveying the liberation and empowerment and the anxiety and loneliness of becoming a widow.

The Joint Center for Urban Studies gave me the best thing possible: a year to write a book about the project. They wanted me in Cambridge, so we moved to a Boston suburb. The schools astonished my children as my rich suburban high school had once astonished me. I spent my days writing in an office off Harvard Square or walking off the writing around the Square.

The View from the Barrio (Peattie, 1968a) was a simply written account of the process of planning and constructing the new city as seen in the squatter neighborhood where we had lived. It was in part a political document, a brief on behalf of those people with whom I had lived and to whom I had become committed, seen both as underdogs and as agents of historical transformation. It also represented my conflict with the planners in being an attempt to define "the problem" in my own terms rather than on theirs. The style owed something to my father's intellectual elegance. The perspective owed something to Pete's politics. The apparently casual style was, I believe, a woman's device for dealing with assertion. It took me twenty years of teaching and lecturing to be able to write another book on the project (Peattie, 1987b), which directly confronted the planners and their planning.

Just as my year's sabbatical to think about public opinion had turned into a decade at the University of Chicago, my year's sabbatical to write a book drifted into over twenty years of university teaching. First, the Department of Planning at MIT hired me to teach a planning studio with a physical planner. Then it was a course called "Planning and Poverty." The chairman always made sure I understood that it would be impossible to renew my contract for another year. Each year, thinking it my last, I tried to figure out how I could break new ground, leaving something behind in the department when I left. I did not bother with faculty meetings; these were not my colleagues. Outside the university I was one of a small group organized to do "advocacy planning" (technical assistance to low-income community groups that had problems with planners, such as urban renewal clearance that was not replaced with new housing, or eradication of dwellings and businesses in the path of a highway). This was my reference group; these were my colleagues.

In the end I received tenure at MIT. I was best known in the planning profession for an article on our advocacy-planning activities that appeared simultaneously in a Students for a Democratic Society (SDS) mimeographed report and the *Journal of the American Institute of Planners* (Peattie, 1968b), from which it was widely reprinted. I received a Ph.D. in social anthropology from the University of Chicago by converting my book into a dissertation, which took three weeks. My department let me teach pretty much what I liked. As a qualitative researcher who needed no computer time and liked to do her own interviews, my research was relatively free of funding constraints. Usually it was simplest to be self-financing. I took unpaid leave, for example, to interview small manufacturers and street vendors in Bogota.

My son says I have done just wonderfully by doing what I felt like doing, and I believe that is true. I had a good early education, excellent sponsorship in graduate school, and a lot of luck. One piece of luck was entering the field of planning just as it was expanding and bringing in more political and social issues. Doing what I wanted has not meant shaping my life toward long-term goals. It has meant seizing hold of, integrating, and interpreting opportunities that appeared. I learned to grow ideas out of engagement with the actual, with all its absurdity, ambiguity, and passion. I think this trust in and capacity to use the serendipitous is what has made my life work; it has, in any event, made it marvelously variegated and interesting.

At the age of sixty I did, at last, make a career decision. I decided to take my life in hand and go on early retirement to retrain myself to work in the peace movement. I gave away my professional books, arranged for my children and old friends to give me a birthday party with dancing, and retired. But I was unable to change my life to the degree I had planned. I work in the peace movement, but not much more than before. Since my university left me my office and secretarial help I spend a good deal of time there. I even help students with their theses. Somehow it seems to work out; it is work which feels like mine.

On my own, after the years of children, I designed and helped build a small, simple, beautiful house in Vermont. As when I first discovered dance, it was an intense experience of moving into a world beyond words. I still "do words." Working without haste on a book about social movements, I have discovered that its subject matter is none other than the publics I thought I would be learning about when, as a young woman, I took my wartime savings to the University of Chicago.

When I retired, my colleagues gave me a splendid party— good food, good talk, and the gift of a little greenhouse for the little house in Vermont. They made a statement that included: "Whereas you have not allowed us to take ourselves so seriously, nor to pontificate nearly as much as we wanted to; whereas you have always managed to keep our sacred cows from consuming most of the pasture; whereas you have named things that no one else would name . . ." I thanked them and said: "This is the last time you will have this experience. You never really hired me. I drifted in. I never felt as if I belonged. The women who come after me will be different. They will take themselves seriously. They will insist that you take them seriously. And, then, they will have to take you seriously. You will never again have someone who is an insider but also an outsider, who need not take any of the conventions of your thought for granted. That is a loss, even if one we must suffer for the gain in justice for women."

References

Lifton, J. L. (1982). *Death in life: Survivors of Hiroshima.* New York: Basic Books.
Peattie, L. R. (1968a). *The view from the barrio.* Ann Arbor: University of Michigan Press.
Peattie, L. R. (1968b). Reflections on advocacy planning. *Journal of the American Institute of Planners, xxx,* 80–88.
Peattie, L. R. (1975). Tertiarization, marginality and urban poverty in Latin America. *Latin American Urban Research, 5,* 109–123.
Peattie, L. R. (1979). Economic anthropology and anthropological economics. In R. Hinshaw (Ed.), *Currents in anthropology: Essays on honor of sol tax* (pp. 85–94). Berlin: Mouton.
Peattie, L. R. (1981). What is to be done with the informal sector? A case study of shoe manufacturing in Columbia. In H. I. Safa (Ed.), *Towards a political economy of urbanization* (pp. 85–94). New Delhi, India: Oxford University Press.
Peattie, L. R. (1987a). An idea in good currency and how it grew. *World Development, 15,* 851–860.
Peattie, L. R. (1987b). *Planning: Rethinking Ciudad Guayana.* Ann Arbor: University of Michigan Press.
Rolland, R. (1913). *Jean Christophe.* New York: Modern Library.
Schachtel, E. G. (1959). (Ed.). On memory and childhood amnesia. In *Metamorphosis* (pp. 279–322). New York: Basic Books.

Chapter 12

Occupation
Sociologist

Helena Znaniecka Lopata, Ph.D.

Introduction to Helena Znaniecka Lopata

The title of this chapter is a take-off on the title of Helena Lopata's first book, *Occupation: Housewife* (1971), which was published — after a long struggle — when she was forty-six years old. Since that time she has published nine more books and has another in progress. In addition, she has published thirty-five chapters in edited books and forty articles in refereed journals. She has presented fifty papers at scientific meetings, many of them international (in Acapulco, Singapore, Windsor, New Delhi, Cardiff, Posnan, Toronto, Vichy, Jerusalem).

Living in the shadow of a famous Polish sociologist father, she felt a debt — familial, intellectual, and emotional — to complete his unfinished work. She helped Polish sociologists understand her father's role in their intellectual history, a role that had been obscured by the post-World War II communist domination of Polish intellectual life. She facilitated the work of Polish sociolo-

Lives of Career Women: Approaches to Work, Marriage, Children, edited by Frances M. Carp. Plenum/Insight, New York, 1991.

gists in this country, particularly those not in favor with the authorities. She held office and then moved to the board of directors of the Polish Academy of Arts and Sciences in America. She benefited in that Poland reminded her of the importance of her father's work and the heritage she represented to Polish sociologists, and that she had every right to her own career as a sociologist. It was only *after* she had made her own mark that she worked as Helena *Znaniecka* Lopata. She established herself before "using" the family heritage.

Her work has been typed as "women's work," but it is this work—on women, on widows—that is the basis for her international acclaim and esteem. Male colleagues say she undervalues this work, much as she understates the difficulty of achieving all that she has while overcoming the obstacles involved in being a woman in a "man's field." Unlike many sociologists, male and female, she did it on her own "through grit and hard work," without a powerful sponsor. One remarked, "It is in the women's movement that she places her advancement." She was a member of the committee that planned and established the professional organization, Sociologists for Women in Society.

Becoming a professor of sociology is a long and arduous process, facilitated and complicated in my case by several circumstances.

The Place and Time of My Birth

The first circumstance was my birth in Poland, in 1925. Both place and time were important. In the years between World Wars I and II and during the 1939–1945 Nazi occupation Poland was politically independent from prior Russian, Prussian, and Austrian occupations of over a century. After World War II the Soviet Union controlled most of the Polish government's activities until the revolutionary events of 1989. Had Poland not been independent, my father would not have returned in 1920 to the country of his birth, socialization, and identification, and I would not have been born there. Had Poland not been invaded in 1939, I probably would have become a Polish scholar—were I not dead. Father was a professor, a sociologist who opened up this field in Poland. That country, though quite patriarchal, did not prevent women who could do so from becoming scholars or professional persons.

I had an advantage over women who were my American age-cohorts in having an intellectual and cosmopolitan background. Father had studied in Switzerland and France before obtaining his Ph.D. in philosophy at the Jagielonian University in Krakow. He came to the United States to work on *The Polish Peasant in Europe and America* (1918–1920) with W. I. Thomas of the University of Chicago. There he married a Connecticut Yankee lawyer, who helped with that book and went with him when he decided to help rebuild Poland. We traveled widely in Europe and received visitors from other countries throughout the years. We lived in New York when I was between six and eight years old while Father taught at Columbia University. The intellectual atmosphere of the "old world" European intelligentsia exuded enthusiasm in the importance of contributing knowledge to a world culture—a feeling of noblesse oblige in which the nobility was of intellect, not of birth.

My parents were older than average, Father being forty-nine and Mother thirty-nine when I was born. Father's first wife had died soon after they had arrived in the United States in 1914. His son, Julek, by that marriage had remained in Poland with his mother's sisters because of the threat of World War I. His aunts kept him with them even after Father married Mother, not trusting an American to raise a Znaniecka. Julek was seventeen years my senior, and we spent relatively little time together. He was a poet and novelist, caught by the Nazis during the Warsaw uprising and sent to Dachau. After release by the American forces he finally made it to America. Unable to forget his experiences, to write about anything but the war or to change languages, he finally committed suicide.

An Only Child of Older Parents

Being an only child of older parents had its pluses and its minuses. The pluses included, in addition to the intellectual excitement, the fact that Father was famous in Europe and, to a lesser degree, in America. Mother considered him a genius. He said emphatically that genius was ninety-five percent work. They both worked very hard. Mother gave up her law career when she married Father, both in order to assist him and because Poland had a Napoleonic code of law for which the University of Chicago had ill prepared her. She was the typical American academic wife. However, the wives of most of my parents' Polish friends were professional women. It was not until I came to America that I saw many women in two-person single careers (Papanek, 1973).

The minuses of being the daughter of a famous man appeared later when I tried to establish myself as a sociologist. I was haunted by doubt of my own ability, apprehensive that sociologists were being nice to me because of my father. For years I feared that I was "given" my Ph.D. on that account, and that Blumer gave me honors in social psychology because he had been so harsh in his review of Father's *The Polish Peasant*. By the time I reached the stage of trying to do sociology, Father's ease of doing it smoothly made my efforts look amateurish.

Another complication helped, in the long run, to encourage my movement into an academic career. At the age of ten I developed osteomyelitis, a bone disease for which there was, and probably still is, no real cure. A staphylococcus bacteria invaded my bone marrow before the age of antibiotics and remained, in spite of an operation to remove the infected area. This prevented my walking for a year then and again, whenever inflammations with drainage occurred. The leg problem was dormant after the first year, until our war experiences. After that attacks occurred almost every spring and fall. I was told not to have children and did not get over the attacks until another major operation after the birth of our second child.

I include this recurrent physical problem because it influenced my life considerably, eliminating many possibilities for the future. Luckily, I ended up with only a scar on the leg and no deformities. After penicillin made the attacks less threatening, I tried to ignore the whole thing most of the time—as is evident by my getting married and having children. However, sedentary reading and writing came more naturally to me than to other girls with the same tomboyish tendencies. In fact, writing became an early pleasure. The Poznan city newspaper had a children's page, and I was frequently published and even plagiarized. (The newspaper was willing to sue.)

The Invasion of Poland

Then the war came. Father was at Columbia University for the summer. Mother and I had stayed in Poland because she wanted to supervise the building of our house in the mountains. That was a mistake. When we got back to Poznan, Mother found out that we were on both the Nazi and the Communist blacklists, simply because my father was an academic. We were picked up with a busful of others one night and taken to what was literally a concentration camp. Although at first we were not aware that this was such a place (people simply were not aware of the depth of the Nazi threat), empty cattle cars were brought in periodically when the camp was filled with Poles, people were packed in and driven around during these winter months until they froze, then their bodies were dumped into mass graves.

By the time the cattle cars arrived after our incarceration, Mother realized that rumors were correct and decided she had nothing to lose by trying to get us out. She lied to the commander, telling him she was an American citizen (she had lost those rights when she married a foreign national before 1924, when the law was changed) who happened to be visiting

Poland when the war broke out, and that she wanted to get herself and her orphaned niece (me) back to America. Being a good American lawyer, she so flabbergasted the man that he did let us out. (This was in the winter of 1939–1940, before the United States entered the war.) She then got us out of Poland through a complicated process that is not germane here. I refer to this experience because of the deep impression made upon me by those events and by the stories I had heard about what had happened to members of our extended family and to friends who stayed behind. The guilt over my survival and my many advantages caught up with me after a visit to Poland in 1966, when the communist government finally gave me a visa.

A Refugee in the United States

After escaping Poland, Mother and I joined Father in Champaign-Urbana, Illinois. Although my English was weak, my education had been very good, and in high school I was placed two years ahead of my peers. I hated Champaign and Urbana high schools, both of which I attended in the two years during which we moved around before settling down. I was younger than the other students in my classes; they had never before seen a foreigner and wanted to have little to do with me. This was another push toward the academic world, which I found more accepting.

Mother had gone to Smith College, which offered me a scholarship, but she convinced me not to accept it for two reasons: She had been unhappy there as a poor relative of alumnae, and she did not wish to spend the money that would be involved. Father had only ten remaining teaching years during which to accumulate sufficient money to last until the end of their lives. She also felt a moral obligation to help people in Poland as much as we could. Mother and I made many speeches around the Midwest, telling of our experiences and of

Nazism in general, usually to unbelieving audiences. We once figured that I alone made over 100 speeches. In return we received money for medicines or used clothing that Mother had cleaned and sent to Poland. My husband's aunt recently showed us the tag from a package Mother sent to her in Siberia.

So, I went to the University of Illinois, where my father was a member of the faculty. Father convinced me to follow a path that seemed surprising in view of his democratic and world-culture views – to join a sorority. However, that move was wise. The pledge year Americanized me in a hurry, and I enjoyed the rest of my university career. I met my husband there during my senior year, and we married at the tender age of twenty. He was a war veteran with the GI Bill, both of us worked part-time, and we rented two rooms in my parents' home, thus managing financially. I finished my M.A. in philosophy and sociology, he in economics, and away from Champaign-Urbana we went.

Graduate School: Introduction to Sexism

I did not become aware of sexism in academia until graduate school. Any experienced discomfort I could blame on American culture, wishing often to return to "civilization" in Poland. Father suggested that I stop judging long enough to learn more about this society. Mother constantly encouraged me to study and do well in school. She saw roles within the academic community as the best for women, in spite of the fact that few women were professors in any scientific field. The women we knew in Champaign-Urbana were faculty wives or taught in the school of social work. Women lawyers whom she knew in this country were doing well – albeit without marriage and children. Mother lived vicariously through Father.

Everyone in my immediate environment assumed that I would become a scholar, probably in sociology, although I tried other fields ranging from chemistry to philosophy. I was the only "girl" in the sociology M.A. program, and I found the six male students compatible. I heard rumors that one member of the faculty, a bachelor, had Friday evening get-togethers for the other students, and I assumed something personal to be the reason for my lack of invitation. It did not occur to me that my friends, the other students, could have done something about the situation. The fact that I was usually the only woman in other academic situations did not surprise me. My background had prepared me for being the odd person around.

In spite of sending letters all over the country, I was unable to get an academic position after receiving my M.A. My husband, Dick, who had not planned on being an academic, nor made any moves in that direction, immediately received a telegram inquiring whether he wanted to teach at the University of Massachusetts at Amherst. We went to Amherst in the fall of 1948. I finally got a job at the Pioneer Valley Association organizing little towns to entice tourists and industry into the region. When, finally, I was asked to teach at Smith College (a great thrill), Dick decided that he had had enough of academia and of the East Coast, and that we were going to return to his home city, Chicago. I told him to go alone—and here I am in Chicago.

The University of Chicago

Moving to Chicago, which I did not like at all from prior visits, proved to be a major plus for me because I was able to enter the Ph.D. program at the University of Chicago, which was a fascinating place at that time. Dick joined a management consulting firm, which paid for my schooling, and I went back to school in 1949. There was a housing shortage and what was available at our price was not especially nice. Therefore, we moved several times, but always near the campus. This was lucky for me because I avoided the larger community's evaluations of my "unfeminine" behavior in doing advanced graduate work. Dick's family tolerated my academic involvement because of him, and I had the full support of my parents.

The sociology faculty of the University of Chicago was relatively small. Although there were many adjunct instructors, the faculty was overwhelmed by the mass of graduate students in those post-war years. Nevertheless, the department was exciting. My dissertation committee consisted of Wirth, Blumer, and Hughes. During the dissertation preparation Wirth died, Blumer moved to the West Coast, and Hughes was supportive but very busy. A major recommendation on my draft was that I get an English editor: "One does not spell 'of course' as 'off course.' "

Most of the 200-plus students were men using their GI Bill benefits. There were very few women students but many wives working to help put their husbands through school. Many of the men students were employed also, as taxicab drivers, musicians, or in other nonacademic jobs. Again, I was not aware of the sexism, except in retrospect. I attributed not being part of the "inner circle" of graduate assistants close to the faculty to my being a wife and being married to a businessman rather than an academician. My closest friends were wives in the doctoral program. Students formed study groups for the preliminary examinations, and in this way I made many friends among the male students. These friendships have lasted throughout my life.

Air Force Officer's Wife and Graduate Student

My sojourn at the University of Chicago was short. It was interrupted because Dick was called into the Air Force during the Korean War and stationed at Langley Air Force Base in Virginia. There I was hit fully by both sexism and racism. My taken-for-granted world was not replicated there. I went to

Chicago for the preliminary examinations and then settled down to work on my dissertation on the Polish-American community, using the inter-library loan system that was available at Hampton Institute. The combination of being a woman working to become a sociologist and going daily to a "Negro college" was too much for many of our acquaintances at the Air Force base. Dick was a lieutenant, and then a captain, so I had to obey the rules for officers' wives and could not avoid contact with other officers and their wives. Their hostility grew as I became increasingly pregnant and continued to go daily to Hampton Institute.

Return to Chicago

Our return to Chicago occurred while I was still working on the dissertation, with the help of baby-sitting by Dick's relatives and encouragement from my parents. Mother typed much of my work, as she had my M.A. thesis on international cooperation in medicine. She finally gave up and sent me a typing book so I could learn how to type by myself. While I concentrated on the final stages of dissertation preparation and Dick started traveling every week as a consultant, we decided that Hyde Park was not a good place to raise a child, and we moved to a suburb. At that time Skokie was a very interesting, culturally but not racially heterogeneous area, and most residents were young couples. Our neighborhood mostly included homeowners with a full-time homemaker, an employed husband, and two or more children. A dog was not a necessity but was ubiquitous.

This was the final blow to my "foreignness" and my "strange" ideas as to what a woman can do. I tried for jobs teaching sociology, the Ph.D. in hand, with no success. The head of the Department of Sociology at Northwestern University stood up when I entered for an interview but did not turn around from his desk, which faced the wall, and declared that he had never hired a woman and never would. Other universities in the area had no openings for me, and I was tied to Chicago by being wife to a man who wanted to work in Chicago. I tried writing, even for popular magazines, but met total rejection.

Occupation: Housewife

So I turned into a full-time homemaker, a two-person career back-up person. My only venture into scholarship was a study of the social roles of suburban housewives in 1956, with the help of a small grant from *The Chicago Tribune*. My background in symbolic interaction and role theory provided valuable theoretical tools for such research. I had become increasingly puzzled by the contrast between self-definition and behavior among women around me, who described themselves as "just housewives" while venturing quite competently to create a new suburban culture and family system. *The Feminine Mystique* (Friedan, 1963) was doing very well in Chicago's suburbia.

I completed 300 interviews with homemakers in the suburbs. Working with a whole-role complex rather than a single-role conception of each person led me deeper into social psychology and the relationship between the individual and society. The research project was exciting. I wrote reports on it and tried to get them published. Even women's magazines were not interested in American suburban housewives! Most of my friends, inside and outside academia, also considered the subject insignificant. Again I put aside my sociological aspirations and returned to full-time housewifery. The tale thus far demonstrates how easily one can become embedded in a local culture, defining the self and the world from the vantage point of that local culture. It changed my life profoundly for over ten years. Gone were the aspirations of being a major sociologist, until I returned to Poland for a visit in 1966. There women were employed, my relatives and former schoolmates mainly in professions and academia. They were amazed that I had given up all the advantages of my background and my gruelling academic achievements—and of the efforts of people who helped us escape from Poland—by not becoming an active scholar. I was informed that the girl whose papers were given to Mother to get me out of Warsaw and Poland had died because she could not get out of the city later. (The Nazis required a paper of permission to leave, and hers had gone with me.) In the view of the Polish intelligentsia, I had an obligation to contribute to science and the world. Believe me, that is a heavy burden, and I had a very hard time dealing with it upon my return to America.

Return to Academia

I added interviews with American urban homemakers and employees to the suburban housewife data and sat myself down to write a book. Father was dead, and Mother was the only person who encouraged me in this venture. My husband and children (born in 1951 and 1955) were accustomed to having a full-time homemaker. My part-time teaching did not really interfere with their lives.

Then I went into full-time teaching at Roosevelt University and began serious commitments to other academic activities in addition to the painful job of writing a book. Dick's business associates warned him that my teaching at a very liberal university would hurt his career. His mother was convinced that my activities would harm his future. My children did not like this whole shift. My son confessed that he found it very difficult having such a peculiar mother—a Ph.D., a sociologist, a working woman, a humanist-atheist, and a foreigner—even earlier, when I taught one evening course and was a full-time mom. Dick was not fully gracious about the inconveniences, although slowly he was socialized back into accepting me as an odd wife. After all, he had married me as a future scholar and supported me, financially and psychologically, through the Ph.D. The problem was that the business community into which he had become absorbed was very negative about my behavior.

Finding a publisher for the book, *Occupation: Housewife* (1971), was another problem. I had so many rejection slips that I quit counting them. Luckily, I finally showed it to a sociologist, Howie Becker, who convinced Irving Horowitz, who convinced Oxford University Press to publish it.

For some reason that I do not understand, I thought I would pay back my debt to society by applying my sociology to the study of widowhood. It was not a pleasant subject because of its obvious connection to death and grief. I spent much time in libraries before talking with widows. Their claim of second-class citizenship appeared to be justified. Few sociologists wanted to deal with this area. There was only one study in the United States (Berardo, 1968) and one in England (Morris, 1958).

In the early 1970s United States government agencies were becoming increasingly interested in the American aging population, and research money was available. I obtained a grant for the study of modifications in basic social roles brought about by the death of a major member of a woman's social circle. This required learning statistics and the basics of computer techniques. The articles and book that came out of that study led to a new, larger grant with possibilities of cooperative work on support systems of widows with sociologists in other societies.

The next major project focused on changes in the social construction of the world and role commitments of urbanites aged twenty-five to fifty-four. The reason I again chose American women to test some basic concepts of role theory and symbolic interactionism was obvious. I had a broad base of knowledge from previous studies that could help in the selection of "sensitizing concepts" (Blumer, 1969), so necessary for the understanding of human beings and their world.

Research on Women

This repeated selection of women as subjects had serious consequences. The feminist movement in sociology picked up on my work, so I have received my share of rewards. On the other hand, I have been labeled by "sociologists of serious sociology" as limited to less than significant subjects. Books and articles dealing with role theory or symbolic interaction generally ignore my work on women. The research on the roles of widows does not permeate any field but social gerontology. Not even family sociologists want to bring that stage of life into their texts.

My other works, on the Polish-American community (to which I returned twenty-five years after the original venture), immigration, ethnic composition of the labor force, the functions of universities, friendships, occupations, even ballroom dance studios, have been noted in their respective fields. The major work is known mainly to sociologists specializing in women's subjects, who are, with few exceptions, women. It is here that I notice most the continuation of sexism in sociology. Of course, I am not the only one to note this fact, but it affects my career and my relationships with other sociologists. I read the work of my "buddies" even in areas of no special interest to me, if they are using concepts relevant to my work; but the same is not true of my male colleagues.

Years back, when Rose Hum Lee hired me at Roosevelt University, she warned that I had better do well because women were not popular in academe of the 1960s. In 1965, students signed a petition asking that I be hired full-time in a tenure position, assuming that my part-time status was objectionable; although at that time I felt I should not take on a full-time job because of my family. The dean insisted that I obey the petition.

I moved up relatively quickly at Roosevelt, reaching associate professorship by 1969. I worked hard, with many more hours away from homemaking duties. Roosevelt became a less exciting institution after a change in administration, and I went to Loyola University of Chicago as full professor. I carried with me a grant, obtained several larger grants in coming years, was asked to fill in as chairperson for a couple of years, and opened my own Center for the Comparative Study of Social Roles. It is not here that I have experienced overt sexism.

Professor of Sociology

I came full blast on the academic scene at the right moment. Pressure from the government, itself pressured by the feminist movement and its leaders, opened some doors for visible women, and I had rapidly become quite visible, getting grants, finally being published, making speeches, and being quoted by the mass media. My continued activity in the discipline paid off with increasing opportunities for national and international travel and contact. I am no longer limited to Chicago. Loyola's sociology department has been congenial, the university cooperative (given an adequate push), and my family increasingly more tolerant of my professional and scientific commitments.

This does not mean I am free from experiences of sexism. My work is labeled as "limited" to women, thus not mainstream. Let me give you one incident as an example. My presidential address at the Society for the Study of Social Problems, titled "Social Construction of Social Problems over Time," dealt with the problems faced by a society, America as an example, in integrating new members, both immigrants and newborns. The society's journal, *Social Problems,* is required to publish presidential addresses, but the editor delayed publication of mine until he had a special issue on the family. The address was not on the family! I asked for some recognition of this fact, but the male editor did not understand the point.

One of the tremendous benefits of my being a woman is that the feminist movement has made me, and others with whom I have talked, aware that many problems we have faced are not due to our "oddness" but to the generic condition of being the second sex in a male-dominated sphere of a male-dominated world. University professorships and scientific endeavors have been male dominated, and the few women who entered those arenas were not taken seriously.

It is interesting to note that disproportionately many of the women of my generation in this country, especially of my sociological cohort, are foreign-born and/or Jewish. American society appears to have been especially hard on such women. As with the situation of blacks (Myrdal, 1944), a democratic society needs to justify structural and personal discrimination by creating a complex ideology, embedded in the culture and socialization, to explain the gap between values and behavior. Anti-intellectualism is ever present, and the Protestant ethic worked fine for men but placed great restrictions on the self- and other-images of women.

Talking with other women sociologists of any but recent age cohorts made me realize how similar are our experiences and self-doubts. Those of us who tried and survived, becoming scholars and loving what we are doing, had very strong encouragement along the way, often from parents. Sociologist Howie Becker refers to the importance of "side bets": Major commitments must be supported with as many side bets as possible. For a woman scholar the selection of a husband, if one is to be in the picture, makes a great deal of difference in life—although even the most carefully selected man must be constantly socialized into changes he never expected during courtship.

My consciousness of my world has been raised mainly by contact with members of Sociologists for Women and by feminist literature. My husband did not have such experiences in the business community. One of the things we had to work out after I became a full-time scholar was money. Reading *The Two-Paycheck Marriage* (Bird, 1979), I became aware that everyone, including our accountant, continued to treat my earnings as pin money. Dick did not take advantage of my paycheck or of my professional tax benefits. He is still unable to function as a proper "wife" at conventions in which I am the main participant. When we appear as a couple, most people assume that he is the sociologist. But then, most scholars now go to such meetings without spouses. My male colleagues complain that their wives do not want to come along because they have independent lives and identities in their own careers. Things are changing.

I sometimes envy younger women going into sociology, as the world is allegedly easier for them; they have more women colleagues, and men appear less likely to look straight through a woman unless they are attracted to her physical features. At the same time, I feel that my believing that obstacles I faced were due to my personal characteristics, rather than due to worrying about the burden of being a woman in a man-made world, may have been an advantage to me.

Above all, however, constant hard work and a thick skin (including the ability to pull the reviews out of the drawer later on and do what was suggested or ignore the impossible) are absolute necessities for sociologists, women and men. My mother was right in saying that academic social roles are rewarding for women—in highly supportive environments when the children are small, in the many decades after the children are past that stage, and in the yet-to-be-frequent "modern marriage and parenthood." I was lucky in my selection of parents and my so easily resocializable husband of forty-four years.

References

Berardo, F. (1968). Widowhood status in the United States: Perspective on a neglected aspect of the family life-cycle. *The Family Coordinator, 17*, 191–203.

Bird, C. (1979). *The two-paycheck marriage.* New York: Rawson Wade.

Blumer, H. (1969). *Symbolic interactionism: Perspectives and method.* Englewood Cliffs, NJ: Prentice-Hall.

Friedan, B. (1963). *The feminine mystique.* New York: W. W. Norton.
Lopata, H. Z. (1971). *Occupation: Housewife.* New York: Oxford.
Morris, P. (1958). *Widows and their families.* London: Routledge and Kegan Paul.
Myrdal, G. (1944). *An American dilemma: The Negro problem and modern democracy.* New York: Harper & Row.
Papanek, H. (1973). Men, women and work: Reflections on the two-person career. *American Journal of Sociology, 79,* 852–872.

Chapter 13

The Once-Reluctant School Teacher

Catherine Scofield Rude

Introduction to Catherine Scofield Rude

In her career as an elementary school teacher Catherine Rude was consistently a learner as well; and she was interested not only in improving class procedures but equally in understanding the theoretical constructs that underlie their operation. Early in her career she was brought to the attention of a consultant to a New York State school system who was working with the administration to identify teachers who would benefit from a process-oriented science program and who would then serve as "change agents" within their schools. Her name was submitted with the stipulation that she was a beginning teacher who was admittedly attempting to master basic management skills, but the principal added: "Catherine Rude already has the respect of the staff because of her commitment to learning, and, what is more important, she has the intellectual honesty and the concept of self to

Lives of Career Women: Approaches to Work, Marriage, Children, edited by Frances M. Carp. Plenum/Insight, New York, 1991.

explore the unknown in the company of students as well as other teachers." The principal's wisdom and perceptiveness were justified; Catherine became a catalyst and support person for the district elementary schools in addition to her own school's staff, particularly in the areas of science and mathematics.

At a later time she and other teachers were working with students to implement various models of teaching based upon a particular theory of learning. Using these models requires understanding of the theoretical formulation as well as mastery of the skills to implement them in a classroom environment. Catherine Rude was the supportive leader of the group of teachers. She also conducted and videotaped microteaching lessons in order to analyze her growth toward mastery of these skills and the achievement of the goals of the lessons. Her commitment to learning, intellectual honesty, and concept of self led her to utilize such self-help techniques and to give her co-workers encouragement and support for their own improvement.

Over the years Catherine Rude earned the respect and admiration of the students with whom she has come in contact and that of her fellow educators as well. She continued to take courses to help her become a better teacher, never to follow a degree plan. Her transcripts show about 200 units of graduate work. Her continuing enjoyment of the domestic side of her nature was exemplified in the recent wedding of her younger daughter at Lake Almanor, California, where Catherine and her husband recently retired. The mother of the bride designed and made dresses for the bride, the matron of honor (her married daughter), the two flower girls (granddaughters), and herself, and shirts for the ring bearers (twin grandsons).

Career Choices for Women When I Was Growing Up

As a retired elementary school teacher reflecting on more than thirty years of teaching in California and New York, it would please me to say I fulfilled a childhood ambition, but that would not be true. During the 1930s and early 1940s societal pressures limited the careers appropriate for women. Teaching was high on that short list. Women could become teachers with broad social acceptance, but teaching was primarily for single women. A woman was expected to give up her position as a teacher upon marriage. Some school districts employed only single women, and a teacher who married was automatically out of a job. Marriage, children, and homemaking were the most acceptable roles. Not many married women sought employment outside the home. Among the choices of careers for university-trained women, education was the one I was sure I wanted to avoid.

Early Influences

There are many influences on a child's life. Family, school, and community, with their prevailing attitudes, are among the obvious. My early life was typical of the time. I lived with my father, mother, and paternal grandmother outside a small town in Southern California. The citrus groves surrounding the business area were the financial base for the town as well as the wider area. My father's family had been in agriculture for a generation, and until high-school graduation I lived in the house in which he grew up. Little emphasis was placed on education. In his family of seven children only one completed college.

My mother's family was not as typical of the times as was my father's. There was a special drive and emphasis on education, which led to my mother and her three sisters all having teaching careers that they continued after marriage. The women of my mother's family were career oriented, though they restricted their choice to teaching. They emphatically believed in acquiring as much education as possible.

In this they were dramatically influenced by my maternal grandmother, who believed that women were capable of handling a career as well as a family, and that they should prepare

Catherine Scofield Rude

themselves to make a societal contribution and to be independent if necessary. She was an immigrant from England who married a French immigrant coal miner. They raised their family in an isolated area of Colorado that did not provide schooling beyond eighth grade. Her drive and sacrifice led her to set up a separate residence in a larger community when her eldest child was ready for high school. All six of her children acquired high-school educations, and her four daughters took examinations to qualify them as teachers immediately upon graduation.

Having commenced teaching careers, the sisters, over a period of time, moved to Southern California. All married men with agricultural ties, and all continued teaching in spite of prevailing social expectations. They also continued to upgrade their formal educations, returning to colleges and universities whenever possible for summer sessions and night courses. Three of the four eventually earned master's degrees.

My memories of family gatherings when I was a child include many discussions revolving around education and teaching. There were Sunday dinners, at which the men discussed the weather, crops, the agricultural market, and the like. My mother and aunts, while performing the domestic tasks for such family meals, talked about textbooks, behavior problems, ideas for achieving curricular goals, and other educational topics. Eventually and inevitably, when the last dish had been dried and put away, attention turned to younger family members. The theoretical discussion that had taken place in the kitchen was put to more practical use.

I particularly remember a Sunday when I was about six. I was directed to demonstrate my handwriting skills. I am left-handed and began to write in the cramped and twisted manner of many lefties even today. That day I learned the proper posture and technique for writing. Other times there were spelling games, discussions of grammar rules, and occasionally an art project. These were pleasant and important times for me. The sisters obviously enjoyed their work and were able to handle the household chores as well, and their husbands supported them in it.

Given these warm memories, I have tried over the years to understand my reluctance to follow in their path. Perhaps my resistance to becoming a teacher was the result of overexposure. It may have been influenced also by my father's less than whole-hearted support for formal education.

Elementary and High-School Years

During school years I was strongly influenced by my mother's family to work toward a college degree. I proceeded uneventfully through elementary and high school. In high school I was on the academic track, as were most of my friends. There were some discussions among us about careers we might pursue, but marriage and children seemed most likely.

When the United States entered World War II many women around the nation were taking jobs outside the home. This was the beginning of a dramatic change in the role of women, but it was too early, and we were too young to see the long-term changes that would take place. Our little town was not affected as dramatically as were more urban and industrial areas. My life continued pretty much as before. Of the girls in my class who were on the academic track, about half enrolled in college. The others married or found jobs. My family expected me to continue my education, with the goal of a marketable skill. Unfortunately, I had no idea what that marketable skill should be.

There was no vocational counseling at our high school. Like most students, I depended on odd bits of random information for that kind of decision making. The closest I came to receiving counseling was a discrepant event in my junior year. A teacher (who probably was taking a course in testing) offered to administer a vocational interest test to me. I accepted, and we had one brief discussion about the results. The test indicated interests in mathematics and art, and she said this combination suggested architecture as a career. I had no idea what training it required and little knowledge of the field, but the idea held appeal. Based on that one test and discussion, I modified my coursework during my senior year and applied to the University of California at Berkeley to begin training as an architect.

College: From Architecture to Liberal Arts

Once enrolled, I quickly learned what being an architect involved and realized that much more talent and motivation were required than I felt I possessed. I could have used counseling at that point but was unaware of it being available; so, on my own, I shifted to a general liberal arts program and stayed there until I graduated. I achieved one of my goals, a college degree; but the second one, preparation for a career, was nowhere in sight.

A Job in Merchandising

In order to become independent I needed to get a job, and the one most available and interesting was in merchandising at the retail level. I was hired as an executive trainee in a large department store in San Francisco. I coped with the requirements of the job and found some phases of it interesting, but realized that I lacked the desire to pursue a career in this area. A friend and co-worker presented a dramatic contrast, illustrating the importance of commitment in the pursuit of a career. She, too, was a beginning employee, but she demonstrated enthusiasm and interest, which forced me to face the fact that I lacked the motivation to establish a career in merchandising.

Working Wife and Mother

During this time I married a man I had known as a student at Berkeley. While it was necessary for me to continue working during the early years of our marriage, it was understood that my work would be in a field other than merchandising. Although we did not discuss it, I think we both assumed that eventually I would stay home to raise children while he provided the income. During the first few years of marriage I worked at several clerical jobs. As my husband became established in the field of engineering my supplemental income was no longer required, and I stopped working in order to start our family.

When our first child was born my husband shifted careers to the field of education. I had planned to stay at home, but as a result of his first teaching job I was willing to work as a substitute when a teacher had to be absent. The school was in a small, isolated community, and substitute teachers were scarce. I taught because I had a degree and was needed but would have preferred to remain at home. This experience as a substitute teacher only strengthened my resistance against the field.

A few years and two children later we moved to a larger community, where I worked as a substitute teacher in order to supplement our income. As I gained more experience as a substitute, I began to view teaching in a more favorable light. My husband's positive attitude toward education and his obvious enjoyment of his work with the students also alleviated my negativism. His example, combined with my own increasingly successful experience in the classroom, eventually reversed my attitude toward teaching. However, with young children at home, I was not ready to commit myself to the full-time responsibility of a classroom. Although I now felt I had reached the threshold of a career decision, I delayed action because of family commitments.

From Working Housewife to Career Woman

As our finances improved and the children entered school, I wanted to qualify as a credentialed teacher. A return to college was necessary. The California State Department of Education informed me that I needed twenty-four credits to obtain an elementary school credential. Fortunately, there was a community college in the area that offered the required courses and that had attracted some outstanding academicians. This became very important to me as I set out to satisfy the requirements. By family agreement I enrolled when our youngest child entered school.

I was now well into my thirties, but, given the information provided by the State Department of Education, I expected to qualify for a credential in one school year. I was aware that a new California state law that upgraded the requirements would be programmed in over a period of time. It was a shock to learn on registration day that the college already had retooled in response to the new law, and that I must fulfill the new requirements. One year of preparation suddenly became two and one half years. This caused new doubts, but after reflection and consultation with my family, I decided to go ahead.

In spite of my frustration at those additional years, the academic focus of the new law and the work with talented people were beneficial for me as a person and as a teacher. I was forced to meet the requirements of a new academic major more relevant to the education of young children. I chose English literature with misgivings, but it proved to be a fine choice. My knowledge of literature was extended and broadened, and I acquired techniques for analysis and appreciation that continue to be a source of enjoyment. The courses I took opened up areas that provided me with new interests. The fascination and the time involved helped me make the transition from a wife and mother who occasionally earned a little money outside the home to a wife and mother who had compelling interests and commitments outside the home.

By the time I accepted my first job as a credentialed teacher, I had had ample time and opportunity to formulate ideas on the overall goals of education and on the way a classroom should be organized. However, my experience and training had not prepared me fully for dealing with the dynamics of a classroom full of live bodies, with all of the needs and problems of the children. In spite of my age and substituting experience, I suffered the frustrations and doubts of any beginning teacher. Frequently, I headed for home at the end of a school day feeling depressed and discouraged by my failure to achieve goals I had set. However, after discussions with the family and given time to reflect, I would shift my attention to the development of alternative approaches to the problems. Attempting to gain some mastery in a new profession, while at the same time modifying family living patterns, was stressful; but teaching was exciting. Time never dragged, and I always felt a need for a longer day.

During these early years, when our children were still at home, I spent many hours in the evenings reading and analyzing student work; but in spite of the demands of teaching, much of my concern and focus remained on the family. I was fortunate because they supported my work and made minimal demands on my time; but meals had to be prepared, the house kept in order, the laundry done, and so on. I had their help, but it was difficult for me to stand back and relinquish control. Home economics was my mother's major in college, and she was a master homemaker as well as a master teacher. The values of early training are not easily discarded.

As our children became more independent and more involved with their own pursuits I focused more time and energy on teaching. I found opportunities to work with educational leaders at a national level and to incorporate new strategies into my classrooms and into schools in which I worked. As my availability of time increased so did my excitement for the learning process and my self-confidence in the role I played. When our children left home my work was a prime consideration in decisions my husband and I made about other facets of our lives. At some point during this period my primary role as a housewife faded, and I realized that I had become a career woman.

The changes in my life coincided with much greater changes in the national workforce. The extent of that became clearer when I read a recent article in *The New Republic* (October 9, 1989), which reported that in the last nineteen years, the percentage of women in the national workforce has increased from 38% to 45%, with a prediction that the number will soon increase to 50%. More significant are the growing numbers of women who are entering previously male-dominated professions. Whereas in 1970 women comprised 8.4% of the medical doctors who were entering the field, in 1989 that number rose to 31%. During the same period the number of females entering the field of law rose from 5.4% to 39%, and the number of new female dentists increased from less than 1% to 22.6%. I cannot help but think of my maternal grandmother struggling to educate her daughters in the isolated coal mining regions of Colorado. Can you imagine the smile she would wear if she could see the roles women play in our society?

Balancing Homemaking and Career

Advantages of the Profession of Education

The institutional nature of the educational system, with its patterned structure, made the adjustment of having both a family and a career easier. I devoted many hours during evenings and weekends to school tasks, but I was able to schedule my hours to suit the varying needs of the family and to do the school work within the confines of my home. Evening and weekend meetings and conferences were usually scheduled far enough in advance for me to avoid major conflicts with home activities. Classrooms create their own crises, but most are afforded the luxury of slower response time. I did not have to respond to health crises as a physician would, nor meet the demands of various groups and agencies as a politician would. However, comparing the demands of various professions detracts in no way from the real stress of balancing the roles of homemaker and professional.

My changing role was eased by the fixed length of the school day and year. The set schedule permitted me to attend courses to upgrade my teaching skills without interrupting regular classroom procedures and student activities. My family accommodated to the demands on my time and energy that came from the teaching day. They became used to doing household tasks and to making other adjustments required by my absence. Additional time in relation to my work, such as more professional training, temporarily disrupted the routine and placed a greater burden on the family. Without their support I could not have taken advantage of these additional facets of my work that were so important to me.

Child Care

As a working couple our major concern was the care and safety of our children. The child care available to me was from friends and neighbors. Our children were raised during the Baby Boom era. Most families had several children near the ages of ours, so I was usually able to find a trusted neighbor who was willing to watch the children during my absence. I knew these neighbors well and felt assured that my children were getting good care, and that they were able to play with their friends in the familiar neighborhood. Unfortunately, there were days when these neighbors unexpectedly were not available. A state resembling panic descended on our house. Good alternative care must be found quickly. Frantic calls were made, and we usually found another neighbor, but the change of routine left me feeling anxious.

From associating with my adult children and their friends as well as younger co-workers, I am aware that today's parents rely on licensed day-care facilities. In selecting a facility, parents may consider specialized learning programs, but usually the selection criteria are credibility of the staff, convenience of location, and scheduled hours, with some consideration of the cost. When our children were small I do not recall any of my working friends worrying about learning programs for their preschoolers other than what the children experienced with neighborhood play and what they received at home. The location of our day care was ideal in that it was next door or close by. Trust was acquired by our close association with our neighbors. Being in a neighborhood where income and family budgets were similar, charges for tending another's child were set easily and comfortably. There were times, however, when we would have welcomed the availability of a day-care facility.

A less common but more stressful problem for working parents occurs when a child is ill or hurt. No illness is minor where one's child is concerned. When my children showed signs of illness or injury I was torn between the need to carry out my teaching duties and the need to stay with the child. There was my need to nurture and nurse as well as the question of imposing an ill or injured child on a neighbor. These crises did not occur often, but when they did the balance I had made between home and work was tipped precariously. If necessary I called for a substitute. That meant that some of the planned school activities were postponed and that it was necessary for me to readjust the school program. It was not ideal, but it was easier in my position than it would be in many professions.

Family Togetherness

Communication that occurred naturally among us as a family was curtailed sharply when I began working full-time. Our way of dealing with this change was to make a greater effort to give each other full attention when we were together and to attempt to keep our family rituals intact. Mealtime was always an important family time for sharing experiences and problems. As family members became involved with various activities it became more difficult to maintain this practice; but as long as the children lived at home we tried to keep at least the evening meal a time for us to be together. My husband and I always have felt that the rituals a family develops are an important facet of family life. We made the effort to maintain ours, from the way we celebrated holidays and went on vacations to what was prepared for Sunday breakfast. While I am comfortable with the way our family adjusted and coped with its problems, I never felt there was quite enough time to do everything.

Being available when children have special events and activities can be difficult when both parents work. I was usually available for after-school programs, but there were times when our children had special events or school functions that neither my husband nor I could break free to attend. I was not happy when this happened. Our children seemed to take it in stride.

I was raised to believe that my worth as a homemaker depended to some extent on how well I managed household chores. While I do not rate housekeeping on a level of importance equal to that of the other concerns I had, it was a problem that I had to deal with. My husband and children helped with the chores, and I learned to accept some compromises in quality, but I never completely relinquished the "helm." My early training was too strong an influence. I see couples now dividing tasks among family members, and each one seems to take responsibility for his or her part. That seems logical and fair. I certainly approve, but it took me a long time to accept it as part of our life-style.

Summary

In choosing a career in education I entered a field dominated by women; but when I started to teach, the fact that I was married and had young children set me apart from the average woman teacher of my time. During the years in which I taught, the field of education evolved into a much more demanding profession. The curriculum was broadened to accommodate many areas of learning once considered provinces of home and church. Dramatically increased teacher-training requirements and more rigid and consistent standards in the earning of credentials were imposed in response to these demands. In addition, schools have extensively expanded the paperwork of record keeping. Demands on the teacher's time and energy have increased with these changes. Although the alterations were functional and necessary, they made it more difficult to hold on to the excitement of working with students. I was lucky because as professional demands on my time grew, demands of my growing children diminished. I do not envy the young teacher of today who must cope with the increased pressure of today's teaching profession while nurturing a young family.

The family concerns that were a result of my time being divided between home and career sometimes were almost overwhelming; but my family was supportive of my involvement in teaching, and we worked out problems without too much pain. Our children, now adults, deal with similar problems, though their solutions are sometimes quite different. Perhaps we all are richer for having faced and resolved these challenges.

As I think about the course my life has taken and the emergence of women as a major force in the professional world I become aware that my attitudes have been affected more, over the years, than I had realized. My values and expectations are rooted in the social mores of the 1930s. I have not completely discarded the lessons of my youth, but they have been modified. Women today have available to them many more choices than I had. They also have acquired all the pressures that accompany a professional life, especially if it is combined with marriage and children.

To reiterate, teaching was initially an unappealing pursuit for me, but gradually it became a fascinating and challenging interest. I enjoyed my life as a homemaker, and it had many rewards. I could easily have chosen to remain in the home—but I am so glad I chose to teach!

Reference

Menand, L. (1989, October 9). Don't think twice. *The New Republic*, p. 20.

Chapter 14

A Woman Physician Looks Back

Nancy McCall Clish, M.D.

Introduction to Nancy McCall Clish

An innovative aspect of Nancy McCall's medical career was her establishment of a joint practice with other women physicians to provide care for women. Though she had had no difficulty in establishing a solo private practice and was busy since the day it opened, McCall was aware that, more typically, young women experience unusual difficulty in establishing medical practices on their own. Many persons, women included, have more confidence in male physicians. Though her career was thriving, she determined to set up a joint women physicians practice to assist young women in those lean and discouraging years after medical school by providing a supportive milieu in which they could gain experience and self-confidence and build records of competence that would enable them to move on in their careers in whatever way

Lives of Career Women: Approaches to Work, Marriage, Children, edited by Frances M. Carp. Plenum/Insight, New York, 1991.

they chose. Her husband, who could "sell a snowball to an Eskimo," helped to recruit young women to the novel practice. Circumstances beyond her control, primarily the skyrocketing of costs for malpractice insurance, which unfortunately coincided with the outset of her venture, limited the size of the group practice. However, turnover was built into the plan, so over the years a large number of young women have benefited. The San Jose Women's Medical Group, Inc. continues to flourish after McCall's retirement, a monument to her innovative idea and her single-minded determination to bring it to realization.

Few could do justice to her multifaceted talents and roles except Jim Clish, who shared devotedly in the career of McCall and the life of Mrs. Jim Clish. The "Dr. McCall–Mrs. Clish" syndrome is exemplified at a party that was given at the Clish home. A group of Spanish musicians were toasting and serenading Nancy. There was singing and laughter and dancing and gaity. The phone rang: a call from the hospital for Dr. McCall. She was instantly cool, collected, factual, and businesslike—completely physicianlike— briskly asking direct questions and dictating quick orders in preparation for emergency surgery.

She was eminently successful at being both wife and physician. Other physicians (mostly men) with whom she worked in hospitals respected her superior ability, integrity, and skill, especially as a surgeon. One says, "I was impressed immediately with the deftness of her hands, the nimbleness of her fingers, the speed and accuracy of her surgery, and I decided then and there to call her to do certain types of operations for my patients." Jim and Nancy amalgamated into a productive and happy together-ness from very different backgrounds: Jim, adaptable from being widely traveled and a "Jack of all trades"; Nancy, who early on "hitched her wagon to a high star" and was dedicated to a life of searching for fundamental scientific truth and improving the well-being of women through medical care, family planning, and birth control. A long-time friend and woman physician commented, "If Jim Clish were alive, he would never stand still for an autobiography of Nancy written by herself. He would eulogize her to the heavens—and she would admonish him for 'exaggerating again.' "

Influences of Female Progenitors

Except for my paternal grandmother, virtually all the women in my family worked outside their homes; so, for me, this appeared to be the norm. Mother was a school teacher. Even after she developed polio and became crippled she tutored pupils at home. My maternal grandmother owned a bookshop, where I early learned the joy of reading and of being surrounded by books. She lived with us during much of my childhood, and her calming influence was important in my life.

Aunt Selene, who never married, used her considerable artistic ability in her position at the Methodist Publishing House and also gave piano lessons. The piano lessons never "took" with me, but her readiness to communicate and to spend time with me were invaluable. Mother's sister Elsie, a bridge fiend, was a missionary to Poland at one time and eventually took over the bookshop for my grandmother.

The aunts by marriage included an interesting variety. Vivacious Lucy, an accomplished amateur actress, was an advertising executive. Lovely Mabel, who sewed beautifully and collected dolls, was a truant officer for the Nashville city schools. Generous Gertie's many philanthropies kept her as busy as those who toiled for money.

Academic Interests and Experiences

My interests in school were always in the sciences, especially biology and embryology, so when career choices began to arise I leaned toward nursing. For this reason, at age sixteen, I took a summer job in a hospital. All of my previous job experience had been in the bookshop. As a nurse's aide I found the work somewhat unchallenging, but I had a chance to make an observation that turned out to have major influence on my career. It was that, so far as I could see, the nurses did little that I did not do except write in records a lot and give medication. The doctors, on the other hand, visited once or twice a day, examined and exchanged a few pleasantries with patients, gave orders to the nurses, and then left the hospital—at least on my floor.

Thus, the doctors appeared to me to have a much easier job than did the nurses. Aspiring to the former sort of work, I entered the premedical program at Vanderbilt University, having completed high school in three years by going to summer sessions. During the Second World War many universities, including Vanderbilt, had an accelerated program combining the fourth year of college with the first year of medical school. This made it possible for me to graduate from medical school at age twenty-three.

On the crest of a wave of patriotism, my father had decided that he could be of more use to his country as a shipbuilder than as an attorney; so he left Nashville and moved to Los Angeles, where he used his carpentry skills in a shipyard. Like many others, he found California and especially the southern part of the state to be near paradise and much to his liking as a place to live. My mother and brother followed him to Los Angeles just before I began medical school.

I needed summer employment and sought hospital jobs as an extern. The only one I found was in San Francisco. I obtained a map of the United States and saw that there did not appear to be much distance between there and Los Angeles and thought that I probably could see the family on weekends; so I took the San Francisco job. Needless to say, the distance was much further than I had realized, in miles and in philosophy, and I found Northern California to be nearer Paradise for me.

There were fifty-two people in the medical-school class of 1951, of whom four were women. The class before ours included seven women, and the class behind ours had only two. These were years when most of the young men had been at war instead of in college, so the pool of male graduate students was not adequate, and opportunities for women were much more numerous than they were in the very early 1940s and would be again for many years.

I have certainly heard tales of humiliation and discrimination during medical-school years from contemporary women physicians, but I have none of my own to tell and have heard none from my fellow students. Perhaps we were too thick-skinned to notice, but I think it more likely that we were lucky to be among southern men who tended to be kinder and more considerate of women than did men in other parts of the country. At any rate, my four years of medical school, while arduous, were stimulating and absorbing and wonderful. On vacations I had many bus trips back and forth to visit the family, and upon completion of medical school I was glad to settle in the San Francisco Bay area for postgraduate training.

The years of postgraduate training were likewise challenging. First came a general, rotating internship followed by a year's fellowship in pathology at San Francisco General Hospital. There I learned how much I enjoyed contact with living persons. I decided to specialize in obstetrics and gynecology because obstetrics is such a happy service and because I loved doing surgery but did not relish the idea of a complete surgical residency. I had met two kind, empathic ob-gyn doctors who convinced me that I wanted to give that kind of care. For further preparation I took an internship at Stanford Lane Hospital, San Francisco (now Stanford University Hospital, Stanford University), a two-year residency at Children's Hospital in San Francisco, and one year of residency at Kern General Hospital in Bakersfield, California, all in ob-gyn.

A New Automobile and a Husband

In the summer of 1957 I was twenty-nine years old and just ready to start my practice when my elderly automobile was damaged beyond repair in a minor accident. It was obvious that a new car was in order. The handsome fellow who sold me the new car was so interested in how I liked it that he phoned or came by several times to check on how we were doing. Never having purchased a new car before, I thought at first that this was just part of the service. Soon I realized that the interest was not solely in the machine. That is how I met Jim Clish, my dear husband and the father of my two wonderful children.

Private Medical Practice and Family Life

In order to establish a practice in San Jose, California I borrowed $3,000 with a brave, good friend as co-signer. With it I rented and outfitted an office and, what with outside jobs (e.g., part-time college teaching) and great good luck, I never had to borrow more money until we were ready to expand greatly.

To my delight I discovered that being a female was a tremendous advantage to an obstetrician/gynecologist. Many women told me that their husbands insisted on their being seen only by a woman. Of course, there were many husbands who did not mind so long as their wives had good care. I was one of only three female obstetricians in the area and was busy almost from the first day I started.

From the beginning Jim was the cook in the family. I tend to cook up a big pot of something and eat it, meal after meal, until it is gone. He did not agree with that approach. Jim had always cooked and, in fact, was a short-order cook at one point in his career. At first I usually planned the meals and was always responsible for cleaning up. Gradually, as I became busier in my medical practice, he took over the planning and shopping. Fortunately for us—or perhaps for me—his work usually allowed flexible hours, and frequently he could work at home.

We were overjoyed when I became pregnant at last, and Sarah (then called Sally) was born in 1963. In Nashville,

Tennessee, when I was growing up, just about everyone we knew could afford household help. I was tended by Alzada Dillard, who was my beloved friend and confidante as well as my caregiver. I deeply mourned her death ten years ago, although I had not seen her for several years. With my usual good luck I had met Bertha Brody shortly after Jim and I were married. She had been recommended to help my mother convalesce following an operation. At that time Bertha said that I should have a baby, and that, if I did, she would take care of it. So four years later I looked her up, and she, then in her late fifties, came every day to care first for Sarah and then also for Jourdan, who was born a year later.

Because my work was completely unpredictable as to time, we had a succession of live-in students and mothers-to-be to fill in the gaps. However, Bertha was our mainstay until the children were old enough to be in school all day, and then she took a well-deserved retirement. Now in her eighties and living in Chicago, she keeps in touch with us by phone.

After our children were born and my father had retired he and my mother moved to San Jose and lived there for several years just a few blocks away; but until his death Dad considered himself to be an "Angeleno."

Group Practice of Women Physicians

After several years of solo practice I decided that a group of female physicians who could support each other professionally would be a valuable resource. Because of the malpractice insurance crunch that began soon after this brainstorm I was never able to afford to subsidize the first few years of practice for as many women as I had hoped. However, the group soon grew to three physicians and two nurse practitioners.

As the practice grew, Jim became the administrator of the group. We loved working together. He learned to use a computer to do the accounts and helped to pioneer the use of computers in medical offices. During the seventies he had two heart attacks and angina severe enough to require coronary bypass surgery. Then he developed diabetes that could be treated only with large doses of insulin. His failing health necessitated semi-retirement in 1985, although he still stepped in to help with problems in the management and business sides of the medical practice. Jim passed away in 1987 to my very great sorrow.

A Look Around and Back

I retired from practice early in 1989 and am living on my own and doing well. Upon retirement "Dr. McCall" was put on the shelf permanently, and I am now "Nancy Clish." This has resulted in some amusing incidents when I come across physicians who had worked with me in hospitals as "Dr. McCall" and were never aware that I had another name. I see the double-take and the look of doubt when they are introduced to "Mrs. Clish." Sometimes I let them in on the details, sometimes not.

There were several reasons for my name decision. I was not yet married when I graduated from medical school, so the name on my diploma is McCall. Perhaps more influential was the feeling, during my working years, that it was important to me to keep my work completely separate from my private life with Jim and the children and our friends. Also, over the years, I have come to like the name "Clish" despite the fact that it is not all that euphonious. The transformation seems nearly complete. Less than a year after retirement, when I attended a medical convention, I was amused that my hand had difficulty in writing "Dr. Nancy McCall" on the registration sheet.

Both Sarah and Jourdan are in the business world, living on their own and doing well also. We three went to Nashville to a McCall family reunion in the summer of 1988. It was strange to me to see all the changes in the city and especially in the

Vanderbilt University campus. Since that visit the reality of the changes is not as clear to me as are my memories of those places as they used to be—but I must admit that when I look in the mirror I am sometimes amazed at the changes I find reflected there also. That aging face and body do not reflect the person I feel myself to be when I do not confront the mirror. Then I remember that I would still be as old as I am had I taken my turn in running grandmother's bookstore or had become a nurse. Then, the reflected face smiles back at me. I am thankful for the wonderful memories of medical practice and especially the joint practice with other women, as well as my wonderful life with Jim and our two fine children, who continue to enrich my life in retirement.

Chapter 15

Serendipity and Adaptiveness
The Lucky Planner?

I. M. Hulicka, Ph.D.

Introduction to Irene Mackintosh Hulicka

A multitalented and gracious lady who combines the traits of
excellence, perseverance, and compassion in generous measures,
Irene Hulicka is a naturalized U.S. citizen who remains fiercely
proud of her Canadian birth and Scottish ancestry. She was raised
on the vast Canadian prairies on a farm in Saskatchewan, and her
life reflects the work ethic and independence of her beginnings.

Hulicka has functioned in a variety of professional roles. As a
teacher she has been successful and popular at both the undergraduate and graduate levels. As a colleague she is highly valued.
As a researcher and consultant she has garnered national and
international recognitions. As an administrator she founded psychology departments at two colleges and served as dean of the
Natural Social Sciences at the State University of New York
(SUNY) College at Buffalo. In recognition of her continuing excellence and professional contributions, Hulicka was appointed dis-

Lives of Career Women: Approaches to Work, Marriage, Children, edited by Frances
M. Carp. Plenum/Insight, New York, 1991.

tinguished professor by the Board of Trustees of the State University of New York. This is the highest honor in the largest system of higher education in the nation. Throughout her professional career she also has been involved in building a long and successful marriage, raising a family, serving her community, and being a valued confidante, friend, and neighbor.

To each of her many roles Irene brings the unique combination of a good scientist's ability to identify and rigorously pursue important questions with the capacity to listen with a clinician's sensitivity and a mother's intuition. She is aware of nuances but does not tolerate nonsense. She is straightforward and honest in her interpersonal relationships and expects no less in return. Those who have known and worked with her say they would be glad to have daughters—or sons—model themselves after her. She is industrious, accomplished, nationally and internationally recognized, and elegant, with an earthy sense of humor and an appreciation of life that have seen her through the tough times. Although her life has been focused on a continuous quest to gain and instill knowledge, the thread that spans her life and ties her to the people who know her is that Irene cares about them.

A friend of mine from more than thirty years ago paid a visit. As we barbecued chicken and admired Lake Ontario in front of our cottage she commented, "Life is not fair. You got the goodies; I got the dregs." She then asked me, "Why were you more successful? How did you combine career and family so they fit together and you have happiness from both? You were blessed with a good brain, but so was I. One difference—you set realistic goals and made plans and timetables for attaining them. I set goals, but often mine were unrealistic. But the main difference," she concluded, "is that you have been lucky. You always get the good breaks."

Professionally, I enjoy a demanding, interesting, rewarding career. In my personal life I am happy. The most wonderful miracle in my life is that my husband selected me and cherishes our love. I fear what life would be for either of us without the other. We enjoy warm relations with our adult son of whom we

are proud. What events, influences, and decisions contributed
to what I am?

Antecedents

I grew up on a farm in southern Saskatchewan, the fifth of nine
children. My mother had been a country school teacher, and my
father had begun a clerkship in law prior to leaving Scotland to
homestead. Ours was a disaster area financially. Crops failed
year after year because of drought, hail, grasshoppers, dust
storms. Everyone was very poor. Medical care was sought for in
only the most dire emergencies. Clothes, even shoes, were
hand-me-downs. A box of Kleenex was a nice Christmas
present.

I attended a one-room school, where one teacher taught
thirty or more children in grades one through eight. In winter
we kept our lunches by the woodburning stove to prevent them
from freezing. Most children quit after the eighth grade. A few
struggled for some high-school education by correspondence.
Money for my education was a severe problem. After I completed ninth and tenth grades by correspondence my parents
scraped together tuition for "town school" and "board" for a
month while I found a place to work. I was timid and shy.
Convinced I would lag academically, I was amazed to be named
outstanding student for both grades eleven and twelve.

Life Goals: Obstacles and Facilitators

As an adolescent and young adult I wanted to marry, have
children and a happy family life, and also have a career that
would be interesting, challenging, and worthwhile for humanity. My role models were farmers' wives and teachers with no

more than one year of post-high-school education. Lacking exposure to nonfarm employment, I had no conception of career options. Far from having well-defined plans and goals, I operated on blind faith. I believed that with a good education and a record for completing well what I undertook, career opportunities would present themselves.

Later, I encountered obstacles due to being a woman. When I was a graduate student a scholarship was awarded to a man whose academic record was not as good as mine because it would be "wasted on a woman." When I was eligible for tenure an administrator argued that it should not be awarded to a married woman, especially to a pregnant one. As a thirty-year-old applicant to medical school, being a woman, married, pregnant, and "old" cancelled out a Ph.D. and a strong professional record.

Fortuitous events by far outnumbered obstacles. As a child and adolescent, of particular value was my parents' expectation that I would "amount to something." After high school I was expected to consider the three opportunities for women: teaching, nursing, and secretarial work. I did not want nursing; my mother pointed out that my unwillingness to carry out instructions I considered unwise would make me a poor secretary; and the Army said to return when I was eighteen. My parents offered to pay tuition to a "normal school," with train fare and a few dollars to establish myself in a "light-housekeeping room" in Moose Jaw, Saskatchewan. I did not want to teach, but in view of alternatives it seemed foolish to reject the offer. In retrospect I am impressed by that sixteen-year-old, travelling alone to the first city she visited and finding lodgings and employment as a waitress. I was enrolled on condition that I not teach until I was eighteen.

Early in the school year we took standardized tests. Because of a teacher shortage, the ten students who scored highest would be authorized and expected to teach immediately. I was one of the ten. Dumbfounded and terrified, I pointed out that I had promised not to teach before I was eighteen, and I was sixteen with only six weeks of training; but they were adamant, and so I went to teach in a one-room country school with twenty-five children in grades one through eight.

Despite my trepidation and inexperience, I was reasonably competent and creative as a teacher. The temporary certificate was my gateway for further education. In a year I saved enough money to start taking university courses. I obtained teaching jobs every summer in remote areas. At eighteen I was principal of a three-room school in a lumbering village. My forty students, ages twelve to seventeen, in grades six to eleven, had helped the previous principal have a "nervous breakdown." I found desks overturned and overtly hostile, sullen students, a few inebriated on lemon extract. If trains had come more than once a week, and if I had not been low on funds, I might have run away. To my luck an old microscope intrigued the youngsters. Their curiosity aroused, they blossomed under fairness and encouragement. Such "difficult" schools enriched my appreciation of human diversity and strength and stimulated my personal growth.

Unpleasant experiences have helped me develop confidence that I can survive injustice and hardship and emerge stronger. When I was fourteen, the most quiet and timid person in grade eleven, working long hours for sleeping quarters and subsistence food, Mr. T, a teacher with acute disciplinary problems, announced that more severe action would be taken against misbehavers. He ignored several infractions of the rules that disrupted the classroom and reprimanded me for doing algebra homework in geometry period. The principal instructed me to appear that evening before the school board.

Trembling with fear, I stood facing the comfortably seated and well-fed principal, Mr. T, and school-board members. It appeared that I was being held responsible for all of Mr. T's problems. Ordered to apologize, I did so for doing algebra in geometry period but claimed I was not causing the other problems. My judges were aghast. Unless I admitted guilt I would be expelled from my three classes with Mr. T. I ran from the room, crying. That night it was about −30 degrees Fahrenheit. I stumbled around the dark streets, frightened, disillusioned, perplexed, and sobbing. I was almost sure the principal and most board members knew I had not disrupted classroom activities. I believed I had been selected as an example who would be subservient.

After a sleepless night I went to school, not knowing what else to do. The principal called an assembly of the entire school and demanded that I apologize for unspecified but obviously heinous sins. I said I was sorry I did algebra in geometry class but had nothing else for which to apologize. He repeated the threat of expulsion from Mr. T's classes. I gulped that I would take them by correspondence. He threatened to expel me from his own three classes. I said tremulously, "I'll take them by correspondence too," and with a little show of courage or defiance quavered, "and I'll pass them." Then he threatened to expel me from school. Very privately, Mr T apologized, admitting that he had picked on me unfairly. I did not hold a grudge against this weak man, but I am almost sure that the principal and school board engaged in blatant and conscious abuse of power.

This experience reinforced my tendency to act on the courage of my convictions and not bow and scrape in the face of superior power. It has precipitated justified animosity against me because of my tendency to attack, usually abrasively, persons who even appear to abuse the power associated with their positions.

When I completed my master's degree in psychology the only position in my field, involving assessment of penitentiary inmates, was considered unsafe for a young woman. I applied for teaching positions and, ironically, benefited from pro-male bias. I signed an application, "Irene M." An enthusiastic response was addressed to "Mr. Ian M." Thereafter, I used my initials. They continued to write to Ian. High-school teachers with three academic degrees were rare. "Ian" was offered a salary higher than that of some full professors at my university. When I arrived, school-board members, aghast that their hireling was not a middle-aged man, said the salary would have been much lower had they known they were hiring a mere young woman. It was useful to repay student loans and save for more education.

Another example of good luck was my dissertation topic. In a Friday afternoon statistics class we studied complex analysis of variance. I thought it a beautiful, elegant technique. The next day I used it in a research-design assignment for another class. During the following week I was complimented by professors for the excellence of my dissertation research proposal. The design I dashed off in less than a weekend was considered sufficiently complex, original, and meaningful for a dissertation.

Not everything was so lucky. I, who knew nothing about carpentry, electric circuitry, solenoids, microswitches, and so forth, had to design the apparatus; worse still, build it with blood (a pint sold every few weeks), sweat (often the room was over 100 degrees Fahrenheit), and tears of frustration. After it was painted, a thing of beauty in my eyes, woes were not over. To hide unsightly wires and switches it had a tunnel through which the rat passed to enter the chamber for food or water. The rats, being nocturnal creatures, tended to remain in the dark tunnel. Some had to be pushed or pulled out, neither being scientific and the latter inviting bites. Consequently, the apparatus was rebuilt without a tunnel. Data collection proceeded through odoriferous ten- to twelve-hour days, seven days a week, until a rat ate a crucial part. A metal structure replaced the wooden item. Such modification could affect behavior, so data collection started again, from the beginning.

The greatest positive influence on my career has been the incredible good luck of having a loving husband who always encourages me, challenges me to respond to new opportunities, and supports my endeavors. Because we value a traditional family life, and because my career had more flexibility than his, my job options have been restricted geographically. Sometimes jobs were less than ideal. No matter. Our marriage has added more to my career than it has detracted from it. The love and support I got at home enabled me to be professionally more competent and daring than I would have been otherwise and made it unnecessary for me to try to obtain from my career values and reassurances that careers cannot give.

Choice Points and Events along Life's Path

I am appalled and amused by the casualness of my career decisions. The year after I became a teacher at sixteen I went to the University of Saskatchewan. At enrollment I was asked my career goal. I blurted out social work because someone had mentioned a college-educated social-worker niece. How different my career might have been had I said plant science (a real interest), or if I had known that I could study medicine, law, or agriculture.

Economics interested me most. My professor conceded that I was doing well but implied that it was a man's field. I took this as a challenge and majored in economics. In most classes I was the only woman. Over coffee and at parties fellow students oriented conversation around economic issues. While I found economics interesting, I did not like to discuss it in social situations. I felt uneasy about my choice. As graduation neared I had to decide whether to find employment in economics, teach school, take graduate work in economics, or change fields. I loved the social and intellectual life of a university student. Finances were tight, but in summers I taught school; in academic years I worked part-time and my scholarship covered tuition and some book expenses; and I was used to living on a shoe-string.

I had not fully rejected social work. The University of Saskatchewan did not have a program. I applied to the University of Manitoba for a scholarship, but that would mean leaving the university where I felt so at home and happy. I had taken a psychology course. It was boring, but I sensed that if I could overlook the dreary textbook and nice philosopher teacher, the study of human behavior might be exciting. An actual psychologist had just been hired to establish a department. My decision rule: If I received a social-work scholarship of more than $500 I would take it, less than $500 I would not. I was offered $500. The pull of my alma mater was strong. After a few coin flips I returned to Saskatchewan and took an honors degree in economics and psychology. Ironically, I have no desire to discuss psychology in nonprofessional situations. I may have given up economics for the wrong reason.

I decided to take my master's in psychology. A visiting professor gave a lecture and demonstration on hypnosis. My thesis was an ambitious project on hypnotizability. But while I was still working on it the chairman of the department left and the department dissolved. He assured me he would continue to be my advisor and told me to send him thesis chapters for critical comment. None was returned. The university did not know what to do with me. The dean, a chemist, sent me from one nonpsychology professor to another for guidance. I received conflicting advice: Use chi-square, do not use chi-square; use analysis of variance, analysis of variance is ridiculous; the thesis must be at least 100 pages long, anything over fifty pages is too long. The dean had difficulty convening an orals committee. One examiner was a psychology instructor with no M.A. Angered by the delays and because a man with less education than I was on the committee, I knitted throughout the exam and on occasion said, "Just a minute, I'm counting stitches," before answering.

As I indicated, after completing my M.A. I obtained a teaching position at a substantial salary because it was assumed I was a middle-aged man. I enjoyed teaching math, English, history, and chemistry where my competency was under my own control. However, because I was the only female teacher, I had to teach all physical education courses for girls. I know of no able-bodied person with less athletic skill. I was also required to teach French. I took grades nine and ten by correspondence, did not take grade eleven because I felt incompetent at "town school," and then, realizing that a foreign language was prerequisite to university, took grade twelve. My performance in an undergraduate course was less than stellar. I could increase my own competency in vocabulary and grammar but not pronunciation. Unless I went to a big city, which did not appeal to me, teaching might always involve subjects in which I could not develop expertise.

Besides, I wanted both marriage *and* career. Marriage in a rural area would afford few career opportunities except in teaching. I opted for more education as a solution. This was easier because I was no longer dependent on a temporary certificate for summer jobs, having completed a Bachelor of Education degree. However, my paper on poetry for an education class was adopted as part of the curriculum. So, had I kept at it, I might have had a good career in high-school teaching.

When I decided on a doctorate I was influenced more by the perpetual-student phenomenon than by career goals. Lacking access to university catalogs or people with advanced degrees, I assumed that universities in major cities in Canada, the U.S.A., and Britain had graduate programs, and submitted applications on a pot-shot basis. My husband has asked, "How could you select the University of Nebraska over Berkeley, especially when Berkeley made you a better offer?" I knew about them only through brochures. Nebraska was one of the first to respond favorably. I have an antipathy for large cities and knew Lincoln was not huge. Nebraska has a nice sound, almost as nice as Saskatoon, Saskatchewan.

It was a good choice. The department was small but faculty members were competent, kind, and interested in students. My first research design was circulated as an example of errors typically made by inexperienced researchers, my second as an example of a good design. My luck with a dissertation topic has been described. During the oral examination I may have confirmed notions about the futility of higher education for woman. Asked what I hoped to be doing five years hence I answered,

"To be a happy wife and mother." That dearest wish would have been fulfilled on time had our first child not died.

Academic positions were not plentiful nor well paid. I decided not to accept less than $4500, which I had been offered for a teaching job prior to studying for the Ph.D. A telegram from the president of a midwestern college invited me to meet him at the International Hotel in Denver for an interview. I wired that I would meet him. The wire was returned; there was no International Hotel in Denver. A phone call confirmed my guess of the Cosmopolitan Hotel as the interview site. I was offered an assistant professorship at a salary of $4500. I accepted.

Colleagues were pleasant, students highly motivated, and research respected. I earned extra money by teaching in a hospital sixty miles away and in extension courses for the University of Nebraska. I started new research and prepared articles based on graduate-student research. But I was not happy. The line between town and gown was firmly drawn by the college. It had hired a number of interesting, young, unmarried women but did not have one unmarried man on the faculty. There was the Faculty Club for men and the Women's Association for female faculty and wives. I visualized what life would be: sixty- to seventy-hour work-weeks and Saturday nights out with the girls. I resigned.

The next year I went to a large southern university. The graduate program in psychology was strong, with competent students and highly qualified faculty. I obtained animal laboratory space from the pharmacy department and had grant support; my research was thriving. I was selected as one of the three outstanding professors in the university. But men with fewer publications and no more impressive teaching records had higher ranks and salaries. In social life there were nice men but no one uniquely important to me. Should I switch to business, law, or medicine, where financial rewards are influenced by effort? Must I relinquish aspirations for marriage and children? If so, I should enhance my qualifications so I could do something truly worthwhile as a scientist. I wrote to graduate schools about summer-school classes and enrolled for credit in calculus.

Deliberations on career change were disrupted pleasantly. On Wednesday afternoon came a knock on my office door. An attractive faculty member invited me to dinner. I did not have a free evening until Saturday. The following Wednesday the chairman of the psychology department of my beloved alma mater offered me a position. I told him I could not consider it because I planned to be married. He was shocked that I had met the man only a week before. I did not tell my future husband this until he told me that, the day after our first dinner, he wrote to his mother about his intention to marry. Three months after we met, we had a lovely church wedding and a reception given by colleagues. On my wedding day I gave three lectures but had time to have my hair done and be at the church for the 4:30 ceremony. Our decision to marry involved no deliberation whatsoever. It seemed right, and over thirty years later we agree that our intuition was on target.

I debated whether to adopt my husband's surname. The only reason for not doing so was my dozen or so publications. It was not important that someone might fail to realize I wrote those masterpieces. My husband slightly preferred sharing the same name. I have never been sorry, but I think the matter is inconsequential.

Husband and wife could not both have tenure at our university. Because I had been affiliated with it first, he could have tenure only if I relinquished it. My department would hire me on a year-to-year basis. My husband opposed this, and I would not be able to inhibit my outspokenness about injustice. The university was in a small town with limited opportunities for employment. We decided that the most constructive way to deal with the rule was for me to take medical training. I took courses in physics and chemistry, while retaining a full teaching load, plus another nine lectures per week. A colleague with crippling depression would ask me to take his classes "just for this one day," but "one day" followed another for over twelve weeks. On the same day he was hospitalized after a suicide attempt and I with threatened miscarriage. Age, gender, and pregnancy were reasons for several medical schools to rule negatively on my admission. We decided that my husband would apply for positions in cities where I might be accepted for medical training, or obtain a position in psychology.

Personal tragedy affected our plans. I should have fired the physician when he made his first mistake and certainly when he made a second. He made still more. While my husband was trying to hire a pediatric specialist to take over our baby's care, a hospital employee informed me, "Your baby is dead. What funeral home do you want to use?" The physician said I was to blame: I was too ambitious professionally and insisted on continuing to work. He had said repeatedly that there was no reason I should not.

Because of the emotional trauma I did not finish the last course required for medical school. My husband accepted a position at the University of Buffalo. The psychology department was unsuccessful in attempts to have the nepotism rule waived so I could be hired. The most appealing option was a clinical internship at the Veterans' Administration Medical Center (VAMC). My final salary as assistant professor five years post-Ph.D. was $5600; my intern stipend on a thirty-two-hour week was $5400. I worked sixty-five hours a week as an academician, so my hourly rate doubled. The internship met my needs for learning, creativity, and independence. The manager said, "We have many elderly patients. Will you try to help them?" Here was a challenge to explore a new field. I had no training in gerontology, little experience with the elderly, and no experience with the hospitalized elderly. My supervisor had an aversion for physical illness and loss. He never visited my patients' ward. I had almost complete freedom. It was an exhilarating growth experience.

During the first week I received impetus for a research project. In a meeting to consider an eighty-four-year-old patient

a physician administered a mental status test. The patient
responded correctly to, "Who is the president?" "Who is the
governor?" and so on, but could not tell what day it was. He was
judged to be disoriented for time and to have a memory
disorder. Later he asked me, "What day is it?" I hesitated. He
laughed, "You had to think, too, before you could answer." He
explained that one day was like another in the hospital; he did
not see well enough to read newspapers or the ward calendars.
I completed a study on aging and memory that took learning
into account.

I was pregnant again and was offered a position at the VA
as the only psychologist affiliated with the Medical Service.
Miscarriage was threatening and tests revealed signs of a rare
form of cancer. We experienced terror and anticipatory grief.
Should I bring a potentially motherless child into the world? I
believed that it was not for me to decide that a child we both
wanted should be denied life. Emphasis moved from dying to
living. I poured myself into work as an opiate for fear and
because I had used all my sick leave and needed vacation days
after the baby was born. I was monitored closely by the cancer
institute. With each passing week I felt better as chances for
carrying the baby to full term increased. I worked until 4:00 P.M.,
the day our son was born. We were elated, though during the
first weeks I did not let myself experience the almost perfect joy
I had felt when our first child was born. I was afraid we might
lose him, too; and we feared he might lose me.

We adapted easily to caring for an infant. I returned to work
less than three weeks after he was born, having used all
vacation time. (There was no maternity leave.) We assumed that
our love for our child was not measured by the number of hours
we spent with him. I had no illusion that I could provide the best
care. An excellent lady cared for him during the day. (Recently
she was the guest of honor at a dinner hosted by our son.) The
next three years were wonderful. I was seen at the cancer
institute and maintained status quo. Our fears receded. Then,

there was no sign of the terrifying symptoms. We were happy to be parents. I was productive in clinical work and research.

The chief of staff said the hospital must reduce its staff. My position was eliminated because "You are not a bread-winner. You have a husband to support you." I could not believe I was victimized simply because I had an employed husband. I told a senior professor, who initiated protests from universities whose graduate students were trainees in our VA. I told a VA official when he requested a report on a project I had underway. Shortly, I was asked to remain as research psychologist. In accepting the position I was rather insulting. When my employer spoke of the time and the long-distance calls he had used to find a way to retain me I said that his time and the calls were a waste of taxpayers' money to resolve a problem that should not have occurred because I should not have been victimized by threatened loss of my job.

The next two years I did clinical work with geriatric and disabled young patients, obtained research grants, published, and participated in regional and national meetings. The central office suggested that I be promoted, but the local manager refused. He was not likely to retire soon, and I was unwilling, for family reasons, to transfer to another VAMC at the higher rank and pay. A Catholic college invited me to chair its small psychology department and design a combined psychology major and teacher training with emphasis on mental retardation. I was much inconvenienced by inadequate support services and facilities. "My" phone, shared with others, was upstairs, over, and downstairs from my office. I issued an ultimatum: There would be a phone in my office or I would not remain. They complied. After the program was developed, the position was not challenging.

My twenty-two years at the State University College at Buffalo (SUBC) exemplify my tendency to change professional emphasis periodically without necessarily moving. I joined SUBC as chairperson of a nonexistent psychology department, with a mandate to develop a strong one. In five years faculty grew from none to thirteen, facilities from two rooms to adequate offices and outstanding laboratories, and classes to a rigorous major and an honors program. I resigned as chairperson to expand my professorial role and begin a new line of research.

Three years later I became dean of the Faculty of Natural Sciences, and a year later dean of a new Faculty of Natural and Social Sciences. I had no desire to be dean and took the initial position for the wrong reason. I had refused until I met a new vice president. I was concerned with his arrogance, egotism, and inexperience. Perhaps with equal egotism I decided that the dean must have personal and professional security such as I had in order to interact effectively with him. The university was reorganized. The position of dean carried little authority. I resigned to return to our psychology department.

Soon after, the president and other ranking administrators appeared at my office with champagne to announce my selection by the State University of New York as distinguished professor. I showed no enthusiasm, thinking, "Wouldn't this happen the one time I postponed preparing slides for my next class, which begins in fifteen minutes." A reception was held in my honor. An hour before, I slipped on ice and hurt my ankle. I clenched my teeth and went to the reception, which was a stand-up affair. I might not have lasted had I not been able to lean on my son and husband. People commented on how my affection for my family showed as we linked arms during the ceremonies!

One evening I told my husband, "I had a call about being research consultant in Southeast Asia." He asked for details. I had not inquired. He recommended that if a second call came I should. It came. During the next six weeks I worked full-time, expanded my expertise in the area of consultation, got my shots, bought tropical clothes, and packed for a twelve-week assignment involving a trip around the world. It was a fascinating experience. I had an interesting collaboration with an eminent scientist-educator-physician in Madrid. At a lunch in my honor I was seated between a count and a duke. This country girl relaxed when the duke said the accomplishment of which he was most proud was a technique for curing ham. We talked about curing meat while I observed the duchess and countess for choice of cutlery.

Another adventure involved a semester in the U.S.S.R. One Sunday, I had a backlog of work and set the goal of completing it by 2:30 so I could garden. The desk was clear by 2:10, except for an application for a Fullbright appointment. I dashed it off and was surprised to be accepted. Before our departure (my husband accompanied me), the U.S.S.R. invaded Afghanistan. It was uncertain whether our government would send scholars and whether the U.S.S.R. would accept them. Selected for expertise in aging, I was assigned to child development. Invited to tea, I was introduced as the lecturer. Professors were cordial; students gracious and welcoming; operas, concerts, and museums outstanding. The airport lost my luggage for thirty-seven days and suggested I pay storage.

Never was there question about which was more important, husband and son or career. Because psychology is flexible, my job choices were secondary to my husband's. When he retired and our son was in college, my foot did get itchy. I looked at positions. When I said employment for my husband was not a condition, I was asked how divorce would affect my work!

Invited to interview for the position of Dean of Academic Affairs at a western university, I did some research, and finding student enrollment of about 12,000 and pleasant geographical features, agreed to go. When my hosts talked of their 37,000 students, I requested brochures. It happened that I was being interviewed by the University of X at Y, not the University of P at Q! Once, after five hours of non-stop interviews and lunch with the president, I asked him to direct me to a washroom before the next meeting. He showed me to his private facility. Almost every square inch was decorated with posters of him: in tennis clothes, a tux, a jogging outfit, academic regalia, his undershirt. One Sunday my husband and I drove to the country to buy fruit and stopped at Lake Ontario waterfront properties for sale. One had a shabby cottage and a view of unsurpassable beauty. We enjoyed making the cottage comfortable and landscaping the grounds. The itch was eradicated.

The Present, Professionally and Personally

I enjoy my present, professionally and personally. My husband has retired, and we both enjoy his retirement. He goes to Europe twice a year during the academic term, when I am fully occupied. We are fortunate with respect to health, although we had a worrisome time when he had four unsuccessful surgeries that left him blind in one eye. We enjoy a mature, rewarding relationship with our son.

As a professional I am as busy as ever and engage in perhaps a greater variety of activities. In my full-time position I offer three courses per semester to 300 to 350 students. In one course of about forty students each is required to submit ten short papers plus a term paper. Each paper is evaluated carefully, and often when it is returned to its author it has more handwritten than typed material on it. I have undertaken to provide a variety of optional educational experiences, demonstration or hands-on involvement for students. Like all academics, I have my share of committee work and expectations for scholarly activities.

Several years ago our local medical school requested my help in designing educational experiences for its students and medical residents. Recently, my primary contributions have been co-instructing a course with a physician and giving occasional lectures or workshops. About five years ago the psychology service in the local VA medical center asked me to serve as a consultant. I conduct a weekly clinical supervision seminar with psychology interns and staff psychologists.

I initiated an extra professional activity on my husband's suggestion. I am openly afraid of how lost I will be if I have to face widowhood. A combination of widowhood and professional retirement could be devastating for me, though retirement without widowhood would, I think, be very enjoyable if our health continued to be reasonably good. My husband's suggestion was that I start a small private practice that would provide professional activity that could be continued after retirement.

In Retrospect: What Changes Would I Make If I Could?

If I were given the power to redesign my life I definitely would not change my family of origin, my husband, or my son. I would have more learning opportunities and career guidance. If health permitted, I would have more children.

Being a psychologist has brought me much happiness, but I could have been as happy and productive in a variety of other professions. I might select one of the plant sciences that involve both basic and applied research. I might select a profession like law or medicine, which, given my proclivity for work, would provide a high income and permit me to expand my private initiatives to help others achieve personal goals.

I would probably structure my career less in the academic mold and more in the eight-to-five mold. In an eight-to-five professional position I gave eight hours of work and, with a clear conscience, had my evenings and weekends. As an academic I am at work from eight to five and, because there is so much that could and should be done and no defined limit that suggests one has done enough, I work five or six evenings a week and most weekends. To me, the touted flexibility of academicians has resulted in a substantial work overload. Yet I think I have balanced home life and professional life in such a

way that my family has not been seriously deprived. My social, recreational, and cultural life has been restricted because of overcommitment to work, but family life, though condensed because of long hours of work, has been the center of my existence. Perhaps because my husband and son know they have top priority in my values, they have been consistently understanding about my work.

Would I be fully employed during my son's infancy and childhood? I think so. He had an excellent baby sitter, always the same one, and he has maintained an affectionate relationship with her. He benefited from her love and creative child-rearing practices during the days and from our love and attention during evenings and weekends. I never felt I was depriving him by taking him to his babysitter. I was giving him a pleasant experience and more people to love. Whatever he might have been had I disrupted my career to spend more time with him, I am very pleased with the person he is.

Would I have devoted more time to research, writing, and scholarship and less time to students, patients, and program development, or vice versa? I think I would maintain the same balance. Research and scholarship enriched my potential to serve students and patients and to develop programs. Conversely, interaction with students and patients was a major source of research hypotheses and interpretations. Although productivity in the academic sphere is assessed by number of articles published or grants awarded, I judge some of my best accomplishments to be the probability that some students, patients, colleagues, neighborhood adolescents, and other associates have been able to lead more productive, happy lives because I was able to help them see their potential or enhance their confidence or identify alternative courses of action.

Could I have been one of those psychologists whose names are known by most other psychologists? That was never my goal, but I probably could have made myself well-known within a subdiscipline had I confined myself to a narrow focus. Do I regret that I did not? No. A narrow focus would bore me, and it would have sacrificed geographic closeness to my husband.

Whenever he expresses regret that I have accepted what appeared to be less than ideal employment in order to maintain a traditional family unit, I honestly answer that whatever I have lost in career advancement has been more than compensated by personal happiness.

Further, I have been lucky and adaptive in modifying positions. If I met the needs of the employing institution, the institution was supportive when I modified the position to incorporate activities of interest to me. My career would have been different, and not necessarily as rewarding, had the nepotism rule not enabled me to discover the challenge of studying the psychology of aging and the pleasure of interacting professionally with elderly people.

As of now I can say that in many basic ways life has been kind to me. My professional and family activities have complemented and contributed to each other rather than produced conflicts. Although my *joie de vivre* has been supported by my own diligence, values, and adaptivity, much credit is due to Lady Luck.

Chapter 16

A Career in Nursing

Beverley L. Thomas, R.N.

Introduction to Beverley L. Thomas

Beverley Thomas' writing of her chapter was interrupted by Hurricane Hugo. She is qualified for nursing services in disaster situations to which the Red Cross responds and is committed to answer a call immediately, at any time to any place.

Retired from a career as a registered nurse, she has a busy schedule. As director of human resources of the county chapter of the American Red Cross she plans and coordinates personnel functions for twenty-six paid staff and 700 volunteers. Two or three days a week she volunteers at a senior center. She drives and reads for the Commission for the Blind; is nursing officer for the county Red Cross team for family assistance and teaches Red Cross disaster classes; teaches 55/Alive courses for the American Association of Retired Persons (AARP); and is a consultant in epidemiology to the county health department and works in its flu clinics. She has received numerous commendations from the various organizations who benefit from her volunteer work and is widely

Lives of Career Women: Approaches to Work, Marriage, Children, edited by Frances M. Carp. Plenum/Insight, New York, 1991.

admired for it in the community. Her funniest story about her volunteer experience is trying to fit a six-foot-four man who could not bend his legs into her Honda Accord. She got him in—sitting crossways on the back seat!

Colleagues during her gainfully employed years remember her outstanding ability to organize her work, her play, her finances: Everything about her seemed well planned and thought out. As director of Nursing Support Services in a large hospital she demonstrated sincere care about her employees. At the same time, she expected the best that they could give, just as she demanded it of herself. She had little patience for incompetence on the part of others—none for less than the best from herself. Perhaps this ability to organize and to give of her best explain the ample "retirement" volunteer activities, which she combines easily with an active social life and travel.

"The best of everything to a girl I know will go a long way," a classmate wrote in my high-school annual. It was 1946. World War II was over. I was going to the University of Colorado, along with thousands of returning servicemen, to fulfill a dream held since childhood. I enrolled in a five-year baccalaureate program leading to a Bachelor of Science degree in nursing.

Why a Nurse and Why a University Degree?

I do not know what determined my choice of career. I now believe that it takes a special kind of person to be a good nurse, but I did not know that when I played doctor/nurse as a child, or even when I was a Red Cross junior nurse's aide during high school. Only after I had become a nurse did I identify the qualities of common sense, compassion, empathy, willingness to give of oneself, caring for other people, and emotional stability as prerequisites. Only then did I realize I had those qualities.

As a high-school graduate I just wanted to be a nurse. In the context of the times I was not constrained to enter the field.

Thanks to World War II, women had discovered that they could do jobs besides teaching, secretarial work, or nursing. A career in nursing was my choice. My mother may have influenced my choice. She had been a teacher, then a legal stenographer. In her sixties, she revealed that she had always wanted to be a nurse and trained to be a licensed practical nurse (LPN) and worked as one. In retrospect, I believe I chose nursing because I had the requisite qualities and abilities, even though I did not know what they were at the time.

Nursing was never my only goal. At one point I wanted to be an airline stewardess, which at that time required one to be a nurse. However, inch by inch I exceeded the 1940s' height limit for airline stewardesses. Inspired by a summer working as a physical therapy assistant, I thought I would like to go into the Air Force, get an advanced degree in physical therapy, and work as a physical therapist.

Why go to a university for a five-year curriculum instead of a three-year diploma program in a hospital? Why did it have to be the state university rather than one of more modest esteem? I was a good student, graduating twentieth in a high-school class of 650. I was an achiever, aspiring to lofty places in my chosen profession, so I wanted a good education. I applied to Johns Hopkins and Stanford, but the cost was prohibitive. My tuition at the University of Colorado was only twenty-five dollars per quarter.

I received a very good nursing education at the state university, and the lack of graduation from an expensive, high-status institution never made a difference in my career. It was twelve years before my having a baccalaureate degree, rather than a nursing diploma, made a difference in my salary. After that it made a big difference. Today an academic degree is essential if one is to progress beyond staff nurse. Ironically, in 1948 my status-conscious mother offered to put me through medical school. I declined and never regretted it. I specialized in public health to help people help themselves to enjoy better health and to avoid hospitals and doctors unless necessary.

Nurse's Training and Marriage

During my senior year I took vocational planning and developed a long-term plan that I hoped would lead to a nursing consultant position with the Joint Orthopedic Nursing Advisory System (JONAS). This was inspired in part by a summer spent caring for polio patients. Those plans never came to fruition.

At the same time I was invited on a rare blind date with two classmates. We were required to live in the nurses' residence, where we had a 10:00 P.M. curfew and only two late leaves a week (until midnight). My date had come to Denver to work as a mechanic in a garage owned by his buddy's father. He had enrolled in a new course through the University of Denver to become an airplane and engine mechanic.

Our backgrounds were quite different. I was an only child from a reserved English family, a city girl, well-educated, somewhat of a loner. He was a country boy from a German family. His mother died when he was five, and his brother was twenty years older than he, so during the remainder of his childhood and youth he had lived alone with his father. Reportedly, he was rather wild and had dropped out of school to join the Navy at seventeen. He was rough around the edges and had a terrible temper. Our relationship was stormy at times. However, he aspired to get an education, and I admired him for his efforts to improve himself. At first my parents did not approve of him because of his lack of polish. However, he was good at working with his hands and could fix anything. They appreciated that ability and in time came to like him.

The day came when student nurses could marry and live outside the nurses' residence. By the spring of 1950 we decided to get married, setting the date for September. My parents were opposed to our marriage. Relatives said it would not last two years. We did not listen to any advice. We dreamed of going to Alaska, where my nursing skills and his mechanic skills would be readily marketable. In retrospect, I realize that the decision was based more on his desire than on mine.

In the summer of 1950 I was assigned to a three-month rotation at the state mental hospital in a town 120 miles from Denver. In July my fiancé came to see me on a Wednesday night. He was in the Navy Reserve. With the outbreak of the Korean War, reserves were being called to active duty. He had been ordered to report for a physical examination and expected to be shipped out immediately. I got emergency leave. We returned to Denver and hastily planned a wedding for Friday night. With my parents' help, we had a church wedding and a reception complete with wedding cake. Our honeymoon was a weekend in a mountain cabin.

Unexpectedly, he did not pass the physical—too myopic. I went back to Denver for my last six months of training. We lived next to the garage where my husband worked. He got glasses and continued with school. We were busy and happy. I graduated with special honors and got a job as a public health nurse.

The Korean War was escalating, and my husband was called up again. This time the Navy accepted anyone with a warm body, never mind if he could see. In April he left for a sixteen-month hitch on a destroyer escort assigned to Korean shore bombardment. I lived with my aunt and her daughter in a small apartment and continued with my job. In December my husband's ship returned to Pearl Harbor for drydock repairs. We decided that I was to come to Honolulu, since the ship would be there at least three months. In Honolulu a polio epidemic was raging. Because of my experience I became a Red Cross nurse, teaching classes in polio nursing and caring for acutely ill patients.

Children

In February we decided to start our family, and in March I became pregnant. I gave up polio nursing but continued to work with the Red Cross, teaching a nurse's aide class in a women's prison. This was the wonderful thing about nursing. No matter where I went, I could always find a place where I was needed.

In August we were still in Honolulu. The ship was having sea trials, and I was five months pregnant. My husband announced that we were to be in San Diego in three days. We took a troop ship to San Francisco. My husband reported to Treasure Island because he was afraid that if he reported to San Diego he would be assigned to another ship, delaying his discharge from the Navy.

While we were in San Francisco, living in a transient hotel, I became acutely ill. I was diagnosed as having polio and was quarantined in the San Francisco County Hospital. Fortunately, I did not have the bulbar type polio, and I was discharged after ten days. My husband obtained a hardship discharge from the Navy. The day I left the hospital, we started driving to Denver. I was lying down all the way. We lived with my parents for six months, during which I had physical therapy and recovered my strength. My pregnancy progressed normally. My husband enrolled in the University of Denver's airport management course.

On New Year's Eve, 1952, our son was born—a scrawny five-pound-and-three-ounce shriveled-up monkey of a baby. I was thankful for my training in caring for premature infants. Our son thrived, and we moved to a rented apartment. Foot surgery confined me to a wheelchair for a while, but I managed our three-room apartment and the baby. Later I did some private-duty nursing to supplement our income.

In 1954 my husband graduated. Two job offers for airline station agents arrived on the same day from two airlines—one in Oregon and one in Arizona. He chose the job in Oregon. We looked at the atlas to see where we would be. We packed our few belongings in a U-Haul trailer and moved. I have often wondered how our lives would have been different if we had chosen Arizona.

Job hunting in Oregon was a disappointment. I wanted to

work part-time, but the local hospital would not consider part-time nurses. So I cared for our home and healthy, growing son and coped with shift work for my husband. In 1955, just as we planned, our daughter was born. We had completed five years of marriage and had learned to enjoy the Oregon outdoors. I taught some Red Cross classes to "keep my hand in." I missed nursing, and the desire to resume my career was growing.

Career and Family Development

In 1958 our third child was born. By then I was really restless and wanted to continue building my career or at least to work in my profession. The decision was made when I learned that Oregon law required a nurse to have worked during the past seven years in order to retain the license. I was not about to lose that license! I did not particularly like hospital work, but out of necessity I tried our local hospital again. I immediately obtained a position as a 3:00 P.M.–11:00 P.M. float relief nurse. I could be called to work on two hours' notice. Actually, it worked well because my husband had rotating shifts and days off; so I usually worked when he was at home.

He was not too pleased about my working, but it did help economically. He was unsuccessful in obtaining a better job in the airline. We had not expected to be in Oregon so long, but we liked the environment and bought our first home. We had fruit and nut trees, a huge garden, and space for active children to run and play. Our marriage was stable. It was hard work to manage a home, three children, and two jobs, but we did it.

My job was a revelation. I felt that I needed to return to training. There was equipment I had never seen, drugs of which I had never heard, and treatments that had been developed in the seven years since I had last worked in a hospital. I coped, learned, and confirmed once again that I was a good nurse.

And, once again, I was glad that I had chosen nursing as a profession.

When our youngest entered kindergarten, I discovered that I was qualified for a job as a school nurse. Although there were no openings at the time, I applied and hoped. School nursing would be ideal with the 8:00 A.M.–4:00 P.M. hours, and school holidays and summers off. The salary was very good for those times. A school nurse had quit unexpectedly, and I was offered the job. When I first worked in public health I had a caseload of 1000 families and six schools. School nursing had not amounted to much. Now I found that school nursing was health-education based and public-health oriented, centered in the schools and reaching out to the community. I had launched a career that gave me satisfaction and positive reinforcement for my nursing skills.

In 1964 my husband's education finally paid off when the city built a new airport terminal and hired him as the first manager. Our improved economic status, busier lives, and growing children motivated us to buy a larger house in 1966. Being a working mother was not easy, and having a hyperactive younger son complicated our lives considerably.

Break-Up of a Marriage

Our affluence and complicated lives affected our marriage. My husband seemed threatened by my job and jealous of the time I spent on professional or community activities after work. My job gave me the confidence, positive self-image, and "strokes" I did not receive at home. For me, life at home was like walking on eggs. After eighteen years of marriage and seemingly out of the blue my husband asked for a divorce. I was devastated. Later I learned that he had been seeing other women.

Divorce was not in my value system and no one in my family or his had ever been divorced. I insisted we seek counseling, and he reluctantly agreed. It was too late and unsuccessful. I filed for divorce after he moved out. We got back together and struggled on until the fall of 1970. My husband was depressed, and it was like living with a zombie. The relationship was destructive to everyone. One day, when he once again beat our younger son, it was the straw that broke the camel's back. I insisted that he move out immediately, filed for divorce, and went through with it.

This was before divorce was accepted in our society and before dissolution of marriage was available. I perceived the failure of our marriage as a tragedy, and the divorce was the most humiliating experience of my life. I felt relieved to be out of the relationship but disheartened that I had wasted twenty years. My family never accepted the situation, and acquaintances avoided me. They did not know what to say or do in our couple-oriented world. However, it was a growing experience that allowed me to become a self-sufficient, independent, successful woman, personally and professionally.

Career Woman and Single Mother

My children (aged seventeen, fifteen, and twelve) and I continued to live in our home. In retrospect, I regret that I did not seek counseling for the children, especially for my daughter. The divorce had long-reaching implications for her. As for me, I made a conscious decision not to waste my energy on bitterness but to use it to keep my family intact.

My career took a step up at this point, which was fortuitous economically. My supervisor had arranged to take a year's leave of absence. She approached me early in 1970 about replacing her for the next school year. I had never thought about going into management, but it was too good an opportunity to pass up. Earlier, I had been working because I wanted to. Now, I had to work. I had no management experience, but I had completed a

Master's Degree in Health Education after working toward it for five years at the rate of one course a term. That effort undoubtedly contributed to the failure of my marriage, but it turned out to be vital to my new job.

Four months before my divorce was final the woman I was replacing for that year decided to retire, and I was offered the job permanently. I was ecstatic. It meant financial security in raising three teenage children and a plus for my career. I missed the contact with the children that I had had as a school nurse. However, I could accomplish things as a program coordinator that I could not even influence as a staff nurse. The school district had 20,000 students in forty-four buildings. I continued successfully in this position for ten years.

During these years I was very much involved in the community and in professional activities. I was appointed by the state governor as the first nurse on the State Comprehensive Health Planning Authority. I was chairman of the County Comprehensive Health Planning Committee, president of the State School Nurses' Association, and secretary of the National School Nurse Organization, the latter of which involved travel all over the country to board meetings. I was Oregon School Nurse of the Year in 1976.

In 1977 I legally resumed my maiden name when my former husband married for the third time. I passed up an opportunity to go to South America with Project Hope. Unfortunately, that opportunity did not come my way again. In 1978 I sold our big house and moved to a rented condominium. I was unsure where I wanted my life to go. Fifteen months later and on a more even keel, I bought a condominium. Condo-living fitted my life-style perfectly. My daughter lived with me, and we found that adult child and parent living together was difficult for both.

My children grew up successfully. No drugs, no crime, and no hippie life-style in the difficult years of the 1960s and 1970s. All three graduated from high school, two graduated from the state university, and one completed a Master of Business

Administration Degree. All hold management-level positions. Both boys married at nineteen. There are three grandchildren. I am proud of and maintain good relationships with all of them.

A Tour in Southeast Asia

By 1980 school budgets were being cut, and programs such as health services were at risk. Program justification and budgets were an annual frustration. When contracts were issued for the 1980–1981 school year, I was offered a half-time management and half-time staff position, which I found untenable. First, it would have meant regressing in my career. Second, staff positions were part of the bargaining unit that management administered, and I could hardly wear both of those hats. Furthermore, I had been in one position ten years, and I needed a change. Therefore, I elected to take a leave of absence for a year to pursue and expand a plan I had been developing for a summer experience.

This was the time when the Cambodian people were fleeing the genocide of Pol Pot. I was accepted by the International Rescue Committee to go to Thailand as part of a U.S. Public Health Service team working in a Kampuchean Holding Center for refugees. There I found 130,000 refugees confined to an isolated camp two square kilometers in size. There were 20,000 school children who exhibited skin diseases, malnutrition, infections, and communicable diseases. They attended school in quadruple sessions—two hours per group per day. Classes were taught by Cambodian refugee teachers.

I established a rudimentary school-health program and selected and trained seventeen young men and one woman to be school health aides. Language was not much of a problem because the refugees were so eager to learn English. Some knew English and acted as interpreters. The aides did health assessments and made referrals to outpatient clinics. Volags (interna tional volunteer agencies) provided services at the camp. It was a different world from the Thai town in which the Volags lived. I am glad I had the experience but probably would not repeat it.

By the time I left, the camp population was down to about 67,000, communicable diseases were under control, and children were healthier; but social problems were beginning to develop, such as drug abuse, wife beating, thievery, and black marketeering. It had been a lonely time for me, and I felt that six months was long enough to be away, so I did not accept assignment to a Lao camp in the north of Thailand.

On the way home I stopped in the Philippines to visit a lady who had been a foreign student and for whom my children and I were a "friendship family" when she attended the University of Oregon in the 1960s. She was vice president of a bank and had a sumptuous home, a maid, a yard man, and a chauffeur. The contrast from camp life was almost ludicrous. She did her best to give me back the twenty-seven pounds I had lost in Thailand and to replace my ragged, sun-faded clothes. The Filipino national pastime seemed to be eating, and I was royally wined and dined.

Coming home was a shock. Eugene, Oregon seemed to have changed. My daughter had moved to her own place just before I returned. I did not want to return to the school district, but it was hard to consider giving up the excellent benefits and security. I applied unsuccessfully for a number of international health positions. When waiting for the mailman became the most important activity of the day I knew I had to do something else.

Hospital Administration

A friend had surgery, and when I visited her at the hospital I happened to see the job-opening list on a bulletin board. There were two new positions in nursing service administration, and

I felt that I could do either of them. I had not thought of returning to a hospital after eighteen years, but I applied for and got one of the positions. I resigned from the school district and started my new job. My mother said I would regret going back to a hospital, and in a way I did.

My philosophy of helping people stay healthy and out of hospitals was in direct opposition to the hospital's goal to fill its beds. In addition, the first two years were very difficult because of the almost overwhelming work. Everything was more difficult because the director of nurses tended to be vague and inconsistent, and to scapegoat her staff. She was asked to leave in 1983, and her assistant became director. She and I worked well together: She was a wheeler-dealer, and I was a detail person. During my third year I received a bonus for my work in the highly stressful, complicated job I held.

An interesting interlude in 1981–1982 was having a Cambodian refugee whom I had sponsored come to live with me for fifteen months. She had been an interpreter in Thailand.

Parental and Personal Illness

The year 1985 was a terrible one. During the previous spring, my father was diagnosed as having cancer of the colon and had surgery, and my mother was terminally ill with oral cancer. They lived 1200 miles away. In January I developed rectal bleeding and had surgery for a polyp. It had a grade 1 carcinoma. This required that I be off work for several weeks. In March my father had an intestinal obstruction and surgery again, then chemotherapy. I flew to Colorado to be with him and to help my mother, though I was not yet completely recovered from my surgery. This was the first of six trips I made to Denver in a year.

My father died in May, leaving my fragile, ill, eighty-year-old mother. She refused to stay in a hospice, so we put their house up for sale and I brought her to Oregon. Her hospital bed was in the living room of my townhouse because she could not negotiate the stairs. I arranged day care and returned to work. Many times I had thought of leaving my position to care for my parents, but they would not hear of it. I was ambivalent since I had to continue with my life after they were gone. In July we moved to a single-level condominium where my mother could have her own room.

Daily care was expensive, but I was making more at the hospital than I would have made with the school district. When my parents' home was sold, two of my children and I flew to Colorado to unload thirty-five years' accummulation of belongings. We had an estate sale on the patio, but it poured rain for three of the six days.

In September my supervisor, in effect, asked for my resignation. We had just hired new directors and I was pleased that we finally had a complete management team in place, but she felt that I did not fit anymore. It was a shock because I had no warning. If circumstances had been different, I would have stayed and fought for my position. However, that same day my mother was admitted to the hospital with pneumonia, and the stress cup overflowed. I resigned my position, at least having the presence of mind to negotiate four months of severance pay.

Amazingly, my mother recovered from the pneumonia, but I stayed at home and cared for her for two months. Again my nursing skills were a blessing. In December I obtained a half-time position as administrative assistant at the local Red Cross chapter for a pittance salary, mostly to give me relief from twenty-four-hour-a-day nursing care. My mother was able to stay alone the few hours I was away. She gradually weakened and died. I continued at the Red Cross, grateful for working only half-time, because it took me months to recover from the physical and emotional exhaustion of the previous year. I kept an eye open for management positions, but nothing had surfaced by February, 1987. Alternatively, I had hoped that a career with the Red Cross would develop, but that did not happen either. Then my part-time job came to an end because of severe budget cuts.

Retirement

I was fifty-eight years old and unemployed. For the first time in my life I used unemployment funds while I searched for a position. My unwillingness to relocate made it more difficult. I found that positions on the level I wanted were not plentiful at best and that no one wanted to hire a management-level person my age. This discrimination was subtle, but it was there.

My ace in the hole was that I could retire. Once I was able to work through the difficult concept that my skills were not marketable in my community, and to assure myself that I had resources to live comfortably, I decided to retire. I applied for my school district retirement and restructured my investments for additional income. My condominium and car were paid for, and I had no debts. It was the best decision I ever made.

Over the years I had planned what I would do with all that time. Now I had to implement those plans. I had always done volunteer work and continued it. I continued to do enough nursing to retain my nursing license, as insurance if I needed more income. I bought the Harvard Classics, since my science-oriented education had not focused on that kind of literature.

I took piano lessons again. I had dreamed of being a concert pianist and had studied for ten years before my nursing career won out. At no time was it more than a dream, though I studied from age seven to seventeen. I am a realist; I did not believe I had sufficient talent or dedication to become a concert pianist, and no one encouraged me. My love of music continues. I listen to music a lot and play the piano occasionally.

Still, I had too much time alone. I needed more contact with people and greater community involvement. I looked for more volunteering opportunities. I was volunteering at the shelter for battered women, and I was on the boards of directors of two non-profit organizations and the Red Cross Disaster Services Committee. Now I began driving frail and elderly people to medical appointments for Special Mobility Services and driving and reading for a teacher for the blind, who is blind. My nursing background is invaluable in both of these services. I became more involved in Disaster Services, and I am qualified to serve in national disasters. I am a certified instructor for the AARP 55/Alive Mature Driving course and for Red Cross disaster courses. I do nursing care for sick friends and neighbors and for senior and disabled services. I work at immunization clinics for the health department. I am busy and involved.

For the fun side of life I travel, read, knit, play cards, and play the piano. I have been to Hawaii, to China, to Florida to visit family three times, and to Colorado. I am going to Australia and New Zealand this year and to Alaska next year. The only thing lacking was a "significant other." Now I have a friend with a boat and camper who fulfills this need.

My friend has a big black Labrador, who is a great pal with my little dog, which my children gave to my mother in the last month of her life. Since she is a gray poodle and was a Christmas present we named her Silver Belle. She was probably my salvation in those months of recovery. Her presence forced me to get out and walk and to laugh at her antics. She was someone to care whether or not I came home. Although it is a nuisance to arrange for her care when I travel, she is a faithful friend, and her relationship with my friend's big Labrador enriches the human friendship.

Looking Back and Ahead

Looking back at my life and writing it down have been painful at times but cathartic, too. I have had it all: education, marriage, children, career, caregiver for my parents, and now retirement.

I am amazed at what I have lived through in a world that saw the Great Depression, World War II, the Korean and Vietnam wars, the dawn of the nuclear age, space science, television, computers, and advances in medical science.

My career included public health, private duty, teaching, hospital staff, school nursing, and nursing management. I have never regretted the decision. Nursing is different than it was when I started but basically still means caring for people—nurturing, fostering, protecting, and developing them.

I realize how important good health is, and I work at maintaining mine. I have learned that circumstances alter goals, and that one must set new goals and risk taking advantage of unanticipated opportunities. A "Y" in the road of life requires a decision of which way to go. Once decided, one must make the best of that decision. However, one can learn from that experience how to make a better decision for the next "Y" in the road.

Most of all, I learned that when the chips were down I was the only one I could really rely on, and that I had to be tough to survive as a single woman. My daughter criticizes me severely for that philosophy. I was delighted to find, "We write our own scripts, live in what we ourselves create, and we're ultimately responsible for everything that happens to us" (Bradford, 1988, p. 391), and "We are each the authors of our own lives—there is no way to shift the blame and no one else to accept the accolades" (p. 431). This philosophy reaffirms my faith.

I feel good about myself as a person and as a woman. I am proud of what I have accomplished and look forward to the future. I am delighted with retirement and, frankly, too busy to work. This year a friend wrote: "Happy birthday to a gal who has mastered the art of staying balanced and on track in this confusing, confounding experience known as life." What more could I ask for than that?

Reference

Bradford, B. T. (1988). *To be the best.* New York: Doubleday.

Chapter 17

This Sho' Nuff Ain't Been No "Zombie Jamboree"

Jacquelyne Johnson Jackson, Ph.D.

Introduction to Jacquelyne Johnson Jackson

Jacquelyne Jackson, a sociologist, was the first black post-doctoral student and first black and first woman on the medical school faculty at Duke University. She always debunked the residents, particularly those whose misguided sympathies stereotype blacks as poverty-stricken. She is quick to point out that she was reared in an intact family, no rats or roaches—in short, that stereotyping is erroneous, however well intentioned.

Her work unites rigorous scholarship with civil-rights activism. Her data-based reports are published in prestigious journals and earn respect in the research community. At the 1971 White House Conference she worked tirelessly for the Black Caucus, ensuring that national data on the multiply disadvantaged (e.g., black, old, female, poor) were not ignored. Her home is a meeting place for social-change agents.

In addition to her command of data on the national level, she

Lives of Career Women: Approaches to Work, Marriage, Children, edited by Frances M. Carp. Plenum/Insight, New York, 1991.

is immediately responsive to individuals. She is one of a small group of black and white professionals who look into complaints regarding mental-health care of poor blacks in the city and county. She interrupted writing this chapter to represent a sixteen-year-old black high-school junior who was about to be expelled from the county school system, which is tantamount to denial of admission to the city school system and the community college. His mother, who earns too little to hire an attorney but too much to receive help from the legal aid program, appealed to Jacquelyne upon learning that her son could be represented by a designated nonattorney. Jackson won at the hearing.

Her view is color-blind. Most distressing to her, in the student's case, was the behavior of a black assistant principal, who indicated in private that he thought expulsion was not warranted, but who contributed to the evidence out of concern for his own job. In explaining the delay Jacquelyne wrote: "I do, of course, understand that kind of dependence, and I remember that if all of those individuals who pretend today that they supported Martin Luther King, Jr. during his lifetime had really done so, King would indeed have had a powerful army, an army that could have withstood any of Pharaoh's troops. But, such is life!"

Her concern is age-blind. Also, while her chapter was in preparation, an author dedicated his book to her for being, "in the forefront of research, writing, and espousing the rights of Black senior citizens. Professor Jackson has done more than anyone in the United States to draw attention to the uniqueness and special needs of the Black elderly" (Davis, 1989, p. xiv).

She has written about role models, influences of current societal context and consequent problems in generalizing from one age cohort to another, and sex, as well as skin-color differences. She is currently preparing a book-length manuscript that will update her earlier research and thinking in this area.

Energy, perseverance, and dedication characterize Jackson as a researcher, a civil-rights activist, and a single mother. A colleague who has known her long and well says: "She marches to that different drummer whom we all would do well to heed."

In writing about my career as a Negro female at a major southern university, beginning shortly after its racial integration, I claim the license of a peripatetic iconoclast. I dedicate this uncovering of myself to my mother who helped make it possible for me to be an independent thinker.

Personal Background

When they married, my mother had a bachelor's degree (English and Latin) from Shaw University, and my father had bachelor's and master's degrees (accounting, commerce, and finance) from New York University. Later he had further graduate training, and my mother received a master's degree. He set up Tuskegee Institute's School of Business. In 1932 Mother went to Winston-Salem to have my twin and me delivered by the man who had delivered her, the first Negro physician in that city.

When I was born far fewer than one percent of Negroes in the United States completed college. Almost none were professionally employed. There was one Negro professor for every 5,541 Negroes, as compared, for instance, to one Negro clergyman for every 475 Negroes (U.S. Department of Commerce, 1935). More Negroes than whites were native-born (99.2% to 87.7%) of native-born parents (99.3% to 73.4%). Most Negro families (97%) had gainfully employed members. More Negro homemakers than white homemakers were employed (37.5% to 10.2%), though more of the Negro (33.9%) than of the white (15.2%) employed housewives did their work at home.

Only Georgia's and Mississippi's Negro populations were larger than Alabama's. The 22,320 Negroes in Macon County comprised 82.4% of the population, far above the 9.7% in the nation. For more than sixty-seven years the county's major sources of employment have been Tuskegee University (formerly Tuskegee Institute, founded in 1881 by Booker T. Washington) and the Veterans' Administration Medical Center (VAMC) for Negro veterans throughout the nation. Until my early adulthood all university and VAMC employees were

Negro, so most whites were economically dependent upon the expenditures of these Negro employees.

Until 1964 local public officials were white. Booker T. Washington (who died seventeen years before my birth) promoted Negro enfranchisement. My parents voted long before Martin Luther King was known, and I years before the Montgomery Bus Protest. The economic upper-hand of Tuskegee Negroes was apparent in the protest of the Tuskegee Civic Association (TCA), begun in 1957, against the gerrymandering of Negro voters from the city. John Nowak and colleagues (Nowak, Rotunda, & Young, 1978) regard the 1960 case as the second major reapportionment case to reach the U.S. Supreme Court.

Tuskegee was "put on the map" by Booker T. Washington (former slave, first Negro to dine at the White House, first Negro awarded an honorary doctorate from Harvard University) and George Washington Carver (former slave, later called "the scientific wizard" or "the peanut man"). I perched on my father's knees at his funeral in 1943. Major artists and entertainers and prominent scholars and speakers came to Tuskegee University. Presidents Taft and Franklin Roosevelt visited there.

Macon County was an oasis for middle-class Negroes. They were far better educated than their white counterparts, many holding undergraduate and even graduate degrees from northern universities. More Negroes were professionally employed. The most articulate speakers of standard English were Negro, not white. In my youth Macon County had a private hospital, an indoor swimming pool and tennis court, football and track stadiums, a private nursery school, an elementary school, a college—all Negro-owned. No such facilities were regularly available to whites. The privileged middle-class in Macon County was Negro, not white.

I was reared in a middle-class family. My parents were respected pillars of our community. They employed full-time, year-round domestic workers. My nursery, kindergarten, elementary, and preparatory schools were private. My private piano instructor was Booker T. Washington's only daughter, who had studied classical music in Europe.

Education and Early Professional Experience

There was no question that I would attend college (although my father allowed that you could lead a horse to water, but not make him drink; you could send your daughter to college, but not make her think). Unlike my father, who earned his way, my mother's father was her "money bags" and my parents were my mine. My academic mentors were white Jewish males who immigrated from Hitler's Germany. I was a natural American citizen, a Protestant, a Negro female. The differences mattered not at all. They tolled the sociological bell for me, and I remain grateful. Universities often hire Negro faculty "for Negro students." Incogitant jargonizing of Negro faculty as role models for Negro students has rendered the concept meaningless. Could educators believe that race automatically bonds Negro students and Negro faculty?

I earned my B.S. and M.S. at the University of Wisconsin, Madison before my first marriage (1955), my Ph.D. in sociology at the Ohio State University the year after my divorce (1960). I remarried in 1962, and Viola was born in 1964. I had seven years of experience as a faculty member at two segregated institutions (Southern University and A&M College, and Jackson State College) and at Howard University. I published articles in journals. My book based on my doctoral dissertation (Clarke, 1962) was mentioned favorably in *The New York Times*. I was consultant to federal programs (e.g., Teachers' Corps), presented papers, and served as officer for professional organizations. I traveled extensively in the United States, Canada, and Mexico.

I.was active in local civil-rights movements. I housed and fed many members of the Congress of Racial Equality (CORE).

I transported a CORE worker across the state line when the police issued a warrant for his arrest. Invited to deliver a lecture at Mississippi's Negro land-grant college, I was "uninvited" on arrival. Mississippi's education board had declared me *persona non grata* because my book spoke favorably of the NAACP. As local coordinator for the annual meeting of the Association of Social Science Teachers (ASST) I was forbidden by that board to hold the meeting at Jackson State University. Jackson State's president forbade holding the meeting in Mississippi. Medgar Ever's alleged assassin was in the county jail, and the college president was alarmed about "my tribe" (Negro social scientists) creating racial unrest. I agreed not to hold the ASST meeting at Jackson State, but said "my tribe" would meet in Jackson in April. Jackson State's president forbade faculty and students to attend our sessions. Some had had an "Uncle Tom" session with him when they asked permission to invite a nationally ac-claimed civil-rights activist to address the Sociology Club. One student said:

> We went to the President's office . . . to get his approval on having Reverend Shuttlesworth . . . speak to us on an objective basis. And . . . the President, hearing the name Shuttlesworth, became angry—he became so frustrated that he ordered us out of the office before we had finished . . . and he told us . . . that if we were to do anything like that again we would have to be dismissed. (Warren, 1965, p. 362)

A cherished recollection of the 1963 March on Washington is meeting friends I had not seen since university days at Wisconsin or Ohio State. After the march several of us went to a well-known restaurant for dinner. Upon ordering cocktails we learned that the city had been declared "dry" for the entire day of the march, another indication of apprehension about gather-ings of Negroes.

In 1963 I removed my stitches, cut my sutures, whatever, in a segregated hospital in Jackson following emergency surgery. On my second post-operative day my roommate was hallucinat-ing, her relatives sitting on my bed. Private rooms were empty, but the few for Negroes were occupied. Informed that I could not leave with intact stitches, sutures, whatever, I severed the whatever, signed the release form, and had a nurse wheel me out before my parents and husband arrived. My white physician was appalled.

Shortly after, I attended Medgar Evers' funeral and joined the march down Lynch Street to a distant funeral home. Months later and pregnant, I skittered from bush to tree, tree to bush, as Jackson's "finest" overreacted to "the Jackson Riot" (1964). A witness wrote that he had: ". . . seen a Marine outfit storm a fortified hill in Korea with fewer men and less fire power . . ." (Warren, 1965, pp. 46–47).

Standard Operating Procedures in Tragic Situations

When I came to Duke University in 1966, with Viola and my domestic, I was not a "po', deprived, disadvantaged nigra." That is how I was often perceived, and not just by "po' white trash." To me, tragic situations are those infested with racism and/or sexism. My criterion for selecting events is that at least four other Negro female professors of my generation experienced similar ones. "Having company" lessens the pain. Similarity of experience points to institutional behavior directed against the class of Negro females who joined faculties of previously segregated southern universities about the time I did. Such events are unlikely to occur to Negro female academics today—at least overtly. They are useful as benchmarks for measuring progress in regard to prejudice and discrimination.

Being First

I was the first Negro woman to receive a Ph.D. in sociology from Ohio State (1960); first female chairman of the Caucus (now

Association) of Black Sociologists (1970–1971); only female founder of the National Caucus on Black Aged (a title I coined) (1970); first female president of the Association of Social and Behavioral Scientists (1972–1973); first Negro editor of a journal of the American Sociological Association, *The Journal of Health and Human Behavior;* first Negro member of the Review Committee on Aging, National Institute of Child Health and Human Development (1973–1977); and the first Negro member of the National Advisory Committee, the Federation on American Immigration Reform (since 1979).

At Duke I was the first Negro postdoctoral fellow in the Center for the Study of Aging and Human Development (1966–1968) and the first Negro full-time (1968) and tenured (1971) on the medical school faculty; and, no doubt, as I was described in a different setting, Duke's first Negro faculty member "perfectly explicit in militant sympathies" (Warren, 1965, p. 362).

Being first typically meant that I was identified as "who I was not," most often a maid. Bound to Minnesota in mink coat, mink hat, and suede boots, I stopped by my office. A white male asked if I could unlock a door. When I said, "No," he told me to send "someone else from Housekeeping." Weeks after paying faculty club dues, one Saturday afternoon, Viola, a nephew, a friend, and I swam in the pool. On Monday the club's president informed me by letter that I had no right to use the pool. This man had told me repeatedly how he and his pregnant wife had protested racial segregation at a Durham theater.

Being first affected my federally funded study on Negro kinship in various ways. My Negro interviewers and coders were subjected to discrimination, and they discussed these events endlessly on "my time." One incident was triggered by a white volunteer at a Medical Center snack bar who informed a Negro male adult, when he ordered grape juice, that he did not want grape juice because it cost more; what he wanted was a grape drink. A conservative estimate of work lost over that event was 250 hours.

When I fired incompetent workers I was overridden by the

department. Mine were its only black clerical and technical workers, and federal funding agencies required data on the race of employees. My workers, aware of this, decreased production. One secretary used my equipment, supplies, and time to type outside manuscripts for pay. Another gabbed instead of checking the bibliography for *Minorities and Aging* (Jackson, 1980).

Being a nonphysician in a medical center and not based in the sociology department had drawbacks. (I refused joint appointment to avoid being a "four-fer," doubly counted by race and sex on affirmative-action reports.) The sociology department planned to admit to its doctoral program a Negro who needed more academic exposure, to be paid over the summer from funds controlled by a member of the sociology department who would be busy. I was asked to place him under my "sociological wing." Never mind that I was busy, professionally and single-parenting.

Recognizing that I should not have been a "first" at Duke because I was not socialized to be "a good nigger," I realized that I must become less trusting, naïve, and open, and more cynical and protective of myself. I learned to cope with unreasonable requests by *just saying no*. No to the minister who wanted to refer to me a Negro freshman grappling with the problem of retaining her virginity under contrary pressure from her boyfriend: If she has to ask, tell her no. No to the wife of a white professor: I will not come to your Sunday school so the children may meet a Negro. No I will not interview a Negro woman for a position on the nursing staff—I know nothing about nursing. No to a Negro doctoral student in history: I will not be "shadow advisor"—if your department thinks you need a Negro advisor, let it hire a Negro historian.

Broken Promises

I agreed to teach "The Negro in America" for one semester in the sociology department. The oral contract stipulated that I would receive pay additional to my salary, half midway and half at the end. I extended my domestic's schedule and paid overtime. I was paid midway, but at the semester's end I was told that Duke did not permit such payments to full-time faculty.

When I became professor I was told I would receive five-percent annual raises. This was last fulfilled over fifteen years ago. I was not told that faculty were to generate their own revenues. In a medical center this is no problem for clinicians, who receive a portion of patient fees. I am not a clinician. Outside research funds *supplant* salary; what I needed was *more* money.

I coped as mother and professor simultaneously. I did not relocate because it would have broken Viola's continuity with friends. I coped by earning additional monies through outside employment. I was Viola's "money bag" from private kindergarten through a Massachusetts preparatory school, a Quaker college, the Ohio State University, and two years as a Peace Corps volunteer. By my decision, Viola's education included travel. Before finishing college she visited most of the fifty States, Canada, and Mexico; various countries on the African, Asian, European, and South American continents; and various West Indian or Caribbean Islands. She spent a high-school term in the Dominican Republic.

I mention Viola's travel because of the marvel and doubt expressed about it. In 1966 she went with her grandparents to Japan, the Philippines, and Hawaii. Whites marveled that a Negro girl had such a holiday. Who would believe it! Returning from Uganda and Nigeria, she was questioned by a Negro playmate. He said Viola lied, that she could not go to Africa. I was generally gentle with those who expressed amazement or doubt. Coping financially was eased by my elderly, widowed mother. She paid entirely for Viola's eight-week Spanish-language session at the Universidad Iberoamericana in Mexico City. We are grateful that our mother and grandmother, who fusses annually about paying income tax on a portion of her Social Security benefits (on which she already paid taxes during her working years), helped us.

When I attended scientific/professional meetings, young Viola often accompanied me. When she did not I paid child-care "around the clock," so I attended only when I was a program participant and stayed only long enough to keep my commitment. After Viola entered high school, funds curtailed participation. Benefits of professional meetings need no listing. The loss is offset only somewhat by more reading of professional journals.

Another consequence was lack of a long track-record of research grants. I cope by accepting the obvious. Recently, the University of California at Berkeley was recruiting minority faculty. Two official letters urged me to apply. I did not, knowing that universities prefer faculty members who obtain external funds. My advice to young female academics, Negro or white, is to obtain written contracts specifying the details.

Outrageous Expectations

I was planning an NCBA conference. The center's director asked that I announce its Aging Training Program and distribute brochures at the meeting. Later I saw the center's application for renewed federal funding. Where the applicant must justify lack of minority participation it stated that *I* had failed to recruit minority applicants. Except for the one request, I was not asked to recruit anyone. The outrageous expectation was that I would accept the misrepresentation without demur.

When I received a grant to make the film *Old, Black and Alive!* I hired a film company of young whites from Boston. The purpose was to provide contrasting examples by socioeconomic status, living conditions, health status, and philosophy of Macon County's elderly Negroes. I had created the content. My father served without pay as local contact for the filming crew. Surprised to find the film focused solely on poor Negroes in ill health, I asked, "What happened to the shots of retired Negro professionals who were not poor, not on welfare, not in poor health, not in substandard housing?" The response was that *all* old Negroes *are* poor, and so forth. Only those that met the young white Bostonians' stereotype were kept in the film.

They had spent most of the grant monies. The best solution was to place footage showing middle-class Negroes at the beginning. My reaction each time I see the film is that it rushes past the middle class in its haste to show "real" Negro elderly. In April blooms burst out in radiant and majestic shapes and colors in Macon County. When the film was shown at the center a white female's comment was that the "artificial" floral setting was out of place. This time, the outrageous expectations were mine. I had not realized how pervasive was the negative stereotype of southern, elderly Negroes among whites—even among social scientists.

Misuse and Abuse

Browsing through an Institutes of Health (NIH) publication about individuals who obtained their doctorates as federally sponsored fellows, I saw that my Ph.D. was listed not from the Ohio State University but from Duke. When I showed the error to a black NIH staff member, she said I should be glad Duke got the credit. An editor who asked permission to reprint one of my articles in a book asked also for the university of my Ph.D. She wrote back that, in effect, I had lied—she knew my Ph.D. was from Duke!

Duke's medical students were required to take a course "team-taught" by a psychiatrist and a behavioral scientist from the Department of Psychiatry. When I became a team member I was the only Negro faculty member in the department. I was teamed with a skillful white psychiatrist. By the time he left, a Negro psychiatrist was on board. Before classes began the white overseer expressed displeasure with an all-Negro team. An exceptionally good Negro student who completed all the work earned a grade of H (H = honors, P = pass, F = fail). A white female who left early in the course, never to return, received an F. The overseer asked us to change her grade. As the senior professor I refused. Her grade was changed and the Negro's was lowered to P. We fought this but lost. I withdrew from the program. Effective teaching is impossible when students know that if they are white, the white overseer will not let them fail.

Coping with such misuse and abuse is nigh to impossible. Even individuals who listen to you are unlikely to believe you unless they are your racial-gender cousins. I coped by expressing my outrage to "significant others," exhausting reasonable remedies, avoiding interaction with my offenders, and/or storing the episode in my "memory kit" to use in reducing subsequent misuse and abuse.

Inadequate Support Services and Supplies

Adequate support services and supplies are sine qua non for professional sedulity. For many years, when the center received requests related to Negroes, they were forwarded to me for reply at my personal temporal and monetary costs. Negro colleagues in professional organizations could not understand that Duke did not cover the costs of my organizational work. When I was asked to contribute original documents to federally funded conferences whose proceedings would be released in edited books my requests for up-front expense monies were denied. It was assumed that I had access to Duke typists and such. For example, lack of advance monies severely limited the scope of a chapter's content (Jackson, 1988). Payment after its completion was too late. I "did the best I could," but my message to Negro and non-Negro female academics is: Include agreements for institutional support services and supplies in your contract.

Standard Operating Procedures in Ideological Conflicts

Years ago, the study of race relations was not "in" in sociology. Until the 1940s and 1950s sociology (as opposed to rural sociology) was verboten in most southern land-grant institutions. (Jackson State College was not alone in fearing what "my tribe" might do.) On the other hand, my majoring in social theory shocked some professors at Ohio State. The proper major for a Negro was race relations. A race relations professor posed this task during my orals: "Explain why Negro athletes and entertainers are more successful in breaking racial barriers than are Negroes in such professions as law and medicine." The answer, of course, must focus on racial ideologies rather than race relations. At Ohio State I learned about the powerful influences ideologies have on social control and social change, as in Gandhi's use of *Satyagraha*, Hitler's reign as *der Führer*, and the Negro civil-rights movements of Alabama. Understanding ideology and ideological conflicts as they affect social control and social change within the academic context is crucial to any Negro professor's understanding of her or his status and role.

Negro Gloating

My first task as postdoctoral fellow was a critique of the gerontological literature on Negroes. A Medical Center study reported that "nonmanual" Negroes and whites were similar by religiosity, whereas "manual" Negroes were more religious than their white counterparts. ("Nonmanual" and "manual" refer to the subjects' occupations.) I found that "manual" covered occupations ranging from skilled craftsmen to day laborers. Most whites were in higher-level occupations; most Negroes were day laborers and household workers. There were no differences in religiosity between upper-level Negro and white manuals, or between lower-level Negro and white manuals. Reaction in the center was that I should not gloat. Until then I had not been aware of ideological biases that arise when Negro social scientists identify as spurious, Negro–white differences reported by white researchers.

Negro Desegregation of Public Facilities

After the Civil Rights Act of 1964 and the Voting Rights Act of 1965 I taught summer school in a Negro public university. My students worked with Negro children in a Headstart project—outdoors because officials refused to open a building. The area had no grass. Negroes were not permitted to use the public city park and its swimming pool. We decided to desegregate the park with a well-planned visit. In addition to contacting local authorities and civic leaders, obtaining parental permission, and reviewing with the children the historical and legal aspects of their undertaking, I arranged in advance for legal services and bond fees. Even the picnic was symbolic (fried chicken and watermelon). The children enjoyed the outing, no arrests were made, publicity was minimal, and the park remained desegregated.

In another poor county, the school system was in its first year of court-ordered desegregation. In a school where Negro and white students were segregated by assigned seating, a ten-year-old Negro male was accused of writing a note, "I love you," to a white female classmate. Her father wanted the child arrested. The white principal, superintendent, and other local officials confronted an explosive crisis. White Duke psychiatrists and psychologists who were consultants to the local officials asked me to join them and prepare a sociological analysis. There was no note: No one could produce it; no one had seen it. The teacher had often told Negro students she hoped to see them all imprisoned.

The father was threatened into accepting his son's expul-

290 Jacquelyne Johnson Jackson

sion or losing his job as school janitor. The mother's job in the mill was vulnerable. They locked the son out of their home. Fortunately, a grandmother took him in. A compromise was reached: The lad remained in school, the overtly racist teacher was given a nonteaching assignment, and the father retained his job. But the child was irretrievably damaged. Years later a Duke medical student and I located twenty-year-old "Herman." He was a high-school dropout; his six siblings were college graduates or in college. His work history was discontinuous, although he scored well on a standard intelligence test (Pinsky, 1970). Negro manhood was wasted by despicable treatment of a Negro manchild.

Status of Negro Women

An outstanding student received a scholarship from Duke. She preferred to attend another university, but her father was totally disabled, and the full scholarship and prestige of Duke increased the pressure. She was depressed and upset when she arrived. Her condition worsened, and she was hospitalized at Duke. Her attending psychiatrist, a white female immigrant from Germany, recommended transfer to a psychiatric hospital. Through the intervention of another white psychiatrist, a more appropriate treatment was set up: "Had Dr. Jackson not . . . acted to bring in the second psychiatrist, the girl might still be . . . receiving 'treatment' for her 'illness' " (Pinsky, 1970, p. 2). The first psychiatrist found the young woman mentally ill because she was Negro, eighteen years old, and a virgin—abnormal because she believed all Negro females lose their virginity long before that age.

I have been involved in many ideological conflicts about the status of Negro women. Examples illuminate what it has been like for me as an expert on demographic, historical, and legal trends. I focus on invited presentations between 1970 and 1980 that grew out of publications (Jackson, 1971, 1972, 1973, 1975,

1979). Most were delivered at universities in thirty-six states and the District of Columbia, usually at three or more universities in each state. Many were based on Bureau of the Census and National Center on Health Statistics data. Comparisons of Negro women to Negro men, white women, and white men on such measures as education, income, labor force participation, unemployment, and occupation showed Negro women at the bottom. Initially, I was surprised that many persons—especially Negro men and white women—were skeptical about this finding.

Stereotypes were common: (1) "Negro women have always been better off than Negro men." Yet unemployment rates during the past eighty years most often show higher rates among Negro women. (2) "Unlike white women, Negro women have always had to work." Until recently, labor force participation among women has been higher for Negroes, but many white women have worked and not always in preferred jobs. Most women in the New England sweat shops, for instance, were white. (3) Many persons would not believe that birth rates of successive cohorts of college-educated Negro women are lower than corresponding white rates. But this is the case.

Many social scientists report that Negro women fare better than Negro men on the basis that the socioeconomic gaps between Negro women and white women are smaller than those between Negro men and white men. I argue that the appropriate comparison group for Negro females is white males, and that comparative analyses of the four race–sex groups yield more information. Let us use earnings as an indicator in a labor market characterized by affirmative action. The table on the next page shows the total mean income and wages/salaries of Negro and white full-time workers in 1980 and 1987 and their component changes. In 1980 the mean total income of Negro females was 52.8% that of their white male counterparts. In 1987 it was 54.6%, a gain of 3.4%. Female Negroes gained in comparison to male Negroes, earning 76.8% as much in 1980 and 80% as much in 1987. Female Negroes lost

Race-Sex Ratios of Mean Total Money Income and Mean Wages/Salaries of Negro and White Year-Round, Full-Time Workers by Selected Characteristics and Component Changes United States, 1980 and 1987[a]

	Race-sex ratios					
Characteristic and year	Negro female/ white male	White female/ white male	Negro male/ white male	Negro female/ white female	Negro female/ Negro male	White female/ Negro male
Mean total money income						
15+ years of age						
United States, 1980	0.5284	0.5866	0.6878	0.9008	0.7682	0.8528
United States, 1987	0.5463	0.6288	0.6828	0.8688	0.8001	0.9210
% change	3.4	7.2	-0.7	-3.6	4.2	8.0
South, 1980	0.5088	0.5793	0.6714	0.8782	0.7577	0.8628
South, 1987	0.5893	0.6751	0.6145	0.8729	0.9589	1.0985
% change	15.8	16.5	-8.5	-0.6	26.6	27.3
South Atlantic, 1980	0.5184	0.5296	0.6194	0.9789	0.8369	0.8550
South Atlantic, 1987	0.5103	0.6173	0.6397	0.8267	0.7977	0.9649
% change	-1.6	16.6	3.3	-15.6	-4.7	12.8
30-34 years of age						
United States, 1980	0.6229	0.6573	0.7546	0.9477	0.8255	0.8711
United States, 1987	0.6209	0.7213	0.7102	0.8608	0.8743	1.0156
% change	-0.3	9.7	-0.6	-9.2	5.9	16.6
Mean wages/salaries						
15+ years of age						
United States, 1980	0.4636	0.4758	0.6513	0.9743	0.7118	0.7306
United States, 1987	0.4989	0.5354	0.6608	0.9318	0.7550	0.8103
% change	7.6	12.5	1.5	-4.4	6.1	10.9

[a]Sources of data: U.S. Bureau of the Census, Current Population Reports, Series P-60, No. 132, *Money Income of Households, Families, and Persons in the United States: 1980*, Table 46, pp. 144–145, Table 47, pp. 150–153, Table 50, pp. 167 and 169–170, and Table 53, p. 181, U. S. Government Printing Office, Washington, D.C., 1982; and U. S. Bureau of the Census, Current Population Reports, Series P-60, No. 162, *Money Income of Households, Families, and Persons in the United States: 1987*, Table 31, pp. 114–115, Table 32, pp. 118–119 and 121, and Table 34, pp. 134–136, U. S. Government Printing Office, Washington, D.C., 1989.

in comparison to white females, earning 90% as much in 1980 but only 86.9% as much in 1987. Narrowing of the income gap was greater between white women and men than between Negro women and white men and between Negro men and white men. Changes in income gaps are more pronounced in the South and South Atlantic. Perhaps of most interest is the change in the white-female–Negro-male gap. In 1987 the mean total money income of white females in the South was higher than that of Negro males, a reversal of an historic trend. Nationally, white women's incomes were 85.3% of Negro men's in 1980 and 92.1% in 1987. These comparisons clearly suggest greater affirmative action benefits to white women than to Negro women or men.

Status of Negroes

Perhaps the most significant difference between Negro scholars, such as I, and Negro organizations and individuals dependent on federal funds is in descriptions of Negro statuses. I contributed an invited manuscript to the National Urban League's *The State of Black America* (1985). Data showed that Negro elders had fared better in recent years. The League's status reports, including the 1990s, all deny improvement. Also, the media typically inform the public that most Negro elders are poor, that most Negro females are unwed mothers before adulthood, and that all Negro mothers are single-parent poor and ineffectual.

Au contraire! Less than two-fifths of Negro elders have incomes at or below the poverty line. The poverty rate of Negroes 65 and older declined by 45.8% between 1959 (62.5%) and 1987 (33.9%) (U.S. Bureau of the Census, 1989). Most females are not "children having children." In 1987 73.5% of Negro females aged eighteen to nineteen had never had a child (U.S. Bureau of the Census, 1987). The public image of single-parenting Negro women is that they are poor and rear wayward children. The solution most often offered is implicitly based on patriarchal authority: They need Negro husbands and fathers.

Hogwash! Coupled with not having more children than they can support, the remedy is full-time year-round employment at reasonable wages. Among Negro mothers not living with spouses, the poverty rate of those who did not work during 1986 was 4.9 times as high as that of those who worked full-time (U.S. Bureau of the Census, 1987).

Standard Operational Procedures in Normal Situations

The repetition of events that I label tragic and ideologically conflicting has almost normalized them for me. Tragic events have lessened over the years. Ideological conflicts are likely to remain. A close friend and Durham County commissioner tells me I "don't think like most blacks." I am dismayed by Negro teachers who do not like the splendidly realistic movie *Driving Miss Daisy* because the Negro male star was cast as a chauffeur. I have disdain for Negroes who reject Alice Walker's powerful *The Color Purple*. It captured a way of life in the rural South a few decades ago. As a child I knew wives of Negro professors at Tuskegee University and professionals at VAMC who always referred to and addressed their husbands as "Mister." And, lest we forget, white masters owned *as slaves* their Negro wives and children.

I do not believe that Negro sociologists are prohibited from unfavorably reviewing a manuscript or publication by another Negro sociologist. The negative reaction of some Negroes to my review of a book poorly edited by a Negro sociologist was unexpected. I cope by continuing to review products by Negroes and non-Negroes by the same standards. I did not support Negro sociologists who petitioned the American Sociological Association (ASA) to withdraw an award to Negro sociologist William J. Wilson for his important *The Declining Significance of Race* (1978). Petitioners believed that Wilson was wrong to proclaim any decline in the effect of race on Negro attainments. I am glad that the ASA ignored the petition.

Conclusion

With help from my significant others and wisdom gained through the years, I have learned to cope quite well with my various statuses and roles. When conflicts occur I shift into the role more important at that time to me. I try to produce competent scholarly work and provide empirical data supporting it. That is one reason why I have included some statistical data in this chapter. If time were to turn back in its flight and remake me a young professor of sociology, I would not accept employment in a university in early stages of racial desegregation. I would be more conscious of the ideal fit between timing of children and careers. I would spend less on Viola and more on myself. A bit of "Don't do as I do, do as I say": Maintain good health habits; always take care of you.

Long ago at Jackson State College, when I was perturbed about the abuse the president was heaping on the few faculty members who aided members of CORE and the Negro lads who marched in the demonstrations, a gift came in the mail—a record made by the Alabama Christian Movement for Human Rights. It contained just the right lyrics: "We've been 'buked and we've been scorned . . . but we're still carrying on." I still play that record.

I am sustained by a favorite cousin who tells me that when friends share "news" about Negroes, she takes pride in saying, "Jackie wrote about that a long time ago." I appreciate Carl Rowan's devotion of over two pages to my work in *Just Between Us Blacks* (1974) and his agreement with me that Negro women had not yet arrived in terms of enhanced social status. I gain new energy when Ruppert A. Downing (with whom I am not personally acquainted) writes that:

> Responsible research . . . is an advocacy service when findings are brought to the attention of . . . decision-makers. The work of Black researchers such as Jacquelyne Jackson . . . illustrate advocacy through responsible research. (1989, p. 292)

I thank Dr. Hans Gerth, Dr. Charles Gomillion, and Dr. Kurt Wolff especially for making me keenly aware that sociological knowledge is in and of itself useless, that its ends should always be practical. Each of them, as I, was victimized by racial hatred and bigotry, and each of us tried to fight against them with faith that "the morrow cometh."

Oh! You may want to know why I returned to "Negro." Over the past century, we Negroes have been from black to colored to Negro to black to African-American without some of us learning to paraphrase Gertrude Stein's "a rose is a rose is a rose." Merely changing labels ain't no "zombie jamboree" either. Amen.

References

Clarke, J. J. (1962). *These rights they seek.* Washington, D.C.: Public Affairs Press.

Davis, L. G. (1989). *The black aged in the United States, a selectively annotated bibliography* (rev. ed.). Westport, CT: Greenwood Press.

Downing, R. A. (1989). Human services and the black adult life cycle. In R. A. Jones (Ed.), *Black adult development and aging.* Berkeley, CA: Cobb & Henry.

Jackson, J. J. (1967). Social gerontology and the Negro: A review. *Gerontologist, 7,* 168–178.

Jackson, J. J. (1971). But where are the men? *The Black Scholar, 3,* 30–41.

Jackson, J. J. (1972). Where are the black men now? *Ebony, 27,* pp. 99–102, 104, 106.

Jackson, J. J. (1973). Black women in a racist society. In C. Willie, B. Kramer, & B. Brown (Eds.), *Racism and mental health* (pp. 185–268). Pittsburgh: University of Pittsburgh Press.

Jackson, J. J. (1975). A critique of Lerner's work on black women and further thoughts. *Journal of Social and Behavioral Sciences, 20,* 63–89.

Jackson, J. J. (1979). Illegal aliens: Big threat to black workers. *Ebony, 34,* pp. 33–36, 38, 40.

Jackson, J. J. (1980). *Minorities and aging.* Belmont, CA: Wadsworth.

Jackson, J. J. (1985). Aged black Americans: Double jeopardy re-examined. In *The state of black America.* Washington, D.C.: The National Urban League.

Jackson, J. J. (1988). Social determinants of the health of aging black populations in the United States. In J. S. Jackson (Ed.), *The black elderly: Research on physical and psychosocial health.* New York: Springer.

Nowak, J. E., Rotunda, R. D., & Young, J. N. (1978). *Handbook on constitutional law.* St. Paul, MN: West.

Pinsky, M. (1970, September 7). For Durham's blacks and poor, mental health disgrace. Durham, NC: *The Carolina Times.*

Rowan, C. (1974). *Just between us blacks.* New York: Random House.

U.S. Bureau of the Census, Current Population Reports (1987). *Fertility of American Women: June 1987.* Washington, D.C.: Government Printing Office.

U.S. Bureau of the Census, Current Population Reports (1989). *Poverty in the United States: 1987.* Washington, D.C.: Government Printing Office.

U.S. Department of Commerce, Bureau of the Census. (1935). *Negroes in the United States, 1920–1932.* Washington, D.C., Government Printing Office.

Warren, R. P. (1965). *Who speaks for the Negro?* New York: Random House.

Wilson, W. J. (1978). *The declining significance of race.* Chicago: University of Chicago Press.

Chapter 18

Implications for Future Research

Jacquelyn Boone James, Ph.D.

Introduction to Jacquelyn Boone James

Jacquelyn James earned her doctorate in psychology from Boston University, Boston, in 1988. While working for it she received a National Institute of Mental Health Family Traineeship. Upon receipt of the Ph.D. she was awarded the Dissertation Scholarship Award from the Boston University Graduate School and the Jeanne Humphrey Block Dissertation Award from The Henry A. Murray Research Center, Cambridge, Massachusetts, for her dissertation "Women's Employment." The Murray Center also immediately offered her a position as research associate, which she continues to hold. She wrote a chapter, "Women's Employment Patterns, Occupational Attitudes and Midlife Well-Being," for *The Meaning and Experience of Work in Women's Lives*, edited by N. Chester, which was published in 1990 by Lawrence Erlbaum.

Lives of Career Women: Approaches to Work, Marriage, Children, edited by Frances M. Carp. Plenum/Insight, New York, 1991.

Currently, she is co-investigator of a Health and Personal Styles Project funded by the National Institutes of Health. Her particular research interest is identification of the antecedents and individual differences in successful mid-life development for women.

James is married to another psychologist, and they are the parents of two children.

Correction of a Misconception and an Oversight

Much has been made of the fact that research has focused on men's lives and not women's, especially in the study of work. As the gap in scholarship has narrowed it has become more and more apparent that generalizing from the experience of *some* women, who serve as research subjects, to make statements about *all* women is problematic as well. Such generalizations are not only a disservice to women for whom they do not hold but may also restrict the range of possibilities available for women's expressions of individuality. Even when, in studies of groups of women, we do find and isolate "normative" behavior for women, we often forget to take note of the exceptions.

One example of this problem is the oft-repeated assertion that until recently ". . . the only women working throughout adulthood were those 'unfortunate' enough to be without a husband—the unlucky spinsters and the widowed" (Betz & Fitzgerald, 1987, p. 4). And even though history records that unmarried women of this era were working, the stories of their career lives are seldom told (Heilbrun, 1988). The life stories that appear in this volume serve as a correction for both the misconception that married women never worked on the one hand and the oversight of unmarried women's careers on the other. The stories of women who chose not to marry can be found here, as can the stories of rare women who, during the middle decades of this century, had careers that were important to them and that were actively sustained over the life course.

What is special about these women? What can be learned by examining the experiences of women who differed from the norms? Is there wisdom to be gained from their hindsight? What do they reveal that researchers have discovered over and again? Do their individual experiences substantiate or refute the findings of research on women and work? In what ways do their experiences suggest new avenues for research about these issues?

Inspiration, Infuriation, and Astonishment

The portrayals of career paths in this volume reveal women with vivacity and verve. Their experiences will, at different moments, inspire, infuriate, and astound. One cannot predict which elements of which stories will inspire (or infuriate or astound) a given reader, but surely no one can fail to be inspired, for example, by the philosophy of Lisa Redfield Peattie, who saw her career as a heartfelt endeavor, a life's mission. In her own words Peattie describes her work as a process of ". . . conducting a life in which a leading component is a strong intellectual drive to learn and to express my understanding in words." She, in fact, refers to her career as a "life" not a choice. Also inspiring is Margaret Schweinhaut's narrative describing her evolving awareness of the way in which one can perform seemingly impossible tasks in the service of some larger, personally relevant goal. In order to accomplish her goals she had to do things she thought she could not do. In reading these memoirs I was most inspired by the sheer number of obstacles Helena Lopata overcame to become the well-read scholar that she is today: an incredible exit from Nazi-occupied Poland, a near-ruinous childhood illness, and the limitations for married professional women in America, to name just a few.

The now familiar tales of discrimination and exploitation are still infuriating as revealed in the lives of these pioneer

women. One is infuriated anew to learn that Irene Hulicka had
to conceal her identity as a female in order to acquire reasonable
pay, and that Lois Mailou Jones had to conceal her race by
mailing an art exhibit for review rather than presenting it in
person, as was the usual procedure. Also infuriating was Ruth
Weg's discovery that there were more rigorous requirements for
women's graduate training than for men's. Most infuriating was
Irene Hulicka's account of how her work was cast as the source
of blame for her baby's death.

I was astounded by the assertion by both Nancy Clish and
Shirley Woods that they had never felt the sting of sexism or
discrimination. Says Woods, who had suffragettes for teachers,
"It never dawned on me that there was anything I could not do
because of my gender." Also astounding was Josephine Hilgard's complete career reversal. After diligently earning a Ph.D.
in psychology she entered medical school and completed the
long process of becoming a physician, when a move for her
husband's career rendered her first degree nearly useless in the
face of an "antinepotism" rule at the university of her husband's new appointment. These are but a few examples of the
intrigue in these portrayals.

Confirmation of Research Findings

Also of interest and reassuring to researchers is the way in
which the authors of these vignettes, without any direction on
the part of the editor, draw conclusions that researchers have
also drawn on the basis of studies of groups of women. Almost
all mentioned the importance in their career development of the
presence of supportive parents as reported by Haber (1980),
Houser and Garvey (1985), and Farmer (1985), particularly
fathers (Nagely, 1971; Turner & McCaffrey, 1974). Several
women mentioned the importance of encouragement from
husbands, about which the research evidence is mixed (see Betz

& Fitzgerald, 1987, for the benefits and limitations of dual career marriages for women's careers). Many of the women placed a great deal of weight upon the impact of the social forces abreeze during the course of both childhood and career development, for example, both World War I and World War II and the Great Depression (emphasized by Elder, 1974, 1979, 1985; Stewart & Platt, 1982). Almost all mentioned the dual responsibility of work and caring for others—whether for children, parents, or both—that is well documented by research on the interplay between work and family (see Long & Porter, 1984, for an extensive review of this literature).

Suggestions for New Lines of Research

The beauty of an individual exposé, however, is the possibility of discerning relatively uncharted territory in research and thus suggesting new avenues for researchers to travel. One of these is the assertion by Wilma Donahue that careers may be effectively started at any time in life. Particularly for women whose socialization discouraged serious career commitment, this is a comforting suggestion. On the same topic, Vivian Wood cautioned that, especially for late starters, the psychological barrier of low expectations in life is a very important obstacle to overcome. More research needs to be directed toward the pleasures and the pitfalls inherent in getting a late start in a career.

Much research has dwelled on evaluating the different outcomes for women involved in traditional versus nontraditional careers. Most of this research has pointed out the higher status and opportunity for growth inherent in the nontraditional career, along with the difficulties of proceeding in a "man's world." Seldom, however, are women who have grown, advanced, and left their mark on the world from the platform of the more traditional jobs, such as nursing and teaching, the focus of study. Beverley Thomas (nurse) and Catherine Rude (teacher) accomplished greatly in these careers, and their portrayals suggest that more research is needed on successful career experiences of women in traditional careers and on changes that social forces have generated in these fields.

Another research agenda suggested by reading between the lines of several of these portrayals is that while work/family conflicts do occur, for some these represent challenge and opportunity, even joy inherent in the combination. Consider Shirley Woods' account:

> The creativity required to produce and nurture a child subverts all other creativity. Would you compose music? A lullaby will suffice. Would you be an artist? Try finger paints. Would you study or write? A child will tug at your skirts, and you will be happy for it. The children were tow-headed and pink and full of cute sayings. They clamored to be fed and rocked and bathed and dressed. Through it all I taught school, graded papers, canned fruit, and even raised chickens.

And the editor's own reflections reveal her conclusions at the end of it all:

> Concentration on career to the exclusion of husband and children might or might not have benefited my career but surely would have left other strong needs unmet and left me unhappy and unfulfilled as a person. Confinement to housewifery would have left strong achievement needs unmet, with similar negative personal results and consequently lessened efficacy as wife and mother.

Finally, Catherine Rude's reminiscences, after many years of combining motherhood and paid work, end with, "Perhaps we all are richer for having faced and resolved these challenges."

Some researchers have begun to explore this phenomenon of the pleasure and reward that come with work that one loves and to which one is committed (see Baruch, Barnett, & Rivers, 1983); but more work needs to be done that explicates the life-giving, as opposed to life-draining, aspect of work. Lynne Cheney (1990) has asserted that success "almost certainly will be connected" with work you love, work that involves you deeply, quite apart from whatever other rewards it may bring. This kind of attachment to work needs to be better understood for both women and men. Surely, this has consequences for whether the work has positive or negative outcomes for the families involved as well.

One point that appeared as a theme in several stories is an unresolved issue for research. Several narratives outlined the casual "falling into a career" that Heilbrun (1988) has called into question, that is, the cause finding the woman and not the other way around. Heilbrun contends that in reality, "Each woman set out to find her own work, but the script insisted that work discover and pursue her, like the romantic lover" (p. 25). Individual discretion and choice is an important issue and should become a focus for research.

References

Baruch, G., Barnett, R., & Rivers, C. (1983). *Lifeprints: New patterns of love and work for today's women.* New York: Signet.
Betz, N. E., & Fitzgerald, N. E. (1987). *The career psychology of women.* Orlando: Academic Press.
Cheney, L. V. (1990, September). The secrets of success. *Self Magazine,* pp. 198–199.
Elder, G. H., Jr. (1974). *Children of the Great Depression.* Chicago: University of Chicago Press.
Elder, G. H., Jr. (1979). Historical change in life patterns and personality. In P. B. Baltes & O. G. Brim, Jr. (Eds.), *Life-span development and behavior* (Vol 2, pp. 117–159). New York: Academic Press.
Elder, G. H., Jr. (1985). Perspective on the life course. In G. H. Elder, Jr. (Ed.), *Life course dynamics* (pp. 23–49). Ithaca, NY: Cornell University Press.
Farmer, H. S. (1985). Model of career and achievement motivation for women and men. *Journal of Counseling Psychology, 32,* 363–390.
Haber, S. (1980). Cognitive support for the career choices of college women. *Sex Roles, 6,* 129–138.
Heilbrun, C. G. (1988). *Writing a woman's life.* New York: Ballantine Books.
Houser, B. B., & Garvey, C. (1985). Factors that affect nontraditional vocational enrollment among women. *Psychology of Women Quarterly, 9,* 105–117.

Long, J., & Porter, K. (1984). Multiple roles of midlife women: A case for new directions in theory, research, and policy. In G. Baruch & J. Brooks-Gunn (Eds.), *Women in midlife* (pp. 109–160). New York: Plenum Press.

Nagely, D. (1971). Traditional and pioneer working mothers. *Journal of Vocational Behavior, 1*, 331–341.

Stewart, A. J., & Platt, M. B. (1982). Studying women in a changing world: An introduction. *Journal of Social Issues, 38*, 1–6.

Turner, B. F., & McCaffrey, J. H. (1974). Socialization and career orientation among black and white college women. *Journal of Vocational Behavior, 5*, 307–319.

Chapter 19

Summary

Frances Merchant Carp, Ph.D.

Patterns of Success

Whether interest is in the decisions of individual young women or in expanding knowledge on the life experience and well-being of women in general, it must be kept in mind that the authors are not ordinary women and had careers when women having careers was far from the norm. Each author is considered by peers in her field to have a successful career. All completed a chapter for this book, a task not every recruit would undertake. A few who were invited to contribute chapters declined because of previous commitments, but the most common reason for refusal ran along the lines of, "I made a mess of my career! I would not hold up my life as an example for anyone!" Some who undertook the task found it impossible to complete. In the words of one: "I have learned a lot about myself, but it is too painful to continue."

Thus, it seems that the authors' lives were successful, not

Lives of Career Women: Approaches to Work, Marriage, Children, edited by Frances M. Carp. Plenum/Insight, New York, 1991.

only in the eyes of peers but also in their own—at least to the extent of believing that their stories are worth hearing. They admit mistakes, bad judgments, and regrets, as well as sound decisions, good luck, and happy outcomes. If they had it to do over again, they would do some things differently. They learned from success and failure—and are willing to expose themselves so that others may profit from their experiences.

Some Common Patterns

In nearly every case, expectations of parents and/or others during childhood set the girls' sights high. Higher education was expected of and by these young women, though it was not usual among their age peers. Parents expected these girls to marry, and most did. The typical pattern was to find a husband during college or university days.

For some, career decisions were clear from childhood. For most, career fields were chosen during college years. Some choices proved wrong and corrections were made. Several of the women stayed at home or worked at other jobs for years and did not find their career niches until relatively late. Both men and women served as role models and mentors. Women, if available, were generally supportive; these authors consistently supported the development of younger women.

After reading of their multiple accomplishments it seems evident that these women had high energy levels and enjoyed generally good health. What is surprising is the incidence of serious illness or injury during formative years or severe enough to justify ending a career. In every case the woman used the words "ignore it" in writing of how she coped with the problem.

Perhaps most consistent among these women are determination, drive, and perseverance—often in the face of hard and persistent barriers. When these women set out to accomplish something they did it "come hell or high water." For one, this entailed expatriate life until her status in Europe enabled her to gain recognition at home. For three, it involved planned pregnancy despite physicians' advice to the contrary, miscarriages, or loss of a newborn.

Some write as if their careers simply dropped in their laps without effort on their own part, but careful scrutiny of their chapters suggests that this was not so. Donahue mentions "luck" but defines her career pattern in terms of serendipity — the ability to take what comes to hand and do one's best with it — scarcely a passive stance. Hulicka pairs luck with personal diligence and adaptiveness in describing herself as a "lucky planner." Others who attribute positive outcomes to "Lady Luck" obviously gave her generous support by their own efforts. Woods' becoming a deacon "without even asking for it" is true only in the most literal and time-limited sense. To Peattie's oldest friend, the credit Peattie gives to luck is part of the "delightful scam" of her life pattern of role playing — getting people to take her seriously "by coming at them sideways with your stance of marginality." The friend concludes, "If anybody every *made* their luck, you did!" No author suggests to career-minded young women that they sit passively, expecting flourishing careers to be bestowed upon them by that Lady.

Some Variations

Some marriages proved highly satisfactory and persisted until the husband's death or the present time. Others failed, and women were left to raise children alone. As with marriage, single-parenting had mixed results. One family sailed unscathed through the "hippy years," while another experienced every facet — drugs, long hair, exclusion, and juvenile court.

World War II touched all lives, but not always in similar fashion. Two of the women joined the armed forces at a suitable age and another served them as a civilian. Three women married men who were in the armed services, but the experiences another had with servicemen were instrumental in her decision not to marry.

Individual differences are clearest in the lives of identical twins reared together. Grandfather, the central figure in Schweinhaut's childhood and source of her career goal and early preparation for that career, is not even mentioned by Thompson.

Age, the single most powerful predictor of retirement for men (Palmore, Burchett, Fillenbaum, George, & Wallman, 1985), is not an accurate indicator of retirement among these women. The oldest is winding up her third gainful career since mandatory "retirement" from a university over twenty years ago—and no one who knows her would be surprised if she came up with another. The next-to-oldest is working at her studio on Martha's Vineyard when not at the one in Haiti or at home in Washington, D.C. One who ties with her twin for third oldest is a hard-working state senator. On the other hand, among the five youngest, three have retired completely and have moved (one within the same city, two across the country) to places that better accommodate their retirement life-styles.

Neither is age consistent in accounting for career field. When the oldest ones were growing up the proper goals for young ladies were marriage and children. Women—if they worked—were expected to select school teaching, secretarial duties, or nursing. These relatively oldest women had careers in fields considered nontraditional for women—institute director in a major university, internationally renowned artist, elected political figure, United States Commissioner. Some of the comparatively youngest went into teaching or nursing because they enjoyed and met the challenges of these fields, not because of societal expectations regarding "women's work."

Most life stories chronicle a career path strewn with obstacles associated with being female and/or discriminatory treatment of the authors as women and of their work as it related to women. Interestingly, some take pains to deny any such experiences. Woods' belief that gender was a grammatical concept

that had nothing to do with what she could accomplish may have been outgrown with childhood. She writes with pride of being one of the first women to be ordained an Episcopal deacon, of the "heady years for women" during which she and a handful of other women deacons met to plan for ordination to the priesthood, and of her priesthood as soon as it became possible for women. Southern gentlemen may have buffered sexism in medical school for McCall. Reluctance to do a full internship in surgery (at which she was apparently adept) and the fact that ob/gyn is a "happy" field were no doubt influential in her specializing in the latter, but she also mentions that it is a "good field for women"; and in recognition of the difficulties of young female physicians, her main life work was the establishment of a women physicians' practice. It is not likely that any of these contributors would advise young women not to anticipate differential treatment. Perhaps the hope of most of the authors is expressed by Jackson—that prejudices will be less extreme and less overt for younger women than those they have experienced themselves.

Reference

Palmore, E. B., Burchett, B. M., Fillenbaum, G. G., George, L. K., & Wallman, L. M. (1985). *Retirement: Causes and consequences.* New York: Springer.

Index

Academia. *See also* Education
  feminist movement and, 205
  historical perspective on, 151-156
  Peattie, Lisa Redfield, 181-182
  race bias in, 282-283
  role models and, 171
  sexism in, 12, 143, 146, 147, 160,
    197-198, 200-201, 205, 238, 242
  Wood, Vivian, 167-169
  World War II and, 279
Adoption
  child-bearing decision, 16-17
  Hilgard, Josephine Rohrs, 94-95
Africa, 52
Age level, 310
Aging. See Gerontology
Alcott, Louisa May, 161
Alexander, Franz, 93
Alienation, Peattie, Lisa Redfield,
  174-175
Ambition, sex differences and, 4
Anthropology
  Peattie, Lisa Redfield, 173-190
  Wood, Vivian, 171
Anti-intellectualism, Lopata, Helena
  Znaniecka, 206
Aquinas, Saint Thomas, 129
Art, Jones, Lois Mailou, 43-54

Auden, W. H., 118
Autobiographical and biographical
  narrative
  commonalities among, 308-309
  historical truth and, 2
  male dominance of genre, 1, 300
  personality studies and, 3-4
  style of, 4
  truth and, 2-3
  utility of, 19-20
  variety in, 309-311
  women's lives, 1-2

Becker, Howard, 203, 206
Bernard, Emile, 49
Bettelheim, Bruno, 183
Biology, Weg, Ruth B., 143-158
Biomedical research and knowledge,
  sex differences, 17-19
Birth control, Peattie, Lisa Redfield,
  180

Career change
  Hulicka, I. M., 246
  Rude, Catherine Scofield, 215
  studies of, 3
Career decision
  child-bearing and, 15-17

313

Career decision (*cont.*)
  college students, 11–13
  marital relationship, 13–15
  race differences, 14–15
  Thomas, Beverley L., 258–259
  two–career marriage, 14
Career development
  Carp, Frances Merchant, 134–139
  Clish, Nancy McCall, 230–232
  Donahue, Wilma Thompson, 30–40
  Hilgard, Josephine Rohrs, 95–97
  Hulicka, I. M., 249–252
  Jones, Lois Mailou, 47–48, 53
  Lopata, Helena Znaniecka,
    198–199, 202–207
  Peattie, Lisa Redfield, 184–186, 189
  Rude, Catherine Scofield, 214,
    217–219
  sexism and, 249, 251
  Thomas, Beverley L., 263–264,
    267–269
  Weg, Ruth B., 147–151
  Woods, Shirley F., 110–114
Career opportunities
  Carp, Frances Merchant, 127
  Donahue, Wilma Thompson, 26
  feminist movement, 205
  limits on, 210–211
  marital relationship and, 6
  politics, 61
  race prejudice, 277–278
  research directions for, 303–304
  role models and, 238
  Rude, Catherine Scofield, 213–214
  sexism and, 9, 154–155, 242
  singleness and, 300
  Thompson, Marie McGuire, 72
  women and, 5–6
  World War II, 213, 228–229, 259
Carp, Frances Merchant, 9–22,
    125–141, 307–311
Carter, Jimmy, 44
Carver, George Washington, 278

Child bearing
  bias and, 238
  Carp, Frances Merchant, 131, 133
  Clish, Nancy McCall, 230–231
  decision making and, college
    students, 15–17
  Hilgard, Josephine Rohrs, 92–93
  Hulicka, I. M., 247, 248
  Lopata, Helena Znaniecka, 194
  Peattie, Lisa Redfield, 181–182, 183,
    184
  Rude, Catherine Scofield, 215
  Schweinhaut, Margaret Collins,
    58–59
  Thomas, Beverley L., 261–263
  Weg, Ruth B., 148
  Woods, Shirley F., 112
Child care assistance and domestic
  help
  Clish, Nancy McCall, 231
  Jackson, Jacquelyne Johnson, 284
  Rude, Catherine Scofield, 219–220
  Schweinhaut, Margaret Collins, 60
Child rearing
  career and, 6
  Carp, Frances Merchant, 132
  Hilgard, Josephine Rohrs, 93–94
  Hulicka, I. M., 248–249
  Jackson, Jacquelyne Johnson,
    284–285, 295
  Lopata, Helena Znaniecka, 202
  Peattie, Lisa Redfield, 183,
    186–187
  Rude, Catherine Scofield, 216,
    220–221
  Thomas, Beverley L., 263–264,
    266–267
  Woods, Shirley F., 114, 115–116,
    117–118
Children, illness of, 220
Civil Rights Act Amendments of
    1974, 154
Civil Rights Act of 1964, 289

Civil rights movement, Jackson,
Jacquelyne Johnson, 279–281,
289–290
Clifford, Clark, 81
Clinical psychology, Donahue,
Wilma Thompson, 23, 25, 31–35
Clish, Nancy McCall, 225–233, 227,
302, 311
College students
career decision, 11–13
child-bearing decision, 15–17
marital relationship, 13–15
Color Purple, The (motion picture),
294
Commitment, career choice and, 214
Commitment scripts, 4
Community planning, Peattie, Lisa
Redfield, 173–190
Concentration camps, Lopata,
Helena Znaniecka, 195
Congress of Racial Equality (CORE),
279–280
Contraception, Peattie, Lisa Redfield,
180
Coons, Dorothy H., 32, 33
Curti, Margaret Wooster, 89

Dance, 179
Darwin, Charles, 108
Day-care facilities, reliance on, 220.
See also Child care
assistance and domestic help
Death of child
Hulicka, I. M., 247
Woods, Shirley F., 118
Death of parent
Lopata, Helena Znaniecka, 193
Thomas, Beverley L., 269–271
Wood, Vivian, 163
Death of sibling, Peattie, Lisa
Redfield, 176–177
Death of spouse
Clish, Nancy McCall, 232

Death of spouse (*cont.*)
Donahue, Wilma Thompson, 40
Peattie, Lisa Redfield, 186–187
DeFora, Assadat, 48
Dillard, Alzada, 231
Divorce
career opportunities and, 251
Thomas, Beverley L., 264–265, 266
Weg, Ruth B., 148
Woods, Shirley F., 115
Donahue, Wilma Thompson, 23–41,
303
Downing, Ruppert A., 295
Driving Miss Daisy (motion picture),
294
Drug abuse, Woods, Shirley F.,
115–116

Education. *See also* Academia
Carp, Frances Merchant, 127–130,
131–132
Clish, Nancy McCall, 227–229
Donahue, Wilma Thompson, 27–30
Hilgard, Josephine Rohrs, 87–90,
92–93
Hulicka, I. M., 237–241, 242–246
Jackson, Jacquelyne Johnson,
279–281
Jones, Lois Mailou, 45–47
Lopata, Helena Znaniecka, 196,
197–198, 200–201
Peattie, Lisa Redfield, 178–185
race issues and, 47–48
Rude, Catherine Scofield, 213–214,
216
Schweinhaut, Margaret Collins, 58
Thomas, Beverley L., 259–261
Thompson, Marie McGuire, 73–74
Wood, Vivian, 165–167
Woods, Shirley F., 105–110,
114–115
Educational opportunity
blacks, 277

Educational opportunity (*cont.*)
Donahue, Wilma Thompson, 26
GI Bill, 165, 199
Thompson, Marie McGuire, 72
Weg, Ruth B., 145–146
Eisenhower, Dwight D., 51
Elderly. *See* Gerontology
Ethnic bias
Lopata, Helena Znaniecka, 206
Woods, Shirley F., 106
Evers, Medgar, 281

Femininity, Lopata, Helena
Znaniecka, 199
Feminism and feminist movement
academia and, 205
career opportunity and, 205
consciousness and, 205–206
Lopata, Helena Znaniecka, 204–205
Flemming, Arthur S., 37
Ford, Henry, 31
French, Thomas M., 93
Friedan, Betty, 201
Fromm-Reichmann, Frieda, 94
Fuller, Meta Warwick, 46–47

Gaither, Edmund Barry, 43
Gandhi, Mahatma, 288
Generalization, representativeness
issue and, 4
Gerontology
Donahue, Wilma Thompson, 23–24
Institute for Human Adjustment
(IHA), 32–35
International Center for Social
Gerontology, 37–39
Lopata, Helena Znaniecka, 203
public housing and, 75, 78–80
race prejudice and, 285–286,
293–294
Weg, Ruth B., 149
White House Conference on Aging
(1971), 37

Gerontology (*cont.*)
Wood, Vivian, 167–168
Gerth, Hans, 296
GI Bill, education, 165, 199
Gomillion, Charles, 296
Gompers, Samuel, 72
Graham, Martha, 179
Grandparents
Carp, Frances Merchant, 127
Clish, Nancy McCall, 227
Peattie, Lisa Redfield, 177
Rude, Catherine Scofield, 211–212
Schweinhaut, Margaret Collins,
57–58
Great Depression
Carp, Frances Merchant, 127
Donahue, Wilma Thompson, 29–30
Wood, Vivian, 160–161
Grodzins, Morton, 182

Haiti, 51–52
Health, Lopata, Helena Znaniecka,
194–195
Heilbrun, C. C., 162, 172
Hilgard, Josephine Rohrs, 85–101,
302
Historical event, life cycle and, 5. *See
also entries under specific historical
events*
Historical truth, narrative truth and,
2
Hitler, Adolf, 288
Homemaker role. *See also* Child
rearing
Lopata, Helena Znaniecka, 201–202
Rude, Catherine Scofield, 218–219
Horowitz, Irving, 203
Huet, J. A., 37–38
Hulicka, I. M., 235–255
Hunter, Woodrow W., 32, 33
Husbands. *See* Marital relationship;
Marriage

Individual differences, biography and, 309–311
Institute for Human Adjustment (IHA), 31–35
International Center for Social Gerontology, 37–39
Isolation, Peattie, Lisa Redfield, 174–175

Jackson, Jacquelyne Johnson, 275–297
James, Jacquelyn Boone, 299–306
Johnson, Lyndon B., 36
Jones, Lois Mailou, 43–54, 302

Kennedy, John F., 36, 80, 81
Korean War
  Lopata, Helena Znaniecka, 199–200
  Thomas, Beverley L., 261

Lee, Rose Hum, 204
Lie, Jonas, 46
Life cycle. *See also* Retirement
  historical event and, 5
  retirement and, 7
Locke, Alain, 50
Lopata, Helena Znaniecka, 191–208, 301, 302
Love. *See also* Marital relationship
  Weg, Ruth B., 145
  Woods, Shirley F., 119
Luck
  Hulicka, I. M., 236, 241–242
  theme of, viii, 5, 309
  Weg, Ruth B., 144–145
  Wood, Vivian, 171

Marginality concept, Peattie, Lisa Redfield, 174–175
Marital relationship. *See also* Love
  career opportunities and, 6
  Carp, Frances Merchant, 131–132, 139–141
  Clish, Nancy McCall, 226, 231–232

Marital relationship (*cont.*)
  college students, 13–15
  Hilgard, Josephine Rohrs, 97–98
  Hulicka, I. M., 250
  Lopata, Helena Znaniecka, 202–203, 206–207
  Peattie, Lisa Redfield, 176, 180–185
  role models and, 9–10
  Rude, Catherine Scofield, 220–221
  Schweinhaut, Margaret Collins, 62, 66
  Thomas, Beverley L., 263–265
  Thompson, Marie McGuire, 72–73, 77
  Weg, Ruth B., 148–149
  Woods, Shirley F., 118–119
Marital status. *See* Singleness
Marriage
  Carp, Frances Merchant, 130–131
  Clish, Nancy McCall, 229–230
  Donahue, Wilma Thompson, 28
  Hilgard, Josephine Rohrs, 89–92
  Hulicka, I. M., 241–242, 244, 246
  Jackson, Jacquelyne Johnson, 277
  Rude, Catherine Scofield, 215
  Thomas, Beverley L., 260–261
  Weg, Ruth B., 148
  Woods, Shirley F., 110
Media, 58
Medical profession
  Clish, Nancy McCall, 225–233
  sexism and, 145
Medical school
  Hulicka, I. M., 246–247
  sexism and, 229, 311
Men, role models and, 9–10. *See also* Marital relationship
Milieu Therapy, 34
Military
  Lopata, Helena Znaniecka, 199–200
  sexual harrassment in, 13
  Wood, Vivian, 163–165, 170

Miscarriage, Carp, Frances Merchant, 131
Motivation, viii

Narrative. *See* Autobiographical and biographical narrative
National Institutes of Health (NIH), research focus, 17–18
National Organization for Women, 160
Newspapers, 58
Nixon, Richard M., 36
Nursing
career opportunities, 238
physician role contrasted, 228
Thomas, Beverley L., 257–273

Old boy network, sexism and, 11–12

Parents
Carp, Frances Merchant, 127, 129–130
Clish, Nancy McCall, 227
confidence and, viii
Donahue, Wilma Thompson, 25–26
Hilgard, Josephine Rohrs, 85–89
Hulicka, I. M., 237, 238
Jackson, Jacquelyne Johnson, 277, 278–279, 284
Jones, Lois Mailou, 45
Lopata, Helena Znaniecka, 191–197, 200, 202
Peattie, Lisa Redfield, 175–178, 183, 184
Rude, Catherine Scofield, 211–214
Thomas, Beverley L., 269–271
Thompson, Marie McGuire, 72
Wood, Vivian, 160, 161–163
Woods, Shirley F., 105–107, 109
Peace Corps, 136
Peattie, Lisa Redfield, 173–190, 301
Personality studies, autobiography and, 3–4

Physicians. *See* Medical profession
Pierre-Noel, Louis Vergniaud, 48–49, 51
Piscopia, Elena Lucrezia Coronaro, 152–153
Plato, 153
Poland, Lopata, Helena Znaniecka, 191–197, 202
Politics
Donahue, Wilma Thompson, 27
Peattie, Lisa Redfield, 180, 185–186, 187
race prejudice, 278, 289
Schweinhaut, Margaret Collins, 55–70
Thompson, Marie McGuire, 80–81
Poverty, Hulicka, I. M., 237
Pregnancy. *See* Child bearing
Prejudice. *See* Ethnic bias; Racism; Sexism
Press release, career change and, 3, 4
Promotion, Weg, Ruth B., 150–151
Psychiatry, Hilgard, Josephine Rohrs, 85–101
Psychology
Carp, Frances Merchant, 125–141
Hulicka, I. M., 235–255
James, Jacquelyn Boone, 299–306
Public housing, Thompson, Marie McGuire, 73–83
Public service
Donahue, Wilma Thompson, 35–39
Thompson, Marie McGuire, 71–83

Rabin, Albert I., 1–8
Race differences, career decision, 14–15
Race issues
education and, 47–48
Jones, Lois Mailou, 50–51
Race relations
Jackson, Jacquelyne Johnson, 275–297

Race relations (*cont.*)
  role models, 278, 279
Racism, 7
  academia, 282–283
  career opportunity, 277–278
  educational opportunity, 277
  Jackson, Jacquelyne Johnson, 280, 281
  Lopata, Helena Znaniecka, 199–200, 206
  Peattie, Lisa Redfield, 179
  politics, 278
  sexism and, 290–293
  Woods, Shirley F., 106
Rackman, Horace H., 31
Rackman, Mary, 31
Refugees, Lopata, Helena Znaniecka, 196–197
Religion, Woods, Shirley F., 103–123
Representativeness issue, generalization and, 4
Research directions, 299–306
Retirement
  attitudes toward, 7
  biomedical research and knowledge, 19
  Carp, Frances Merchant, 138–139
  Clish, Nancy McCall, 232–233
  Donahue, Wilma Thompson, 39–40
  Hilgard, Josephine Rohrs, 98–99
  Hulicka, I. M., 252
  Peattie, Lisa Redfield, 189
  predictor of, 310
  Thomas, Beverley L., 271–272
  Thompson, Marie McGuire, 83
  Wood, Vivian, 160, 172
Role models, vii, viii
  Hulicka, I. M., 237
  need for, 9–10, 17
  race relations, 278, 279
  variety of reaction to, 301–302
  Wood, Vivian, 160, 168–172

Roosevelt, Franklin D., 59
Roosevelt, Theodore, 27
Rowan, Carl, 295
Rude, Catherine Scofield, 209–223, 304

Salary. *See* Wages and salaries
Schweinhaut, Margaret Collins, 55–70, 301
Secretarial work, career opportunities, 238
Serendipity. *See* Luck
Sex differences
  biomedical research and knowledge, 17–19
  commitment and, 4
  Weg, Ruth B., 145
Sexism, 7
  academia, 143, 146, 147, 197–198, 200–201, 205, 238, 242
  career decision and, 11–13
  career development, 249, 251
  career opportunity and, 9
  Carp, Frances Merchant, 128–129
  historical perspective on, 151–156
  Lopata, Helena Znaniecka, 199–200
  medical school, 229, 311
  military service, 164
  race prejudice and, 290–293
  Weg, Ruth B., 143, 151
Sexual harrassment, United States Navy, 13
Singleness
  career opportunity and, 300
  teaching profession and, 211
  Wood, Vivian, 171
Single parenting, Thomas, Beverley L., 265–267
Smith, Albert, 49–50
Social work
  career opportunities, 242
  Wood, Vivian, 159–172

Sociology
  Jackson, Jacquelyne Johnson, 275–297
  Lopata, Helena Znaniecka, 191–208
Strong Vocational Interest Test, 153–154
Students for a Democratic Society (SDS), 188
Suicide
  Lopata, Helena Znaniecka, 193
  Woods, Shirley F., 118
Sullivan, Harry Stack, 94
Swing, William E., 103–104

Tanner, Henry O., 49
Teaching
  career opportunities, 238
  Hulicka, I. M., 239–240
  marital status and, 211
  Rude, Catherine Scofield, 209–223
  Weg, Ruth B., 146
Terman, Anna, 91
Terman, Lewis M., 91
Thomas, Beverley L., 257–273, 304
Thomas, W. I., 193
Thompson, Marie McGuire, 71–83
Tibbitts, Clark, 32, 33, 38
Truth, biography and, 2–3
Two-career family
  career decision, 14
  Carp, Frances Merchant, 127, 132–139
  Hilgard, Josephine Rohrs, 85, 90–92, 99–100
  Lopata, Helena Znaniecka, 198, 206–207
  Woods, Shirley F., 111

United States Air Force, Lopata, Helena Znaniecka, 199–200
United States Marine Corps, Wood, Vivian, 163–165, 170
United States Navy, sexual harassment in, 13

Urban studies and planning, Peattie, Lisa Redfield, 173–190

Venezuela, 185–186
Vision, Woods, Shirley F., 121–123
Volunteer work, 67
Voting rights
  race, 289
  women, 111–112
Voting Rights Act of 1965, 289

Wages and salaries
  attitudes toward, 206–207
  career decision and, 11
  Hulicka, I. M., 247
  Jackson, Jacquelyne Johnson, 284
  persistence of, 154–155
  race prejudice and, 291–294
  teaching profession, 241, 243
  Weg, Ruth B., 150–151
Walker, Alice, 294
War. *See* Korean War; World War I; World War II
Washington, Booker T., 278, 279
Weaver, Robert C., 81
Weg, Ruth B., 143–158, 302
White House Conference on Aging (1971), 37
Williams, G. Mennen, 36
Willkie, Wendell, 60
Wilson, William J., 294
Wirth, Louis, 182, 199
Wolff, Kurt, 296
Women
  biomedical research and knowledge, 17–19
  career opportunities and, 5–6
  work force and, 218
Women's studies
  Lopata, Helena Znaniecka, 204–205
  Wood, Vivian, 168
Women's voting rights, 111–112
Wood, Vivian, 159–172, 303

Woods, Shirley F., 103–123, 302, 304, 310–311
Work force, women in, 218
World War I, Donahue, Wilma Thompson, 27
World War II
academia and, 279
career opportunities, 213, 228–229, 259

Carp, Frances Merchant, 130–131
Clish, Nancy McCall, 228
Donahue, Wilma Thompson, 30
Lopata, Helena Znaniecka, 191–197
Peattie, Lisa Redfield, 180–181
Rude, Catherine Scofield, 213
Wood, Vivian, 163–165
Woods, Shirley F., 109